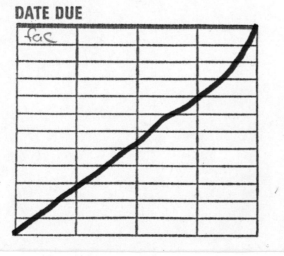

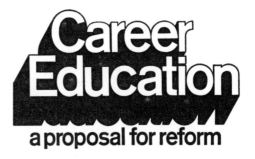

Career Education

a proposal for reform

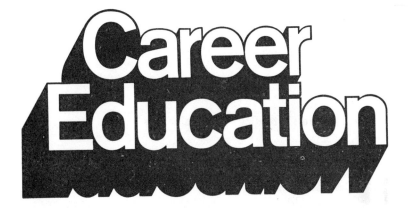

Career Education

a proposal for reform
by
Sidney P. Marland, Jr.

McGraw-Hill Book Company

New York   St. Louis
San Francisco   Düsseldorf
London   Mexico
Sydney   Toronto

Book designed by Marcy J. Katz.

56789BPBP79876

Library of Congress Cataloging in Publication Data

Marland, Sidney Percy.
  Career education.

  1. Vocational education—United States. I. Title.
LC1045.M28   370.11'3   74-11044
ISBN 0-07-040454-2

The author is grateful to the following for permission to quote passages from copyrighted material:

Agathon Press, for Frank W. Parsons, *Choosing a Vocation,* copyright 1909.

American Association of School Administrators, for Grant Venn, "Man, Education and Manpower."

American College Testing Program, for Richard M. Millard, address before Northwest Association of Secondary and Higher Schools, and for D. J. Prediger, J. B. Roth, and R. J. Noeth, "Report No. 61: Student of Student Career Development."

American Personnel and Guidance Association, Paul M. Peters and Joseph T. McGhee, for "Career Education in California." Reprinted with permission.

American Vocational Journal, for "Task Force Report on Education"; for Henry Borow, "Shifting Postures toward Work: A Tracing"; for Kenneth B. Hoyt, "What the Future Holds for the Meaning of Work"; and "Selected Current Definitions of Career Education"; and for Dale Parnell, "Our objective is . . . Vigorous, Viable Society."

Chicago State University, for Elizabeth Jane Simpson, "Career Education: Challenge to Teacher Education," in *Challenge,* Vol. 1, No. 5.

Chronicle of Higher Education, for Paul Lautner, review of Sidney Hook's *Education and the Training of Power;* and for excerpts of materials by Richard Kuhns, Robert T. Keily, Richard Lyman, and Erwin Steinberg.

College Entrance Examination Board for Warren W. Willingham, Richard J. Ferrin, and Elsie P. Begle, for "Career Education in Secondary Schools," 1972; and for Patricia Cross, "The Learning Society," 1974. Both reprinted with permission.

Columbia University, for excerpts from *Columbia Reports,* April 1973; for excerpts from an article by Dr. W. Theodore DeBary in *Seminar Reports,* October 22, 1973; for David Rogers, "Vocational and Career Education: A Critique and some New Directions," in *Teachers College Record,* May 1973; and for excerpts from *Columbia University Directions,* February 23, 1973.

Comment: Women's Education and Development, Radcliffe Institute. for Peter Drucker, "What Education Needs."

Harvard Graduate School of Education Association Bulletin, for Nathan Glazer, "Conflicts in Schools for the Minor Professions," in Vol. 18, No. 2, Spring/Summer 1974.

Houghton Mifflin Company, for E. L. Tolbert, *Counseling for Career Development.*

Kenneth B. Hoyt, for "The Case for Career Education."

Intext Press, for Ralph Tyler, *The Unfinished Journey.*

Love Publishing Company, for Robert L. Darcy and Philip E. Powell, *Manpower and Economic Education.*

Massachusetts Institute of Technology Press, for United States Department of Health, Education and Welfare, *Work in America.*

Carnegie Commission on Higher Education, for "Toward a Learning Society," copyright © 1973 by the Carnegie Foundation for the Advancement of Learning. With permission of the McGraw-Hill Book Company.

Charles E. Merrill Company, for Robert E. Taylor and Keith Goldhammer, *Career Education: Perspective and Promise.*

National Association of Secondary School Principals Bulletin, Reston, Virginia, for Cas Heilman and Keith Goldhammer, "The Psycho-Social Foundation for Career Education"; and for an article by Lowell Burkett, March 1973.

National School Public Relations Association, for "Career Education: Current Trends."

Guidepost, the American Personnel and Guidance Association, for an article by Frank Burtnett, November 23, 1973.

The New York Times, for an article about the Yale School of Music, February 10, 1973, copyright © 1973 by The New York Times Company. Also for an article by W. Theodore DeBary, January 16, 1974; for Ernest L. Boyer, "Higher Education for All, through Old Age," April 8, 1974; and for a quote by John Carusone, February 24, 1974; all copyright © 1974 by The New York Times Company.

Olympus Publishing Company, Salt Lake City, for Kenneth B. Hoyt et al., *Career Education: What It Is and How to Do It;* 1973) and for Kenneth B. Hoyt, *Career Education and the Elementary School Teacher,* 2nd ed., (1974).

Phi Delta Kappa Educational Foundation, for a pamphlet by Fred Wilhelms, 1972, "What Should the Schools Teach?" and for an excerpt from *Kappan,* September, 1973.

Time Magazine, for an excerpt from "Shelves of Learning," December 3, 1973.

United States Department of Health, Education and Welfare, for report by James S. Coleman and the Panel on Youth of the President's Science Advisory Committee, "Youth: Transition to Adulthood," June 1973.

University of Chicago Press, for *School Review,* Vol. 82, No. 1, November 1973, Willard Wirtz, "Education's National Manpower Policy"; and for an article in *School Review,* Vol. 82, No. 1, November 1973, by T. H. Fitzgerald.

Walker and Company, for Judson Gooding, *The Job Revolution.*

to
Virginia
whose patience, wisdom, forbearance,
and kindly criticism have sustained
me through a career of educational adventuring

Acknowledgments

Many people have assisted in the development of this book. Those who had more than ordinary interest in it, and who were especially valuable as contributors of data, counsel, and criticism, include Corinne Reider, Kenneth Hoyt, William Pierce, John Alden, Elizabeth Simpson, Robert Worthington, Walter Coyne, Mary Hallisy, Storey Morefield, Sidney High (all of the Education Division, HEW), Gene Bottoms (Georgia), Ann Raymond (Georgia), Dale Parnell (Oregon), Edwin Petrie (Ohio), Joe Tokash (Texas), Robert Sampieri (California), and William Stamps (Texas). Maryann King, a talented secretary in the College Board staff, has been much more than an off-hours typist. She has managed my deadlines, shuttled efficiently and gracefully between McGraw-Hill and me, and has altogether been an active and contributing partner in the enterprise.

I am especially indebted to John Coyne for his assistance in serving as researcher and creative developer in the preparation of the manuscript.

Contents

Introduction

This is not a scholarly work. I am not a scholar, but rather a practitioner of the profession of education. I have tried to write this book for parents and students and teachers and school administrators as well as for those scholars who may find it of interest. The book is addressed also to persons in business and labor and in government at all levels.

In these pages I try to speak to the people who are concerned about education in America. I have tried to give an accounting of a concept now taking form in its schools and colleges. It is called *career education*. I believe deeply that this concept, properly understood and supported, can change for the better the entire spectrum of education, from the elementary school through college and adult education.

The ideas described here are not new. They go back at least as far as the great twelfth-century Jewish scholar Maimonides and have been reiterated by such thinkers as Benjamin Franklin, Jane Addams, John Dewey, and many more recent scholars and practitioners. But a large idea seems to need the cumulative thrust of other forces at a moment in time to make its way into general acceptance. Some of the forces that have lifted career education to a place of professional and public interest, if not yet general acceptance, are discussed in this book. They include the widely recognized need for our schools and colleges to regain their historically high level of public trust and respect, which has diminished in recent years; to provide more meaningful educational offerings for young people and adults, in response to *their* individual needs and aspirations, as distinct from solely institutional expectations; to remove the destructive effects of the isolation of academic learning from occupational development and real world experiences, a schism which American education has allowed to fester for so long; to concern ourselves as a society with the development of people in all their facets, practical as well as intellectual, and to honor good work of any kind; to redress the aimlessness of many college-going young people, and correspondingly to redress the enormous waste of human energy reflected in the high dropout and unemployed populations among our youth. One could go on citing the numerous forces coming into confluence in the mid-seventies which ask for change in our educational institutions. Not the least pressing is the search for the elusive solution to educating our disadvantaged and illiterate citizens. Work itself, and contemporary American attitudes toward work, have become an increasingly challenging social issue, commanding the sober attention of educators, social scientists, labor and industry leaders. Our commitment to "equality of opportunity," long a platitude, has begun to take on urgent meaning for women, minority citizens, the handicapped—and the nation is looking to our schools and colleges for solutions. Altogether, then, it may well be, as some have declared, that the time has come to put into place this idea called *career education.*

In some ways this book is an album of snapshots. It records the vignettes of educational movement during the early 1970s. A better simile perhaps would be a motion picture made up of many impressions of a swiftly changing scene. In putting these vignettes together, I have drawn heavily upon the work of others, with footnoted attribution and respect. The book is a synthesis of numerous pieces, suggesting the beginning of a whole. Yet as this book goes to press, I am frustrated by the continued emergence of new evidence, new personalities, new legislative action surrounding career education that this "album" will not record.

While I was writing this book, a publication came into circulation that encouraged me in my task. The National School Public Relations Association had conducted an intensive survey of the condition of career education during 1973. In January 1974, their seventy-two-page booklet was published, giving a balanced and lucid report under the title, *Career Education: Current Trends in School Policies and Programs.* Its concluding paragraph follows:

> But in spite of the pitfalls, the criticisms and the continuing dialogue about how to define the concept and implement it, the evidence all points to a strong possibility that career education is the major redirection of the entire educational system.

This book seeks both to define the concept of career education and to report on its current implementation. A score or more of definitions will be found here, along with numerous examples of programs being implemented. The definitions are varied and of mixed transferability, illustrative of the vigor and creativity with which responsible professional people at all levels of education and governance are addressing the theme. In a way, this book is an unfinished piece of work, for career education shows promise of becoming the major reform movement of our entire educational system.

Reform does not come easily to education. But if it comes at all, it emerges slowly and laboriously from the work of many people—especially teachers. In the end, our schools reflect the American society—its values, its hopes, its needs and its diversity. Educators turn slowly in the directions toward which society points, not all of a piece, but person by person, over years, by individual choice. Our society is asking that our schools and colleges sustain our heritage of academic rigor, and concurrently adapt teaching and learning more explicitly to the useful pursuits of the economic and professional world. This slow turn is now beginning.

part one

The
Beginning

The Setting

One of the startling and embarrassing discoveries concerning educational change came from Paul Mort's well-documented research of the 1940s: there is a fifty-year lag between theory and practice in the implementation of a new educational concept.[1] And even after fifty years, Mort noted, only a few schools are actually engaged in the "new" activity. If we still trust Mort's findings, and if the same condition of lag obtains in the 1970s, the concept now called career education must have had its headwaters in the 1920s. For a "practice" of substantial educational change called career education is now being carried on, perhaps hesitantly, perhaps by fits and starts, but nonetheless earnestly, throughout the United States and in several European countries.

One could trace the genealogy of career education back for more than Mort's fifty years, if that were important, for the "theory" deals with very fundamental propositions that have been intrinsic to American education from the start. Career education speaks to the admonition of Alfred North Whitehead in *The Aims of Education* (1929): "Education should turn out the learner with something he knows well and something he can do well."

Yet the present use of the term *career education*, apart from the long-established generalization of a theory, is quite recent. Present usage of the term may have begun around an address I gave before the National Association of Secondary School Principals in Houston, Texas, on January 21, 1971. Some observers cite that event as the beginning of the career education "movement." Not so. If I were party to its advancement, well and good, for that was my intention as Commissioner of Education and subsequently Assistant Secretary for Education during 1970–1973.

There may be some useful threads of autobiography that could explain the circumstances of my commitment to the career education concept. As Superintendent of Schools in Pittsburgh, I came face to face with the dichotomy between the vocational schools and the general high schools. We made some significant gains in the conversion of all secondary schools to *comprehensive* high schools, offering both academic and occupational curricula. The affirmative difference made in the lives of young people and teachers, and indeed in the community, gave me a baseline of confidence in the proposition that all young people should have equal access to occupational and academic learning. We did not use the term *career education* at that time, but we were beginning to nibble at the edge of the idea.

I was influenced, I am sure, by respected educational theorists and thinkers of the time. Conant's work of the 1960s, especially his challenging *Slums and Suburbs*, weighed heavily on me. Conant wrote: "I must record an educational heresy, or rather support a proposition that many will find self-evident, but that some professors of the liberal arts will denounce as dangerously heretical. I submit that in a heavily urbanized and industrialized free society the education experiences of a youth should fit his subsequent employment. There should be a smooth transition from full-time schooling to a full-time job, whether that transition be after grade ten, or after graduation from high school, college, or university."

About this time (1963) I was called by Frank Keppel, then Commissioner of Education, to serve as a member of what became known as the "Gardner Task Force." This group of about ten men and women formulated the bases of what became the Elementary and Secondary Education Act of 1965, with its Great Society initiatives for educational reform. Both as a member of the task force and as a practicing city school administrator, I came to perceive the federal system, beginning for the first time in history to attempt major educational reform. I was torn philosophically between my well-learned doctrine of local control of the schools and the large, clumsy, well-intended intervention of federal force. The evolution, over the ensuing ten years, of Title I and the other lesser parts of the Elementary and Secondary Education Act of 1965 has not resolved my ambivalence. But it has given me a base from which to weigh the respective roles of federal, state, and local authority in any major educational reform. And career education, whatever its refined and sharpened definition may ultimately be, is *educational reform at all levels of the enterprise.*

President Lyndon B. Johnson, to whom much credit is due for his personal engagement in the advancement of education in the United States, said in 1968: "Yet for all our progress we still face enormous problems in education—stubborn, lingering, unyielding problems. Our schools are turning out too many young men and women whose years in the classroom have not equipped them for useful work."

Another leader who influenced the course of education during his distinguished career is Ralph Tyler. I am sure he influenced me, in many of his writings and in our infrequent but always stimulating conversations. Tyler wrote in 1967: "Throughout American history, technology has been gradually affecting American life, but since 1925 and particularly since World War II, the rapid rate of technological development in agriculture, industry and defense has so changed the occupational distribution of the total labor force that the chance for a youth or adult without high school education is becoming increasingly small. . . . Unskilled labor represented 20% of the labor force in 1920 and now only 6%. For most uneducated youths no jobs will be found. . . . A large number of people now are, and many more will be, changing occupations during their working careers, and many of these changes require education and training to obtain the necessary understanding and skills for the job. This is another educational task for which we have meager experience and no tested doctrine to guide us.''[2]

Tyler's words, read in the context of the mid-1970s, seem commonplace and not so very startling. They were, in their time, new challenges to those of us in school administration, and their current familiarity reveals the swift pace of change in attitudes and perceptions of education's function. Yet, in truth, as recently as the late 1960s there was a tacit acceptance of the high school dropout as a normal condition. The dropout, numbering 30 per cent or more, was an assumed element of our ecology; his death in the job market was greeted with a whispered "good riddance."

In any case, whatever influences may have pushed me toward the career education concept by the late sixties and well before it had ever crossed my mind that I might hold federal office, I had developed convictions about the responsibility of the total educational system to develop all learners for useful and satisfying employment, as well as for intellectual and academic effectiveness. In 1968, while serving on the Commission on Tests of the College Entrance Examination Board (without the remotest notion that I would later be serving as the Board's president), I was asked to prepare a paper dealing with the future role of the Board as a voluntary standard-setting agency, serving high schools and colleges. At that time, with very few earnest listeners, I wrote:

> A very large proportion of young people are excluded from the select society that the Board has unintentionally constructed. . . . The great virtue of the College Board is its systematic design for facilitating entrance to varying colleges by students of widely varying school and geographic backgrounds. It is this important virtue that suggests the need for developing a corresponding arrangement for systematically matching high school students with a variety of jobs.
>
> It is here proposed that an institution be created that will give to [occupational] study the same level of respect and prestige that the liberal arts studies now have, and will recognize excellence in areas that are not primarily intellectual. . . . It is emphasized that a student is not

obliged to follow one "track" or the other, as there are no fixed tracks. Most likely he or she will find fulfillment in a combination of academic and vocational-technical studies, whether the goal is college or a job.

This notion had very few advocates in the late sixties when I wrote it. It was received by the College Board staff with something less than enthusiasm. My present colleagues who were there at the time look back and chuckle. But they have since come to look upon career education as serious business.

When the Secretary of Health, Education and Welfare, Elliot Richardson, invited me to become Commissioner of Education in the summer of 1970, he asked me what things in education were important to me. Among other topics I cited my concerns about disenchanted college and university students, unemployed youth, academic discrimination between things of the mind and the world of work, the aimlessness of many high school and college students whose motivations, if any, were circular (to be in school or college because that was what was expected of them). I told him of my notions about the comprehensive high school and the need for greatly increasing the post-high school opportunities for young people and for people in midcareer. I alluded to my still-very-fluid concept of a design for introducing awareness of work and the motivation intrinsic to the work idea, from early childhood education through the self-evident, work-focused functions of the graduate professional schools. Secretary Richardson listened very closely. He is a good listener.

Soon afterward, we spent a day together talking about the opportunities for a federal initiative in education. A full day for this alone, under the conditions of his bone-crushing schedule at that time, was exceptional. But we had it, in relaxed, discursive, and constructive dialogue. He questioned sternly the looseness of my still-untitled conceptualization (and probably still would). His lawyer's mind and his Yankee wit probed the issues of legislative authority, budget, state control, needed research, and the absence of concrete operational objectives. But he gave his general endorsement to the idea, and turned me loose to do what I might. He declared his interest and qualified support at a general staff meeting of all HEW officers, which set off some sparks from the skeptics, notwithstanding Richardson's very high place in their loyalties.

Only a few weeks later, a call came to me from the Domestic Council Chairman, John Ehrlichman, asking me to give immediate attention to increasing the place of "vocational education" in the federal role. He wanted a concrete plan and a systematic design for a major administrative initiative, *with no increase in the budget*. This was in the late fall of 1970.

The planning staff of the Office of Education, together with leaders from the Bureau of Adult Vocational and Technical Education, gathered to formulate a response to the White House. I did not push the larger idea at first, being still an unanointed Commissioner-designate awaiting Congressional confirmation. The staff had trouble mounting anything that looked like a worthy "administration initiative" with no additional funds. Finally, as days passed and the White House called again, I tried out the idea of a total reform that would embrace vocational education as a significant element but would relate the occupational aspects of human development to all levels of learning and all relevant parts of academic instruction.

This took a little time to digest. We finally produced a working draft of what we thought we were talking about, and forwarded it through the Secretary in late December. By that time I had been confirmed, and was able to take my part officially in the planning exercise.

We labored over a name. The idea had to be distinguished from the term *vocational-technical*; it had to imply a sequential system affecting all formal education. It had to be brief, hopefully shunning the mouthfuls of titles that would include Occupational-Academic-Manpower, Elementary, Secondary, Post-Secondary. We tried Liberal and Technical Education; we tried Education for the World of Work; we tried others with equal dissatisfaction.

One day the task force working on the White House response was gathered in an uncomfortable closet called euphemistically "The Commissioner's Conference Room." We hammered out the term *career education*. The *Oxford Universal Dictionary* defines career as "a person's course or progress through life." That was what we were talking about. We settled.

It was only a few weeks later that the Houston address was to be delivered. It seemed as good a time as any, and a most fitting audience—the annual assembly of the nation's several thousand high school principals—to take the plunge. And so it was that the rough idea, the name, and the decision to establish a new high priority for the Office of Education came about.

As I write this in January 1974, it seems that much more has happened during these past three years than one could have expected, especially when one considers the disappointing history of educational reform notions during the preceding decades, none of which had caught fire with measurable results: Life Adjustment Education, The Core Curriculum, Education for Gray Areas had come and gone, without mourners. The signs during these recent years suggest that career education is more than a passing fad.

The term *career education* now has wide usage: publishers such as McGraw-Hill, Scholastic Magazines, Science Research Associates, Singer Corp., General Learning Corporation, Houghton Mifflin, and many others are investing very substantially in instructional materials bearing the career education message. The American College Testing Program has developed significant guidance materials under the career rubric. The College Board before I joined it launched the Comparative Guidance and Placement instrument, especially for high school and community college uses, giving heavy attention to the career planning implications of the counseling function.

Apart from experimental models launched by the Office of Education, hundreds of school systems throughout the country are developing their own models and curricula.

While community colleges have long been engaged in greater or lesser degree in the career concept, four-year colleges and universities are beginning to look seriously at their role in the career education movement.

Business, industry, and labor, with varying levels of conviction, are joining the schools in the search for an appropriate share of the work.

Before concluding this chapter, which has sought to illuminate the setting in which career education is emerging, one significant action should be reported. Some say that the January 1971 Houston meeting of principals was the key point in career education's emergence. Perhaps so. But a far more basic event occurred the following summer.

There is a tradition in the Office of Education that calls each June for the gathering of all chief state school officers in Washington in what is known as "The Commissioner's Conference." I faced this meeting with some trepidation. While I knew many of the chiefs and had found them supportive of my work, I also knew of the skepticism with which they viewed the Office of Education in any role that appeared to preempt the fundamental authority of the states in matters of education. I happened to agree with their position, and still do. But the chalkline of federal "leadership" and state "control" runs through a sticky wicket under the best of conditions and even among friends.

But I knew that if career education were to amount to anything it would have to be a conscious and deliberate decision by each state, operating under the leadership of the chief state school officers.

On June 16, 1971, I put the notion before the chiefs in a hotel meeting room in Washington. We spent a day talking about it. I was examined and crossexamined. There were a number of leaders there who themselves had come up through the vocational-technical system. They knew, probably more than I, the large implications of what we were proposing—a total new system that would elevate occupational development to a par with academic development. There were strong voices, for and against the idea.

At issue, apart from the large philosophical implications for education, was of course money. I had proposed that a certain component of the OE budget that under the Vocational Education Act was discretionary as to its allocation be turned over to the chiefs if they would use the money, together with direct federal allocations under the same authority, for the development of career education models within each state. This was, in a sense, bargaining. But I was bargaining with nearly all parties on the same side of the table by the time the day wound down. One by one each chief state school officer made his commitment, and we reached a unanimous resolution.

There were only $18 million at issue—I say only, because in what was a $5-billion-dollar budget at the time, $18 million is modest. But the key aspect of the money issue was that these dollars, under the law, were *discretionary* dollars. They were not allocated by fixed categorical programs. Hence, they had more usefulness for reform purposes than federal dollars which simply sustain the status quo.

Of the $18 million, one half is allocated by law to the states for discretionary uses in vocational education development. The remaining $9 million were to be used by the Commissioner through such allocations to states as his discretion prompted. Our proposition was that if the chiefs would *all* agree to use *their* discretionary $9 million for career education model-building, I would double their risk money by allocating the remaining $9 million to the same enterprise.

This happened. Subsequently the Office of Education sent out very general guidelines describing the conditions of the model-building activity and, following receipt of assurances from each chief, the money was delivered.

Educational change does not come easily. It does not come solely from money. Money, however, even in small quantities— $180,000 on average per state in this case—is a very powerful federal persuader. But money would not have bought the commitment of any chief state school officer in that room. They knew they could have rejected the career education proposal, and that in one form or another they would have been granted the same dollars, by law, for some other purpose consistent with federal regulations.

That *was* an important day. It is not very productive to argue about when career education was born, but some could say it happened that day.

Of course, one might argue that the idea had been born long ago, and had been here all the time:

> Anticipate charity by preventing poverty; assist the re-
> duced man by teaching him a trade, and putting him in the

way of business so that he may earn self-respect and a livelihood. . . . [Maimonides, about 1200 A.D.]

While career education is by no means solely concerned with "preventing poverty" and "teaching a trade," these goals are certainly a part of our message. How long have the impulses of career education been around? I will settle for 1200 A.D. as a good starting point.

2

A Time for Change

"Pedants sneer at an education that is useful," Alfred North Whitehead observed. "But if it is not useful, what is it?"

One of the central assumptions of career education is that the learner should perceive learning as *useful*—to himself and to society. For whatever reason, we have made little of this basic proposition in designing our curricula and organizing our schools. We have not related it concretely to the individual learner's aspirations.

Whether we acknowledge it or not, our society expects our schools and colleges to equip young men and women for successful entry into the world of work. Abundant evidence points to this conclusion. In 1973 the Phi Delta Kappa journal *Kappan* reported a Gallup survey of attitudes toward the public schools.[1] This survey, the fifth in a series, conducted under the sponsorship of the Kettering Foundation, introduces its finding with the comment: "The CFK [Kettering]–Gallup education polls are now established as a major source of information concerning the status and trends of opinion about significant school questions."

The polls' findings give spreads of opinion, over the period 1969–1973, about many educational issues, among them desegregation, curriculum, school size, budgets. Typically the responses reveal a spread of judgment that might show 60 per cent of the respondents for something, 30 per cent against, and 10 per cent with no opinion. This is not surprising, but the following question and the tabulation appear to show a remarkable consensus:

Should public schools give move emphasis to a study of trades, professions, and businesses to help students decide on their careers?

Yes, more emphasis	90%
No	7%
No opinion	3%

Dr. Gallup offers this comment in the survey report:

More Emphasis to Career Education

Few proposals receive such overwhelming approval today as the suggestion that schools give more emphasis to a study of trades, professions, and businesses to help students decide on their careers. Nine in 10 persons in all major groups sampled in this survey say they would like to have the schools give more emphasis to this part of the educational program.

And most of those who vote for this greater emphasis say that this program should start with junior and senior high school, although many professional educators think it should start even earlier—in the elementary grades.

While the Gallup poll cited above dealt with a universal audience of adults, it is noteworthy that young people, too, look for more attention to their career needs. ACT (American College Testing Program) conducted a survey of student attitudes toward career education with the following results, drawn from a larger array:

Favorable adult attitudes toward career education in the schools are reinforced by the students themselves. A survey by American College Testing Program, published late in 1973, reports: "One of the most striking findings of this study is the apparent receptivity of students toward help with career planning. . . . More than three-fourths of the nation's high school juniors would like such help."

While this survey sought student attitudes toward career *guidance*, the evidence was that, among the numerous "needs for help" as revealed by students, career planning headed the list.[2]

More recent information that addresses public attitudes toward this subject comes from a January 1974 preliminary report of a survey conducted by the National Institute for Education. An abbreviated summary by NIE staff states:

A nationwide survey conducted by the National Opinion Research Center reveals that public views on the objectives of secondary education indicate that most segments of the population rank the possession of job skills far ahead of most other objectives. Job skills were ranked twice as important as respect for authority or academic skills; more than three times as important as keeping students out of trouble, or providing a setting for making friends; and more than four times as important as awareness of cultural identity.

There seems to be little doubt about the expectations of our society, or the expressed needs of our students, as to the significance of careers in their values as a function of education.

A precept of the career education idea is that all young people upon leaving the education system, whether during high school, upon graduation from high school, or upon leaving or graduating from a post-secondary institution, should be ready immediately to enter satisfying and useful employment in a field of the individual's choice. This is a large and demanding ideal. But because it makes us reach high is no reason to shun it. Not only does the school and college have the responsibility to equip the learner, at any age, for job entry, but also there is a new and difficult role of facilitating the job search and providing follow-up surveillance after the individual is placed.

The role of the high school counselor is central to the effectiveness of career education. The concept leans heavily upon the assumption that the student will make increasingly significant *decisions affecting his personal, educational, and occupational goals.* Accordingly, the skills of decision-making, as well as sound information leading to individual decisions, become an enlarged component of the counseling process. Decision-making has begun to find its way into the curriculum as a process to be learned, and, as students and counselors or teachers take on this new dimension of school services, they reflect enthusiastic response to the process.

The College Entrance Examination Board has published the findings of a survey of student and teacher attitudes toward CEEB's "Deciding" program. The key question of the survey was "Are students interested in applying decision-making skills to the personal, vocational and educational decisions that they encounter in school and life?"

Dr. Gordon Miller reports upon his findings from sixty leaders (counselors and teachers) and three thousand students: "Seventy-one per cent of the leaders said the students reacted more enthusiastically to *Deciding* than to other curricular materials they had been taught." Drawing data from original field trials of the decision-making procedure in middle schools and high schools across the country, Miller states: "From our total evaluation population of over 1500 students, more than 95 per cent have felt consistently that it is important to *learn* how to make good decisions."[3]

If we acknowledge that the American people expect these tasks to be performed by our institutions, we must take a very hard look at how our institutions are now organized and how we must ourselves be a part of the change that we propose to bring about.

To enable schools to achieve this emerging expectation, we must begin by purging ourselves of academic snobbery. While we have served well the 50 per cent or more who are college-bound, the other 50 per cent get short shrift. Of the college-bound, I must ask what we have done to help them shape their reasons for going to college, apart from simply going. And what are colleges doing to make their offerings responsive to students' career needs?

One of education's most serious failings is its self-induced, voluntary fragmentation, the strong tendency of education's several parts to separate from one another, to divide the entire enterprise against itself. The most grievous example of these intramural class distinctions is, of course, the false dichotomy between things academic and things vocational.

Contrary to all logic and all expediency, we continue to treat occupational training as education's poor cousin. We are thereby perpetuating its social quarantine. Vocational education teachers are scorned by academic teachers, and vice versa.

Since the original vocational fields were defined, shortly before World War I, as agriculture, industry, and homemaking, we have too often taught those skills grudgingly—dull courses in dull buildings for the benefit of what we all knew were young people somehow prejudged not fit for college, as though college were something better for a select number. What a pity and how foolish, particularly for a country as dependent upon her machines and her technology as America.

The legislative history of vocational education has regrettably contributed to the isolation of this scorned segment of our public schools. The terms of the Smith–Hughes Act of 1917 were constraining and severely categorical, forbidding the larger implications of total human growth that the schools should serve and want to serve. Smith–Hughes prescribed vocational education for "instruction of less than college grade" and "for pupils of 14 years of age or older." The message of the law was "to fit for useful employment."

Over the years the original law has been modestly liberalized in scope beyond support of curriculum in agriculture, trades, and home economics. In 1936 the George–Deen Act authorized the addition of distributive education. In 1946 further extensions were allowed to afford vocational counseling and more general approaches to vocational education. These were tremendously important statutes, giving the first real federal attention and support to a segment of public education. The evolution of these laws to this very day remains a very important part of the federal government's attention to a categorical need that probably would not have been met by states and local jurisdictions without the federal initiative and stimulation. Yet the very substance of categorical differences as viewed by teachers and students has fostered and sustained the unhappy discrimination implicit in the separateness that history has constructed. Smith–Hughes was a blessing and a curse. There were "different" funds to be administered; the programs were quite categorically "different"; the teachers, required to meet separately conceived certification criteria, were necessary "different." We have, for all the good things that have come of the Smith–Hughes Act, created a "different" system within the system, and young people are quick to perceive it. Regrettably, the simple product of the "difference" is that favored young people go to college preparatory classes and *different* young people go to vocational-education classes. This dreadful dichotomy still permeates our secondary schools and, perhaps even worse, attaches its snobbish depressive values and perceptions to many colleges and universities.

An ugly by-product of the separation of academic and occupational programs, faculty, curriculum, and facilities is the general curriculum. This euphemism is a term applied to the academic offerings afforded those students not preparing for college or enrolled in vocational education. It includes upward of 30 per cent of our secondary students, and much larger proportions in our big cities. I judge that the subtle, unspoken, and possibly subconscious reason for the general curriculum is the acceptance of the proposition that vocational education is not very acceptable socially, and if one is not going to college, then the general curriculum is at least not *vocational!*

This is a bitter commentary for me or any other American school teacher to make. Yet it has to be stated, for here again is a part of the reason for career education—a part of the reason for change.

The ancient Greeks could afford such snobbery at a time when a very short course would suffice to instruct a man in imitating a beast of burden. We Americans might even have been able to afford it a half-century ago, when a boy might observe the full range of his occupational expectations by walking beside his father at the time of plowing, or by watching the farmers, blacksmiths, and tradesmen who did business in his home town.

How difficult it is for a child growing up today to perceive *work,* and fit it into his awareness, at age eight or ten or twelve—those critically important years of human development! My children at about those ages used to ask me what I did at work. They knew I was the local superintendent of schools, because they unfortunately could not escape that fact among their fellows and teachers. But I learned to expect the question from them one by one as they grew into age nine or ten: "What do you do in your office, Dad?" My office was my place of work, and there or thereabouts I spent about ten hours a day managing schools and trying to be a head teacher, but what could I tell my children concretely that would answer their question?

A superintendent of schools has a fairly simple task to describe, compared with many workers. Try to tell a child what a banker does, or an insurance man or an accountant, in ways that are meaningful to children interested in work. My children were denied what in an earlier generation would have been direct and concrete participation in the work of the household, the farm, the small family industry, the shop, the art and craft, the service performed by the parents. They could not *participate*.

As a child I could dust boxes and burn rubbish in my father's store. As I took on higher rank, I got to wash the windows and sweep the sidewalk. The day I waited on my first customer, at about age fifteen, I knew a lot about that store and a lot about my father as I watched him work, whether buying, selling, or responding courteously and alertly to the needs of friends and customers. Near our home I could watch Mr. Long, the blacksmith, and sometimes fetch new shoes from the bin when he called. And down the street I could marvel as a ten-year-old at the magic of Mr. Peche's bottling-company operations, and sometimes wash bottles with the spinning brush when he would let me. Later I could ride with the veterinarian on his calls to attend sick cows and horses, and sometimes earnestly carry his bag. But these vistas of work and friendship with a variety of workers are largely denied our young people today. If I were to let my speculation roam, I would attach some importance to the proposition that many older adolescents today are cynical about our economic system because they are frightened by it. They have never had a chance to be close to it or close to people whom they love and respect who are a part of it. But that *is* speculation, and I have no evidence.

Things are different today for the young as they approach work, and how grave our need to reshape our system of education to meet the career demands of the astonishingly complex technological society we live in. When we talk of today's career development, we are not talking about blacksmithing, but about the capacity of our people to sustain and accelerate the pace of progress in this country in every respect during a lifetime of learning.

The question seems fairly simple, if we have the courage and creativity to face it: Shall we persevere in the status quo, sustaining the traditional practices that are obviously not properly equipping fully half or more of our young people, or shall we immediately undertake the reformation of our entire education system in order to position it properly for maximum contribution to our individual and national life? This includes the intellectual and personal fulfillment of all learners at all ages, as well as their development for occupations useful and satisfying to themselves.

Only one choice is apparent. Certainly continued indecision and preservation of the status quo can only result in additional millions of young men and women leaving our high schools and colleges, with or without benefit of diploma or degree, unfitted for employment, and carrying away little more than an enduring distaste for education in any form, unskilled and unschooled.

We need to break down the barriers that divide our educational system into parochial enclaves. We must blend our curricula and our students into one flexible, comprehensive system, especially in secondary schools and colleges. Let the academic preparation be balanced with the vocational or professional program. Let one student take strength from another. And, for the future hope of education, let us end the divisive, snobbish, destructive distinctions in learning that do no service to the cause of knowledge and do no honor to the name of American enterprise.

There are alternatives to the present lock-step system that must be developed—alternative arrangements that provide every young person with equally valued options, both occupational and academic. He or she may go on to higher education, or he or she may become equipped for a technical job through a community college, or one may spin off from the system, say at sixteen, whenever ready and equipped to hold a job. That kind of arrangement would, of course, have to be so flexible that young people could always change their minds and reenter the system, not only as the young but as mature adults. Let us think of a zero-reject system, in which there are no dropouts—where students enter and leave the system at will, provided they are equipped to work, and are assisted in entering the work force.

The present discontent with our system of education is reflected in these data showing approximate annual numbers in the 1970–1973 period:

Leaving high school before graduation	850,000
Completing high school in the general curriculum	800,000
Leaving post-secondary institutions before graduating	900,000
	2,550,000

In other words, roughly 2.5 million of our young people each year for a variety of reasons are voting with their feet, to say that schools and colleges are not meeting their needs. These young people do not possess the conventional credentials from their institutions; moreover, they are not equipped to enter our economic system with salable skills. If we take a very rough average of $1000 per year (which is low) for the investment that our public treasury has placed in their development, we would find the following cost calculations:

Leaving high school after 10 years at $1000/year	$ 8.5 billion
Completing high school in the general curriculum after 13 years	10.4 billion
Leaving post-secondary institutions without credentials	12.6 billion
	$31.5 billion

We are talking about a $30-billion-a-year investment in education, from kindergarten through the leaving level, that has dubious merit for those who, through taxes, tuition, or both, should expect a better outcome. Our society cannot absorb two and a half million disenchanted and underdeveloped young people a year, economically or psychologically. The latter is probably more grave than the former.

Conscious intervention with new arrangements, changes in the teaching and learning environment, liberalization of the conventional day, year, or age of schooling can redress these awesome conditions.

As Stephen K. Bailey has pointed out in an essay on career education, ". . . a variety of social forces and technical developments are pushing American education in the direction of flexible space/flexible time/externally credentialed study that hold enormous promise for individuals and for society as a whole. External degrees, universities without walls, new-style correspondence programs, high school and college equivalency for life-experience, semesters abroad, credit for service-connected courses—these and similar innovations are popping up like mushrooms after a spring rain."[4]

There is, I believe, a readiness for change among teachers and administrators in our schools and colleges. It comes as no surprise to educators that we are performing less effectively than we should, as we examine the total data cited above. Dale Parnell, Oregon's Superintendent of Public Instruction until recently, has pointed out that "one major reason for incomplete performance by schools is that many of our educational traditions stem from the first quarter of the 20th century and even earlier. Far too many of our educational requirements, including those for high school graduation and teacher certification, are based on the needs of a society 40 and 50 years ago. Children, indeed, have outgrown present-day schools."

Dr. Parnell agrees with what James S. Coleman has pointed out in his widely acclaimed 1972 article in *Psychology Today*, "The Children Have Outgrown the Schools," that students have moved from an "information poor but experience rich" society of fifty years ago to a society overly rich in information only. No one watches blacksmiths any more.

How can schools, asks Parnell, "provide experiences that will enable students to relate information to living, to the real-life roles that constitute a part of living for all but a few of the most handicapped"? The answer, Parnell agrees, is career education.

One of the basic principles of career education is that it is student-oriented. It uses knowledge, values, and skills as a means to the *students'* ends, not as ends in themselves. Our education system has always said it was concerned with the welfare of each individual student, but the reality is far short of that mark. Why else do we have so many failures in the schools, so many casualties? Schools have not lived up to the expectations of our students. These expectations—either expressed or felt—are based on the innate practicality of young people. These young people have a sense of their time and the world in which they are becoming adults. It is our task to give them schools and colleges where they can develop the competencies they need and want to negotiate adult life. Not to do so leaves them without emotional or intellectual or occupational resources in the technological world they are about to enter.

The way toward change, then, begins with a new curriculum for all our schools, a curriculum that places the student at the center of all learning. We need to be truly committed to giving every student the opportunity to develop himself or herself to the fullest capacity.

This new curriculum, taking into account the lack of work experiences available today for young people and the need to make the whole learning process more responsible to the realities of our society, must provide "hands-on" opportunities for all students. They need to be introduced in a variety of ways to the world outside the classroom. For schools and knowledge are not synonymous, and man must learn much of what he needs to know about living outside the classroom. Schools must provide more of the knowledge required to enter the work force, at whatever level, with confidence. The level may be that of a hospital orderly or a surgeon, a carpenter, a hairdresser, a political leader, or an architect.

We need a curriculum more open and daring, more imaginative, with new kinds of learning opportunities. Such a curriculum will give students utilitarian skills that have a market value while providing full attention to the humanities. Too often, students wander from one academic year to the next, blindly following schedules that make little sense and which seemingly have no visible connection with their future life.

By placing students at the center of learning and giving them "hands-on" experiences and exposure to the world of work and the economic realities of their future life, they will begin to comprehend the complexities of our society and begin to find a place in this society as working and social members. They will start to tie together the reasons for learning, the reasons for basic skills, the reasons for general knowledge. The motivation implicit in the individual's own determination of career goals and the corresponding academic and vocational skills gives high promise of far better learning effectiveness for all learners. They will not only have the basic requirements to cope with a technological society, but will also be able to control their own entry to that society by having the knowledge and skills leading to their usefulness to themselves and their community.

With the student at the center of education—really for the first time in spite of our traditional rhetoric—and a curriculum that then faces outward toward the community and the world of work, it is necessary that the community be drawn into the school and share in the development of students. It is not possible to have "hands-on" experiences, to expose the students to other sources of knowledge, or to know what industrial society wants in the way of occupational competences, without literally engaging the business community in the schools.

More will be said later concerning industry's relationship with the schools. Suffice it to say for the moment that career education, wholly perceived, calls for a major change in the place industry occupies in education. There is a readiness on the part of industry for this larger responsibility. Strong commitments extended in recent years by the U.S. Chamber of Commerce and many individual corporations make clear the willingness of industry to take on new responsibilities in the development of the young. But school leaders ultimately must be in charge, and public funds must be viewed as more flexibly related to services performed by industry. School leaders and teachers must rise above their present inclination to attempt to have the schools be all things to all students during their developing years.

As we speak of change in education, apart from the declaration of lofty goals, there is the very essential issue of teacher education, which will be treated in a subsequent chapter. But to contemplate a change of the scale envisioned here without the deep involvement of teachers is to be totally unrealistic. Teacher development, both in-service and preservice, will be essential to the enterprise. Further, teachers must believe in and care deeply about the enterprise or it will fail. No board of education and no school administrator will bring off this change unless the faculty agrees. I believe most teachers will find increased fulfillment and success themselves in a design that brings to the classroom a larger dimension of motivation heretofore left to the teachers' desperate and often lonely devices.

We have noted briefly the place of the teachers, the administrators, the industry and business sector as a part of a new design for education. An equally prominent and crucial component is the community at large, particularly the parents of children in school—who must be a part of any change process that will move toward career education.

Parents want a part in the making of decisions relating to major educational change directly affecting their children. Parents are concerned about what the schools are teaching, how it is being taught, and the effects of this teaching. To leave parent representatives out of the process of developing the career education curriculum would probably spell the early dismissal of this educational philosophy. Not only should parents share in the curriculum design, they should also be explicitly engaged in the presentation of career examples, whether postman, doctor, secretary, mayor, or nurse.

There are other reasons for involving parents in the development of this comprehensive reform. Much of what most young people learn is learned in the home, from parents and friends. The schools have no monopoly on teaching. Nor should they. When parents are aware of the objectives of career education, they can reinforce the work of the school and encourage students to take advantage of the opportunities presented to them in the classrooms, in both academic and work-related programs. Strong evidence from national polls indicates that the parents closely associated with the school tend to be strongly supportive of the school.

The Los Angeles schools have published a manual for parental involvement cited by the Center for Career Education in Los Angeles. Excerpts follow:

- Parents learn more about the goals and methods of the school and are better able to support their children's educational efforts at home.

- More realistic ideas about the community are incorporated into on-going courses of study and activities since many different people with differing ideas provide a corrective to single-minded individuals or special interest groups.

- Uncounted hours of volunteer labor and special expertise provide services to students and teachers that few schools can afford to buy.

- Financial support for taxes and bonds is more generous because participating parents become positive voters.

- Shared goals result from parents and teachers learning about each other's expectations for youngsters in school.

- Cultural differences between school and family become an opportunity for enriching educational experiences instead of a problem creating conflicts.

- Children, particularly in elementray school, see their own and their friends' parents taking education seriously and model themselves in like fashion.

- Through the participation of adults who do the work of the world, the "world of work" influences career education programs in a helpful way.

"The influences of parents on children," according to Dr. Barbara J. Shade of the University of Wisconsin at Madison in a paper presented to the Center for Vocational and Technical Education, "are pervasive and long lasting and have overwhelming implications for the career education program." The parent as a "working model" for a resource to the teacher is a natural part of career education, especially in elementary and secondary schools.

The way toward change, the way toward a career education curriculum, begins with a joint effort of all those who are involved with the education of our young. The way toward change begins with the awareness that what we are now teaching in our classrooms is not enough. The way toward change is the realization that our schools must provide for all our students the knowledge and the skills and academic competencies that will, at whatever level they move from the school, permit them to enter appropriate and satisfying work.

James S. Coleman, in his introduction to *Youth: Transition to Adulthood*, writes:

> As the labor of children has become unnecessary to society, the school has been extended for them. With every decade the length of schooling has increased, until a thoughtful person must ask whether society can conceive of no other way for youth to come into adulthood. If schooling (as it is) were a complete environment, the answer would properly be that no amount of school is too much, and increased schooling for the young is the best way for the young to spend their increased leisure, and society its increased wealth. . . . But schooling, as we know it, is not a complete environment, giving all the necessary opportunities for becoming adult.[5]

part two

_The
Need_

Work and the Human Condition

Without work, all life goes rotten. But when work is soulless, life stifles and dies.—ALBERT CAMUS

Mankind, in all its societies and throughout its history, has measured much of its life in terms of work. Archeologists calibrate the development of early man by the discovering and articulating of his primitive tools; anthropologists use a society's relationship to work and its varied forms in determining the discrete cultural characteristics of a particular people. "When social psychologists like David McClelland attempt to account for root differences between technologically and economically advanced nations and those less sophisticated, they speak of work-relevant motives and of achieving versus nonachieving societies."[1] Presumably twentieth-century people will be correspondingly assessed by the scholars of subsequent eons.

Man at first placed a negative value on work. "The institution of slavery in antiquity . . . was not a device for cheap labor or an instrument of exploitation for profit but rather the attempt to exclude labor from the conditions of man's life."[2] Therefore, the

Greeks and Romans arranged for slaves' work, and only the citizen was a man of leisure. The Hebrews, on the other hand, saw work as an unsavory necessity, but having some spiritual worth. The early Christians also put value on work. St. Paul wrote, in a letter to the Thessalonians, "If any would not work, neither should he eat."

It was in the Middle Ages of Europe, however, that work took on positive values; productivity was elevated to worthy status, and indeed became a moral obligation. Martin Luther, and then John Calvin, advanced the dictum that to do work was to do God's will. Thomas Carlyle, preaching social reform, would write, "Blessed is he who has found his work; let him ask no other blessedness." The Protestant Reformation was well founded in the belief that work, wealth, and capitalism all went together; and from that heritage, with a further modification by the English Puritans and their emphasis on ascetic living, has come our Protestant work ethic. Max Weber has pointed out that the spirit of capitalism has been around since ancient times, having an implicit connotation for the significance of work as a "good thing."

The term *Protestant work ethic* currently carries a derogatory overtone with some, notably the young and some social scientists. It appears to attach itself to subtle meanings of self-righteousness, possibly greed, possibly compulsive attachment to work for work's sake. Whatever current shadows may fall over the term, however, work of one kind or another is essential to the well-being of all mankind. *Work* as distinct from the *work ethic* remains an inescapable and ever-present condition of life. Perhaps the term *ethic*, as seeming to carry moral or spiritual obligations apart from the worth of work in itself, is the issue.

Kenneth B. Hoyt calls for a shift in the terms, with *work ethic* being replaced by *work values*. "The work ethic carries strong connotations of societal obligations imposed on the individual; the word *values*, on the other hand, carries strong connotations of individual choice and self-determination."[3]

The change in attitude toward work began around the turn of the present century, when the work place became ill-defined as the family role in providing work experiences declined. The

United States had had a long period of growth, through the time of the Industrial Revolution, where the work of children and young people was important to the economic condition of the family. "While the advent of the Industrial Revolution in the latter half of the eighteenth century brought changes in the nature of work roles within the family, the work of children remained highly important to the economic survival and comfort of the kinship group."[4]

"With the Depression in the 1930s, however, nationwide unemployment reached 25%, and attempts were made by organized labor to keep the fresh crop of new graduates off the labor market. This was done by heightening the educational requirements needed for work. At the same time, the traditional role of the family in preparing youth for work began to decline."[5] This phenomenon is central to the *raison d'être* of career education. Borow continues: " . . . today, adolescents are commonly regarded as superfluous commodities in an adult-operated economy. In the 1960s alone, unemployment among those in the 16–19 age range shifted from 3.5 to 5.5 times that of the 25-and-over segment of the labor force."[6] For minority young people the rate was double the general population's rate.

While the presence of youth on the labor market declined, it increased in the schools. A hundred years ago, less than 5 percent of the high-school-age group were in school; today, nearly all stay in school through the high school diploma.[7] ("Nearly all" overstates the ratio, but the report is correct in noting the high rate.) James Coleman, in his introduction to *Youth: Transition to Adulthood*, adds significant insight to the relationship between youth and work. "This absorption of adolescent time by the school has contributed greatly to the dominance of the student role among the many roles that a young person might have. . . . The delaying of work until after the completion of schooling gives the adolescent no place in the work force."[8] This condition has created among the young an *occupational illiteracy* where they know little about the world of work; though, as Marcia Freedman pointed out at the 1960 White House Conference on Children and Youth, *work is still the psychological way that youth come of age in America.*

This basic issue is central to the message of career education. The systematic and institutionalized isolation of students from work apart from the classroom is a phenomenon of considerable importance to our society. Career education among its several goals seeks to redress this condition.

Because they are not able to find work when they leave school and are ignorant of work possibilities while in school, it is not surprising that some young people seek to escape the system. We have a situation where children do not know what work is for. Arnold Toynbee has contemplated this phenomenon, suggesting the reason youth have rejected material things is because work does not seem as meaningful or as real as it once was. The work that many people do does not show. "The farmer who brought in crops, the wheelwright or blacksmith, the clockmaker, they did meaningful tangible work, but the papers in the briefcase signify nothing."[9] Neither does the family head who "goes to the office," with or without a briefcase.

There are other issues that signal a change in our attitude toward work. We have larger welfare rolls, demands for shorter work weeks, increases in absenteeism and turnover. A Department of Labor conference report describes the problem as one involving workers with more education than was customary in the past, "whose occupational achievements do not equal their original aspirations."

Yet, while the *work ethic* appears to be in trouble for a variety of reasons, the *value of work* has not diminished. Work is being seen by many not as something needed to be done solely for the good of society or even as a source of income, but as experiences to be gained and tasks to be achieved for personal satisfaction and psychological fulfillment alone. "Most people know today that they don't have to work to survive."[10] Yet nearly all people work.

Men want to gain pleasure from their occupations. We are now able to ask: "Do you like your work?" This question was not a consideration to men in the Depression or to those coming of age in time of war. It was not a question for immigrants arriving in America at the turn of the century, desperately in need of any employment. It is only security and affluence that allow the luxury of choice. We are perhaps returning in a fashion to the circumstances of the Greeks and Romans, as citizens of our time, able to choose those things in which we wish to invest our energies.

When our parents and grandparents went to work, they did not presume that the work would necessarily be satisfying or meaningful. The workers of those generations did not ask if the work was relevant, interesting, or psychologically fulfilling. They only wanted to know if they would be paid and how much the pay might be. It is doubtful that they devoted much concern to the expectations for upward mobility. That was a matter to be left to individuals' competences, not the institutions' guarantees. Today's young worker does not accept this condition. These young people assess critically the impact of the work place and the nature of the work, on themselves and on the community. These workers feel that they have a right to find satisfaction on the job, and they are increasingly demanding that right.

Such a privilege—and it is a privilege as we compare ourselves with the rest of the world—is not without its difficulties. We are not only concerned with finding work, but finding work that is agreeable. A study by the Survey Research Center of the University of Michigan questioned 1533 American workers at all occupational levels. When these workers were asked how important they regarded some twenty-five aspects of work, they ranked in order of importance:

1. Interesting work
2. Enough help and equipment to get the job done
3. Enough information to get the job done
4. Enough authority to get the job done
5. Good pay
6. Opportunity to develop special abilities
7. Job security
8. Seeing the results of one's work

We have been helped in our relationship to work because our definition of work is broad and the possibilities for jobs are many. Today we also volunteer our labor, receive no pay, yet are rewarded by our own satisfaction at having done a job. Youth, housewives, retired technicians, and prominent corporate executives find their place in the work force of volunteerism in increasing scale and scope. This phenomenon may have very great significance for future definitions of work, and for future investment of human resources as a product of decreasing hours and days of compensated work.

Work in our society, however, has traditionally meant paid employment, but that term is too limiting. *Paid employment* only accounts for one measurable aspect and ignores the personal and social parts of work. Work has been defined as "an activity that produces something of value for other people";[11] but that, too, limits. We all engage in "work" that is pleasurable, personal, and necessary only for ourselves. Kenneth B. Hoyt defines work as "one's efforts aimed at the production of goods and/or services that will be beneficial to one's fellow human beings and/or to oneself."[12] This is a definition wide enough in its scope to fit our society and our lives. It also fits our purposes in searching the theme of career education.

Besides letting individuals contribute by their production, work also makes communities possible. Work brings people together, allows them to share skills and talents. It gives people a place and an identity in a community. "The work-place has always been a place to meet people, converse, and form friendships."[13]

Charles A. Reich in *The Greening of America* gives further insight to this theme:

> The new way of life proposes a concept of work in which quality, dedication and excellence are preserved, but work is non-alienating, is the free choice of each person, is integrated with a full and satisfying life, and expresses and affirms each individual being. [p. 19]

Work is also an achievement. It tests a person's competence. It gives a worker a sense of satisfaction, having mastered his job and his environment. A very large component of a person's feeling of importance and worth comes from his job. "If an individual cannot live up to the expectations he has of himself, and if his personal goals are not reasonably attainable, then his self-esteem, and with it his relations with others, are likely to be impaired."[14]

Once having mastered the job, the job then matters because the person becomes that occupation. "I'm a lawyer," we say. Or "I'm a truck driver." Identities are shaped by the occupation; life styles are shaped by what one does. Not to allow a person to work or to deny him the means to qualify himself for work is to cripple him. To equip him for satisfying and useful work is to give the means for lifelong pursuit of happiness.

We have moved from an age when almost everyone did comparable or similar work in order to make a living to an age of specialization and mechanization where "a person . . . had a job and traded his specialized efforts for goods and services which someone else produced."[15] There has also been a shift in the kinds of work man does. The mark of a man once was his physical power, the amount of labor he could endure; now his mark is his skills. By 1975, only 5 percent of the needs of the labor force will be left to the unskilled. It is almost impossible to exist in the United States today without a skill of some sort that can be bartered in the market place.

A variety of studies have indicated that people do not want to live useless lives. One recent Labor Department study on work orientations of welfare recipients found that people on welfare are as committed to the work ethic as middle-class people. "Work," as Charles Winick has written, "has a profound role in establishing a person's life space, emotional tone, family situation, object relations, and where and how he will live."[16]

The need to work has also been explained as the desire humans have to order their lives and to establish in their corner of the working world some structure they can control. This term *control* is important. It also has direct bearing upon the career education concept. "The greatest source of dissatisfaction in work results from the inability to make one's own sense of order prevail—the assembly-line is the best (or worst) example of an imposed and, for most workers, unacceptable structure."[17] Correspondingly, the classrooms of our schools and colleges should be critically examined under the spotlight of the assembly-line research. Career education must remove any lingering symptoms of assembly-line teaching or learning.

The problems in the work force appear to lie not in the work ethic (or work value) itself, but rather in the type of work. The new work force is sophisticated and challenging and will not tolerate insignificant labor. Social scientist Abraham Maslow has theorized that the needs of humans are hierarchal, and man has progressed from requiring basic wants of food and shelter to a desire for self-fulfillment.[18] Our educated work force today wants employment that is *meaningful*. They bring more learning, social and environmental concerns, and expectations to the work place, and they want to take more than money away from their jobs.

It is overwhelmingly clear from all of the worker studies done in the past twenty years that man wants to control his environment and feel that his work and he are important. When this is not possible, dissatisfaction sets in.

Dissatisfaction in the work force is not limited to blue-collar jobs. A study done by Robert Kahn in 1972 indicated that, in a cross-section of white-collar workers (including professionals), only 43 percent would choose again the work they were doing. Matters are worse within blue-collar fields. Only 24 percent of a cross-section of blue-collar workers would choose the same job again.[19]

The Health, Education, and Welfare study *Work in America* showed two major sources for job dissatisfaction.[20] The first was termed the anachronism of Taylorism. Frederick Winslow Taylor wrote *Principles of Scientific Management* earlier in this century. In this book, he fathered the time-and-motion studies that organized work into tasks to allow for maximum productivity. The worker's rewards depended on doing as he was told and increasing his output.

Taylor's philosophy of scientific management went something like this:

> For success, then, let me give one simple piece of advice beyond all others. Every day, year in and year out, each man should ask himself, over and over again, two questions. First, "What is the name of the man I am now working for?" and, having answered this definitely, then "What does this man want me to do, right now?"

Taylorism in industry—according to *Work in America*—is

anachronistic. We now have a work force that is educated, native-born, and affluence-minded. This is not an old-world labor force nor one of "rural and peasant origin and resigned to cyclical unemployment."[21] This is a work force that is challenging traditional values and institutions. And it is a work force of more than 85 million, with 22.5 million under the age of thirty. It is also a work force that must accommodate some 4 million maturing young people each year, not all of whom will work at economic tasks, but must live as housewives, students, and citizens at large.

It is fair to say that the system of free public schools, unique in America, has been at the root of our discontent with Taylorism. The liberating effect of learning has brought our younger generations to a realization that they *can* influence their environment and that knowing "who I am working for and what he wants of me" is not enough. Americans are equally concerned about "what do I want to be, and how do I get there?" Tocqueville stated well the implicit effect of the liberalizing influences of education a century ago:

> The evil which was suffered patiently as inevitable seems unendurable as soon as the idea of escaping from it crosses men's minds. All the abuses then removed call attention to those that remain, and they now appear more galling. The evil, it is true, has become less, but sensibility to it has become more acute.

Our modern work force is mobile, and workers regard a job as part of their lives but not their whole life. Recent strike negotiations in the auto industry, as an example, dealt with the issue of forced overtime at the plants. The workers did not want to work overtime on demand. "The incentive to work today is not fear and compulsion as in the past, but rather a search for participation and fulfillment."[22]

Industry is attempting to adjust productivity to accommodate the desires of this new worker, but the attempts so far have been modest and experimental. The work place must be made more humane for the worker. The work force needs more variety, more autonomy, and more intrinsic pride in the job. We who teach in and administer schools and colleges may well take a leaf from industry's self-scrutiny. If indeed the dichotomy of Taylor (what do they want me to do?) is being found anachronistic for adults, it may well be considered as applying to the young in classrooms. For all of our pious rhetoric concerning individualization, creativity, child-centered curricula, it is fair to say that many children, especially in high school, are still putting in time under the rules of Taylorism. Gooding notes, returning to industry, "The young worker is asking such questions as 'Why am I doing this?' and 'What is my life going to be?'[23] He writes that the young workers "are concerned fundamentally with exploring life and with actively living life, not with going through a set of predetermined motions that lead simply toward death." The central message of Gooding's *The Job Revolution* speaks to the schools. The schools are also work places, and the young in school are workers.

The *Work In America* study has pointed out that the automation revolution that was to increase the demand for skilled workers (while decreasing the need for humans to do the worst jobs of society) has not occurred. Jobs such as teacher aides, medical technicians, and computer key-punch operators have developed, but the automation revolution has not produced jobs with "professional" characteristics. The problem lies in our static occupational structure. We need to "infuse middle- and lower-level jobs with professional characteristics, particularly if we plan to continue offering higher and higher degrees of education to young people on the assumption that their increased expectations can be met by the world of work."

One day in the winter of 1972, while having my late afternoon quiet hour with HEW Secretary Elliot Richardson, I cited for him some recent data drawn from our National Center for Educational Statistics and from corresponding data from the Department of Labor. The conversation went something like this. "Elliot, you and I, and nearly everybody else are pushing hard to get our young people to finish high school and go to college. The mark of a 'good' high school is how many graduates enter college." He agreed, and kept on doodling on his yellow pad. I then showed him a digest of a Department of Labor forecast of the employment market. "It says here," said I, "that by 1980 only 20 percent of the manpower needs of the United States will require a four-year college education. Eighty percent of our work force will require something less than the A.B." He stopped doodling. (His doodles are extraordinarily artistic, symmetrical, and precise.) Then I said, "Elliot, we are now sending about 52 percent of our high school graduates to college, and pushing hard for more. Major federal statutes and budgets as well as President Nixon's firm policies are dedicated to making college available to all who want it."

He looked at me with his friendly inquisitor's look. "How many people are we graduating each year from high school?" "About three million," said I. "Figure one-and-a-half million entering higher education each year."

"How many is that by 1980?" asked the Secretary. "About twelve million with some college and about eight million completing college between now and 1980, provided the present rates remain stable," I said, "but we are pushing to improve upon the present rates, and get more people into college, so the figure may be higher by 1980."

"How many college graduates, at present rates, will be surplus to the manpower forecast by 1980?" he asked. "At a million graduates a year, for eight years, at 20 percent needed for the task," I calculated, "about eight hundred thousand a year for eight years, yield six and a half million, not to mention the years after 1980." These were projections of college-educated people whose education would not be needed in the work force.

The Secretary's response was concise: "Christ!"

This conversation had no immediate affect on federal policy, nor has it to this date. It was one of those speculative, idea-sharing sessions that raise issues, true or imagined. But it was a small vignette in the system of government in the early 1970s that helped to structure the base for viewing career education seriously. It leads to this very serious observation, which I offer without validating documentation. (See Chapter 4 for more precise data from the Department of Labor on this subject.)

We should view the future generations of learners in America as coming to maturity at a time *when society may not require all their intellectual and developed capacities in the work force*. But this does not mean that public policy should turn away from the encouragement of all individuals to seek all possible formal education. Career education does address the need for dignity and worth in all, regardless of the work place and the level of compensation. It does not discourage entry into successive levels of higher education. But it does suggest that higher education is by no means exclusively bound to occupational development. While realistic occupational development in postsecondary education is central to the career education philosophy, it is quite probable, in the light of the data cited above, that many people will enter the work force after college at levels of employment now (1974) viewed as beneath their qualifications. Part of the message of career education is to make the educational development of our young so rewarding in personal, cultural, civic, and humanistic ways that economically measured employment, or rank-status measured employment, will be only a part of our human fulfillment. I concluded the conversation with the Secretary by noting: "It is not unlikely that by 1980 we will have table waiters at the Hilton who are M.A.s in French or nutrition or social science, happily engaged in intellectual, civic, and social pursuits, quite apart from their work site. Whether or not they are happy depends a great deal on how our attitudes as a society and our respect for our fellow men and women, irrespective of their economic rewards, change with the reality of manpower changes."

I believe that we will necessarily mature as we view work, and that economically related work of all kinds will have a decreasing place in the value systems relating to prestige or self-esteem, and that other more satisfying and more prestige-related accomplishments by individuals—work, unrelated to economic differences—but still work, will prevail.

According to *Work in America*, the lack of opportunity for self-employment is a major problem. "Our economic, political and cultural system has fostered the notion of independence and autonomy, a part of which is the belief that a hardworking person, even if he has little capital, can always make a go of it in business for himself."[24] This was once quite true. In the middle of the nineteenth century, less than half of all employed people were wage and salary workers. But, by 1970, the number of wage and salary workers had jumped to 90 percent. Self-employment had dropped from 18 percent in 1959 to only 9 percent in 1970.

The growth in America points us toward large corporations and more employment by government. Such institutions "typically organize work in such a way as to minimize the independence of the workers and maximize control and predictability for the organization."[25] The organization is in conflict with the individual who seeks a much more democratic working environment and resists a job that he feels is dehumanizing and leads nowhere. Yet we do know that redesigning of the work place and the jobs themselves not only makes certain kinds of employment more livable, but it also increases productivity. Discontent with much of our present working conditions crosses all ethnic lines, exists for both sexes, and does not single out only minorities, though minorities are typically at the bottom of all scales of justice.

There appear to be creative ways to halt this spreading malignancy in the world of work. We must begin—in the many forms that it will take—to *humanize* work. The task belongs to business and industry to recognize workers as humans and provide the services, opportunities, and advancements that will support the individual worker, even for jobs that may at one time be satisfying but which can in time become dull. To begin to make the work more human, we need, at the very least, to have more flexibility on the job, in terms of hours and specific tasks; a greater voice by the workers in the decisions of the company; a sharing in the profits; and some feeling of pride, on the part of the employees, that their tasks contributed to the finished product. Industry is facing these issues. Industry is also giving strong support to career education, as will be noted in a subsequent chapter. The message here is to help young people in schools and colleges view work affirmatively, knowing that the work place is changing and that they can contribute affirmatively to that change.

A worker should have the feeling not that he holds a job, but that he is involved with a career. Too many people do not have the satisfaction of knowing that their occupation is really their career, having status and importance in itself. All work makes up a career, and an ideal career, as Kenneth Hoyt has written, "will

be generically defined as one that is of maximum meaningfulness
to the worker as part of his total lifestyle."[26] Careers will also be
different in that they stress certain elements, Hoyt noted:

> For one individual, this may be a career consisting of work
> that he most enjoys doing. For another, it may consist of
> work aimed almost entirely at meeting societal needs as
> he sees them. For some, the ideal career may be one that
> brings the greatest possible economic return. For most, it
> will probably be a mix of several work values that combine
> to bring personal meaning to their lives. It will, more and
> more, be an individual matter.

We know that as trends continue most people will have more
than one job, in a long career, possibly in different occupational
fields. We are confronted, then, with midcareer changes, for one
of the keys to worker satisfaction is the ability on the part of the
person to continue to learn and face new challenges on the job,
to "control his environment." We have a dynamic economy in the
United States. The introduction of new products and techniques,
the discarding of old methods, indicates that solely for economic
reasons workers should be systematically upgraded. And this
means—in our highly technical age—that the retraining for career
change needs to be done more than once and with more
sophistication. This is often a responsibility of the corporation.
But it is also a responsibility of the education system—at all levels.

We know from enough studies that workers—blue- and white-
collar both—have to advance on their jobs to gain psychological
fulfillment and self-esteem. This is now viewed, also, as rewarding to the corporation. Advancement may mean career change.
The rate of change and the mobility of our society, the longer
working life, and the higher aspirations of workers all indicate the
realities of midcareer change for most workers.

Midcareer change means midcareer retraining. Here again it is
necessary for industry to work closely with schools and colleges,
for retraining programs on any scale will need to utilize existing
institutions; and, with stabilized or declining enrollments, colleges particularly will be seeking new sources of students. There
is already strong evidence of the education system responding to
this need.

The swift emergence of the midcareer student is typified by Triton College, a public community college near O'Hare Airport in Chicago. Serving a cross-section of exclusive suburbs and inner-city Chicago neighborhoods, Triton's enrollment has leaped from 1243 students in 1965 to 16,681 in 1973. *Time* magazine (December 3, 1973) notes: "Triton . . . attracts adults who are trying to fill gaps in their education. More than half of the students attend part time . . . many combine their studies with full-time jobs."

Triton calls itself "The Career Center of the Midwest." At each level, including the liberal arts program as well as such utilitarian offerings as Auto Technology and Restaurant Management, the emphasis is on practical application of the learning going on. One instructor, according to *Time*, "a former Playboy Club manager who runs Triton's restaurant training school, says, 'There's no dabbling here. Everyone knows where he is going.'"

Extending the notion of "facilitating access," the College Entrance Examination Board's services are used to assess the unconventional students at Triton. *Time* notes, "Through the College Level Examination Program (CLEP), older students can get credit at Triton for learning acquired outside the classroom."

The *Work in America* study suggested a model for midcareer retraining that involves worker sabbatical programs to gain new skills:

> *Worker Self-Renewal*: A program that would provide training and a living allowance for a small number of workers who wish to move from declining industries or job categories into growing industries or higher skill levels (and would be made available to other workers only if there were a surplus of funds). This minimum effort would be designed to have the optimum effect on inflation; it would also have some positive effects on unemployment. The second type of Worker Self-Renewal Program would be closer to a true "sabbatical" program in that it would offer workers financial support to take off as much as a year for anything from skill upgrading to a liberal arts experience. It would be open to all workers and would be, perhaps, six times as expensive as the smaller program. It would have a much larger effect on unemployment and would bring social benefits to a much wider segment of the population.

European nations already have many such programs under way, claiming successful outcomes. The benefits are many: increasing skills and earning power for the individual, giving everyone a new chance in the working world; and providing industry with up-graded skilled workers. For people who "missed out" on their education—either in skills development or liberal arts—this is also another chance for self-improvement. Such midcareer train-ing programs would stretch out the learning process in our society. It would add a significant dimension to the face of postsecondary education. We would cease to have a front-loading system of education, and people would be able to advance with the dynamics of our economic and industrial system, learning new skills as technology changes and the de-mands for knowledge increase.

Career education asks that we set aside the traditional "years of schooling." It may well be that a young man or woman is ready and determined, for whatever reason, to enter the work force at age sixteen. This should not be viewed in the pejorative context of "dropout," provided the choice is rational and the individual is ready. On the other hand, the tradition of enrolling in postsec-ondary education during the years eighteen to twenty-two, or for graduate school, say from twenty-two to twenty-five, should be equally suspect. All learners and workers should be facilitated in leaving the formal system of instruction at any time, and reenter-ing it at any time. The society page would no longer report that the bridegroom "concluded his education at Princeton in 1948."

The inescapable relationship between *education* and *work* is the essence of the career education theme. Yet, as this chapter has shown, we have much to learn, and probably much to change, about that relationship. The National Institute of Education, established by the Education Amendments of 1972, had by mid-1973 developed a broad array of research tasks. The Institute has given career education a very high priority. A staff paper from NIE, published in June 1974 for internal policy planning within the Education Division of HEW, acknowledges the need for much more information on this subject:

An important goal for American education is to enable its

citizens to choose and advance in careers that reward them with acceptable levels of income and satisfaction. The purpose of NIE's research and development activities are (1) to better understand what education's role can be in reaching this goal and (2) to develop ways to improve an individual's chances for career success and satisfaction through education.

To meet this goal, four problem areas have been identified for purposes of research and development. These are:

A. To improve the understanding of the relationship between education and work.

B. To improve access to careers, specifically,

  1. to increase career opportunities for women and minorities

  2. to improve the quality of career choice for youth

  3. to improve the contribution of educational programs to the career development needs of children.

C. To improve progression in careers, specifically, the contribution of education in meeting the career needs of adults.

D. To improve career satisfaction.

The solutions to these problems are not in the hands of educators alone. Growth rates in the economy, availability of jobs and the policies and practices of the labor market are among the other factors to be considered. The Institute is studying what, if any, are the *most* appropriate outcome measures or methods to apply to improvements in the relationship between education and work. It is important that further research enable us to more precisely define the contributions of these various factors, to establish the causal/interactive relationships between them, and to develop the instruments which test the effectiveness of educational interventions.

The interdependence of work and formal education is reinforced by Peter Drucker in *The Age of Discontinuity: Guidelines to Our Changing Society*:

The systematic acquisition of knowledge, that is, organized formal education, has replaced experience—
acquired traditionally through apprenticeship as the
foundation for productive capacity and performance. . . .
[The] productivity of the worker will depend on this
activity to put to work concepts, ideas, theories—that is,
things learned in school, rather than skills acquired
through experience.

One of Georgia's leaders in the career education movement,
Dr. Gene Bottoms of the Georgia State Department of Education,
sums up the message of this chapter:

"A career is what you live to do, not what you do to live."

Growing Up to Work

As early as 1911, George Kerschensteiner, then Director of Education in Munich, Germany, wrote when touring the United States, "We are far too much inclined to assume, both in the old world and the new, that it is possible to educate a man without reference to some special calling. This assumption is erroneous."[1] Kerschensteiner and others saw the answer to preparation for work in vocational training:

> Vocational education was viewed as a means of conservation of our natural resources, of efficiency in the use of our human resources, and of each individual's effectiveness in the economic world leading to dignity and power in the social world. Drifting from school to job, and from job to job, was regarded as a costly human waste that the nation could ill afford.

Among the young there is still the belief in the American dream. The cynics to the contrary notwithstanding, most young people today want to work, believe in work, and find work satisfying.

Daniel Yankelovich, in several national attitude studies of college students from 1968 to 1971, found that 79 percent believed that commitment to a meaningful career was an important part of a person's life.[2]

Other assessments of student attitudes, reinforced by parent attitudes, place the occupational component of education very high among our society's expectations. The Gallup survey conducted annually for Phi Delta Kappa revealed what Gallup called an extraordinary degree of consensus around the objectives of career education (see Chapter 1).

Yet the attitude of the young people toward work has changed in important ways. Yankelovich found that in 1968 over half—56 percent—of all students indicated that they didn't mind the future prospect of being "bossed around" on the job, but by 1971 only one out of three students—36 percent—saw themselves willingly submitting to such authority. Yankelovich also found that students surveyed in 1960 had shifted their values from job security and opportunity for promotion to valuing, in 1970, "freedom to make own decisions" and "work that seems important to me."

What is clear from these surveys is that young people, not unlike their elders, as noted in Chapter 3, want to take more control of their lives. They want to achieve on their own terms, having set standards that are high and demanding. These are not young people evading responsibility, but young people asking for more responsibility. They are, unfortunately, ahead of the times in which they live and are frustrated in their schools, in their job search, and on the job.

The Social Research Group of George Washington University under an HEW grant analyzed the present conditions of transition from school to work.[3] They observed, after examining many pieces of data, "the age of adolescence has been recognized generally as a time of uncertainty and frustration, at least in advanced modern societies. But there is an increase in the expressed intensity of these frustrations as evidenced by . . . social phenomena (increasing drug usage, displays of campus unrest, reprisals of military service, runaways from home, and the growth of a distinct youth culture)." These suggest that change is urgently needed in the institutions used in the past to assist young people in making the transition from youth to adulthood. Changes are not only needed for the young people themselves to lead better lives, but for the national well-being.

James Coleman, predicting a changing role for the schools, in response to the needs of "youth in transition," urges a more flexible learning environment than that presently implied in the wholly individualistic institutional modes, implicit in the modern classroom. "Working with others, under the discipline imposed by a common task and purpose—should provide both a direction to life and the motivation to learn how to implement it. . . . This principle does not mean that new educational institutions should neglect the child's learning. It means rather that a much broader conception of learning is necessary: a conception in which the roles, constraints, demands and responsibilities of adulthood in a complex society are central; a conception that includes general strategies to make use of the environment to accomplish one's goals."[4]

The emergence of *youth* as a force in all our lives deserves some comment. It was Kenneth Keniston who first drew attention to the "phenomenon of youth" in 1970, describing it as a "period of life after adolescence and before full adulthood."[5] Youth have become important in our recent history mainly because of their numbers, combined with the social and political motivations that have moved us to take them seriously. Between 1890 and 1960 the population of ages fourteen to twenty-four in the U.S. rose from 14.2 million to 26.7 million. This was an increase of 13.8 million, resulting from the 1946 baby boom. According to the U.S. Bureau of the Census, every other decade of this century the proportion of persons fourteen to twenty-four relative to those twenty-five to sixty-four has declined, and it will decline again in the succeeding decades of this century. But in the decade of the sixties, the proportion of the fourteen to twenty-four group—and their absolute numbers—increased enormously.

This population of youth, possibly by reason of its size and the attention that size attracted, began to look for direction not outwardly, to their institutions such as school and family and church, but toward each other. No longer did one emerging generation necessarily adopt manners and habits from an older age group. Regardless of whether they were students or workers, youth took their cues from each other. This affected dress, grooming, hair styles, social and moral values, and recreational trends, to name a few.

These young people are growing up in a highly "crowded" climate. The sheer numbers in their age group places pressures on the individual and the institutions where these young people occupy themselves: the schools and colleges, and the work places, the job market, the playgrounds, and, for many, their homes. This has been occurring at a time when schools themselves were becoming larger. The Conant Report of 1959 called for the elimination of small high schools on the premise that they could not economically provide the specialized courses appropriate to contemporary learning needs. Many communities had no choice but to pack their high schools with more children than intended. Double sessions became common in the late sixties, with all the attendant adversities of "crowdedness."

Colleges, too, were growing. A college before the Civil War was considered large if it had five hundred students. By 1900 a large university enrollment was only a few thousand; in 1960 large campuses had 20,000 students and many were larger. But then the college population jumped from 3.8 million to 8.5 million, and we had multicampus systems such as Pennsylvania State University with over fifty thousand students; Northeastern University with forty thousand; and two-year institutions such as Chicago City College with forty thousand. Nearly half of all college students—4 million students—attend only 230 large institutions.

The growth of these institutions was driven by the size of this segment of the population and the belief by parents and young people that a college education was the only way to prepare for a "good" life. But, according to studies on the job outlook for college graduates by the U.S. Department of Labor and by the Carnegie Commission on Higher Education, we know that, between 1974 and 1980, approximately 9.8 million people will graduate from college, but only 7.3 million will be required to fill jobs replacing those college-educated men and women who will leave the job market by 1980. Having to look elsewhere for work will be 2.5 million college graduates whose college training will not be the specific need of the employer, except for newly created roles for the college graduate.

Looking at statistical information available today, we can make a few cautious predictions of what the occupational outlook in higher education will be in this decade. These generalizations are drawn from current Department of Labor studies with the comment that manpower forecasting is a very slippery business.

- The job opportunities will remain relatively steady or improve somewhat in the professions of medicine, law, engineering, dentistry, but the increasing competition for the available school openings will rule out any except the outstanding student. These professional graduate opportunities, however, represent no more than 9 percent of the new openings for college-trained people and require several years of postgraduate training. The competition for professional training in these areas will intensify as a result of increased interest from students in other fields with deteriorating opportunities.

- One field that will expand is that of health-care services. A substantial number of these jobs will require college-level preparation. The college bias of the medical profession will cause many jobs to have this requirement, but the rising costs of health care will push for doing just as much as possible with noncollege paraprofessionals.

- The new opportunities in teaching will vary by subject area, but generally they will decrease in the 1970s. The lower birth rate and its effect on elementary school-age groups will make the prospects for elementary school teachers the poorest of all. In 1973 alone, 300,000 graduates were looking for teaching jobs; the oversupply of high school teachers will soon be almost as large as for elementary teachers.

- At the college level, the U.S. Bureau of Labor Statistics predicts an average number of 22,000 teaching openings per year, but the annual number of masters' and doctors' degrees awarded in 1972 was over 273,000. There were over 34,000 doctoral degrees awarded, and at least half of the recipients traditionally seek teaching positions in colleges or universities where surpluses already are a serious economic and morale burden on trustees and administrators.

- Even though this oversupply in advanced degrees varies widely from one department to another, the oversupply is clear. Perhaps the most serious imbalance will be in the relation of Ph.D.s to available jobs. This, in turn, will encourage administrators to replace teachers having lesser credentials with Ph.D.s or hire Ph.D.s for new openings, thus reducing the opportunities for those holding master's and bachelor's degrees.

- The opportunities for college graduates in business management jobs will show some growth in the next decade. Although the Carnegie study and the U.S. Bureau of Labor Statistics predict a 15 percent net growth in management jobs between 1970 and 1980, in the business sector this is viewed as too high by some social scientists. Most of the net growth in the number of jobs is likely to occur in specialist, technical work, and many of these will not require a college education. The pressures of business competition and the need for efficient, economic operations will push managers to look for new ways to keep costs down. One way is to keep management costs down. Although the economy will grow to meet the needs of a growing population and expanding consumer buying, technology and efficient management will slow the growth of management jobs.

Most of the growth in business job opportunities will occur in nonmanagement work of a technical, service nature which requires a high school or postsecondary technical education short of a degree.

What will very likely happen is that employers will upgrade the educational requirements of "other" jobs and hire more college graduates for work not now classified as requiring a college education. The data collected imply that we may be able to digest more highly educated people in our economy by redefining the credentials for employment, if not the job itself, and thus, with mirrors, make the content of work what we say it is. This regrettable turn of events, while possibly ameliorating the college-graduate surplus, will offset the gains made in recent years to remove artificial educational barriers to jobs—especially those affecting the poor, minorities, and women.

To add artificial educational requirements to jobs creates poor morale for all workers—noncollege and college graduates alike. It also establishes discriminating employment requirements for those people lacking the degree but able to do the work. Further, the jobs become filled with college graduates who have greater expectations than can be realized by the work. We then have such situations as this, a report from a young college graduate who wrote to me as Commissioner of Education to plead for swift progress in advancing career education, especially for the colleges:

> I didn't go to school for four years to type. I'm bored; continuously humiliated. They sent me to Xerox school for three hours. . . . I realize that I sound cocky, but after you've been in the academic world, after you've had your own class (as a student teacher) and made your own plans, and someone tries to teach you to push a button—you get pretty mad.

Even if business and industry wanted to provide challenging and interesting work for all their employees, there are limits to how far they can or should go in upgrading the educational requirements of jobs. It is just not possible to "fit" all college graduates —at the rate they are being turned out—into business and industry as we know it today. College enrollment ten years ago was 3.8 million; it leaped to 8.1 million in 1971 and, while leveling off, remains very high. In 1953, only 48 percent of the high school students finishing at the top quarter of their classes entered college. By 1960, that figure had reached 80 percent. The proportion of the college-enrolled group, as well as growing in absolute numbers, has risen in less than a decade from one-third to 45 percent of the college-age population.

The reason in large part is one of *credentials*, both economic and social. We have created a widely held belief that only by way of the bachelor's degree can a person be truly whole, truly worthy. Colleges quite properly responded vigorously to this expectation, building and hiring and expanding curricula through the teeming sixties. The mid-seventies find many colleges searching urgently for enough students to sustain the budget. The spring of 1974 is a time of faculty curtailment and shortening sail for many colleges and universities. Some young people have sought a different way from their elders to continue "growing up to work." I think the colleges will respond to this, not merely to attract students but also to serve students more realistically, while sustaining their academic values. In *Education and Jobs: The Great Training Robbery*, Ivar Berg cites a speech by James W. Kuhn that outlines the problem at the postsecondary level:

> For those who want to do more than pass through to a career . . . college has much to offer for its cost. The offering takes the form of perspectives, understanding, and insights rather than lucrative techniques and productive skills. . . . [However] not all persons find such an education to their taste or in their interests; some may wish to pursue a career as immediately as possible, postponing until later, or doing without, the contribution education might make to their lives. At present, choice is denied. Entrance to a career (in our economic system) is through college, where schooling all too often is masked as education. Would not the colleges, teachers, students and those who look forward to professional careers be better served if other entry ways were open, available, and used?[6]

We also get indications that business is beginning to look "elsewhere" for employees just as students are looking "elsewhere" for their development. The Bell System, for example, cut back its college recruitment program 40 percent in 1971 and 13 percent more in 1972. Although this was partly the result of the economic downturn of 1969–1971, it also reflects a reappraisal of how many college graduates are needed by the industry, and indicates a lower level of college recruiting in the future. It also reflects an enlightened management policy that pushes the Bell System to help the disadvantaged.

Students of college age are also looking "elsewhere" for different types of advanced training after high school. Students are taking a different view of the occupational importance of a college education. Increasing numbers of students are attending two-year colleges and proprietary schools, taking courses that lead directly to careers in particular fields. There were about 2600 four-year institutions and two-year community and junior colleges in the U.S. enrolling about 9 million students in 1973. This is more than double the number in 1963. To the increasing concern of conventional colleges, there are now an estimated 9000 proprietary schools (not all accredited) enrolling up to three million students, and drawing a gross revenue of about $1.5 billion. These schools are *all* engaged in occupational teaching.

Thus we find that, while students and society want schools and colleges, *in addition to other institutional objectives*, to equip the young for work, there remains a gap between the expectations and the performance of our educational system. There is little doubt that the history of education expresses a central expectation that the schools shall provide significant support for occupational training. This has been what vocational education sought to achieve, as clearly expressed in the literature and the great legislative thrusts of 1919, 1963, 1968, and 1972. And for those relatively few students who have persisted in the traditional vocational courses in high school, the record is reasonably satisfactory. I say "relatively few," for if we set aside the students counted in home economics classes and typing classes, who are not planning to develop their economic vocations around these fields, we can count perhaps less than 10 percent of the high school enrollment in fully structured vocational programs. (This is not to diminish the importance of home economics and typing, for these elective offerings in high school provide useful skills and personal enrichment for the student, quite apart from a vocation.) But the numbers of young people developed for occupations in the high schools remain short of our society's hopes, as expressed by the cited Gallup survey. Current figures from USOE indicate a total enrollment of about 3 million students in "gainful employment" vocational programs, against a population of 16.5 million in the high school age group.

Having looked at the limited numbers enrolled in vocational education, let us look at the other parts of the high school. For some years I have denounced the general curriculum, and have sometimes felt quite alone in my discontent with that pedagogical euphemism which engages fully 30 percent of our young people and up to 60 or 70 percent in some of our big cities. I was reassured to find no less an authority than Fred Wilhelm, former Executive Secretary, Association for Supervision and Curriculum Development, taking equal or stronger exception:

> One of the best things that could happen in American education would be for every secondary school to abolish the despicable general education curriculum, and set out to meet the needs of the group now held in custody therein.[7]

After the vocational curriculum and the general, there follows in some schools the business curriculum, though this is frequently contained under the *vocational* title, causing our statistical data to skew. But remaining is the college preparatory curriculum, now reaching over half the young people. Some of the students in the college curriculum have goals and aspirations for purposeful career development in college. Most do not, for they have had little chance, except by coincidence, to learn much about the world of work. All of these conditions—the low number of vocational students, the ill-served general students, and the career-illiterate college preparatory students—are what career education addresses at the elementary and secondary school level.

Students of the history and philosophy of education still view with considerable respect the Seven Cardinal Principles prescribing the objectives of secondary education in the United States. Developed under the auspices of the National Education Association in 1913–1918 by scholars, the principles establish the following objectives to be served by our high schools:

1. health

2. command of fundamental processes

3. worthy home membership

4. vocation

5. citizenship

6. worthy use of leisure

7. ethical character

We may quibble today, sixty years later, with the precise meanings of these objectives, and we may question the degree to which the schools have addressed adequately their implicit charges. But there is little doubt that vocation was, and remains, one of the Cardinal Principles.

As long ago as 1907, Frank Parsons, generally accepted as originator of the counseling and guidance concepts in American education, declared: "Book work should be balanced with industrial education; and working children should spend part time in [cultural and scientific curricula]."[8]

The work of Stephens in 1970, in drawing upon the work of Parsons in 1907 and 1909, brings special insights to the circumstances we face today. They appear to be not greatly different from those which stirred Parsons to write in *Choosing a Vocation*:

> First, a clear understanding of yourself, aptitude, abilities, interests, resources, limitations and other qualities. Second, a knowledge of the requirements and conditions of success, advantages and disadvantages, compensation, opportunities and prospects in different lines of work. Third, true reasoning on the relation of these two groups of facts.[9]

Edwin L. Herr of Pennsylvania State University has constructed an excellent synthesis of the evolution of vocational education into what is now the career education concept.[10] This work was prepared under a grant from the U.S. Office of Education in 1971 and 1972, through the Center for Vocational and Technical Education at the Ohio State University. Since I drew heavily on this work in furthering career education policies and programs in Washington, I shall do so in these pages, trying to give proper attribution without cumbersome footnoting. Those who seek a brief and lucid statement of the scholarly and historical base for career education should see Herr's *Review and Synthesis of Foundations for Career Education* (Washington, D.C.: U.S. Government Printing Office, March 1972; see ERIC Bibliography).

Returning for a moment to Parson's admonitions, as he put the first words to "vocational guidance," it is useful to examine the contemporary expressions of scholars who were not likely to have come under Parson's tutelage. The National Institute of

Education brought together in 1972 researchers in the social sciences not steeped in the customs, literature, and practices of conventional educators (and surely not Parsons), and laid out the statement of the career education design as they saw it, afresh (compare Chapter 3):

> An important goal for American education is to enable its citizens to choose and advance in careers that reward them with acceptable levels of income and satisfaction . . .
>
> - to improve the understanding of the relationship between education and work
> - to improve access to careers . . .
> - to improve progression in careers . . .
> - to improve career satisfaction

While today's scholars and planners use different words from those of Parsons in 1907, we are tempted to note *Plus ça change, plus c'est la même chose.*

Herr, drawing upon Stephens, has traced the early impulses of career education to a national joint meeting of the National Society for the Promotion of Industrial Education and the National Vocational Guidance Association in 1914 in Grand Rapids, Michigan, where the keynote address declared that the schools should be refocused to provide for *each learner* a "conception of his industrial obligations and opportunities." The message called for the "entire curriculum [to be] shot-through-and-through with the meaning, history, and the possibilities of vocation."

John Dewey addressed the same 1914 convention, undoubtedly reflecting his observations and experiences at his occupations-oriented Laboratory School of the University of Chicago: a democratic education, he said, required no "separation of vocational training from academic training."

Many other citations from the early years of this century can be offered to make it clear that career education, by whatever name, is not a Johnny-come-lately to American educational theory. The term is new, but many of the ideas which the concept embraces have been around a long time, albeit dormant for the most part.

There are reasons for the failure of the schools to hear Dewey,

Parsons, Whitehead, Conant, and many others as they pled for unity between academic and occupational teaching and learning. Stephens gives serious weight to a decision made in 1918 by NEA which established singular *crafts* as the direction for vocational education to move, as distinct from the more generalized and comprehensive *technical education*. Further divorcement was encouraged, according to Parsons, when NEA established professional policies pointing the guidance counselor toward "educational" objectives rather than vocational objectives. This dichotomy remains strong today, and not necessarily for reason of any insidious determination by NEA. In fact, NEA has given formal and supportive endorsement to the career education concept, and has participated in its advancement during the early 1970s.

But the profession of counseling has been driven, especially in post–World War II years, to turn its principal energies to getting young people into college. That has been what parents, especially the more powerful and influential parents, wanted; that has, therefore, been what the principals and school superintendants wanted; that was what the more intellectually attractive students wanted. Therefore, counselors, like most people, do what they are expected to do in a system that rewards those who comply. The drive for college entry is clearly a product of social values which have, for a variety of reasons, intensified over the past twenty years. Our percentage of high school graduates going on to postsecondary education was about 30 percent in 1950. The latest figures from USOE indicate about 60 percent.

Today's counselors are mindful of the problem which career education raises, not only for their own value system, but for the necessary additional professional development that the larger task demands of them. Writing in *Guideposts* (November 23, 1973), the journal of the National Vocational Guidance Association, Frank Burnett states:

> Many early leaders of our Association are identified as pioneers in the research and practices that have provided the base for career education. . . . Contemporary leaders were writing and teaching these concepts long before they were popularized by the speeches and writings of Marland. . . . Counsellors have acquired a fresh identity

> as members of the career education team. . . . Other
> American Personnel and Guidance Association directors
> are also involved in the groundswell for career education.
> . . . The effective implementation of career education
> programs will require that counsellors join with teachers,
> administrators, colleagues in non-school settings, and the
> general public in placing a collective shoulder behind
> career education.

I have sought in these references to past and present theorists
and observers of American education to draw a profile of how we
have arrived at the point where we now are in helping our young
people "grow up to work." While much of the history of
vocational education has focused on the secondary schools, the
message implicit from the literature is addressed to all levels of
education. This includes elementary education, as well as postsecondary.

"Growing up to work" is not an objective to be limited to the
lower schools. Historically, both in America and abroad, higher
education had its origins and reasons for being in the development of individuals for vocations. In a recent essay, Stephen Bailey,
Vice President, American Council on Education, observed the
unity of vocation and the liberal arts in Harvard's early years.[11] He
notes that Harvard was not only a theological school, but "the
founders provided for the teaching of the arts, sciences, and
good literature as well as theology. But educating clergy was
surely the essential purpose of the early Harvard. . . . Seventy
percent of Harvard graduates in its first century went into the
ministry." This was career education at the postsecondary level.

But between the time of Harvard's founding in 1636 and the
present, there has developed in our colleges and universities an
isolation of occupational offerings from the more respected
academic offerings. While a number of very important colleges
and universities are now attempting to redress this dichotomy,
the separation is deep and pervasive in most institutions. Clearly,
the professional schools, such as law, medicine, and the like, *are*
dedicated to occupational development. But here again, as in the
stigmatized and isolated vocational schools of the secondary
system, the isolation of "pure" occupational learning from gener-

al education is, I believe, dangerous snobbery, now being addressed by some universities.

W. Theodore de Bary, Provost of Columbia University, has given much attention in recent years to the elevation of the general education curriculum in harmony with occupational teaching. Columbia is undertaking a major curricular reform under de Bary's leadership. He writes:

> A liberal education is viewed as consisting equally of general education and specialized (occupational) training, the two complementing one another from the freshman year of college to even the level of post-doctoral training.[12]

Richard Millard, higher education specialist with the Education Commission of the States, is even more insistent in his criticism of the colleges and universities for their disdain for occupational education. Acknowledging recent change in community colleges, Millard observed:

> . . . colleges not only ignored vocational and technical education [in their curricula] but so influenced the secondary curriculum that vocational and technical programs became second class programs in the secondary schools. . . . As states and as a nation, we have become progressively more aware today of the central role vocational education must play in the total educational picture if we are to meet the diverse needs of citizens and the manpower needs of the country.[13]

Millard notes the compelling call for *change* and flexibility in higher education. He offers thoughtful guidelines:

> (a) I suggest that the key to reasonable and effective flexibility to meet the educational needs at all levels for the citizens of the country in the last quarter of a century may well lie in the very concept of vocational education itself. It is too easy for some of us in higher education to forget that the origins of higher education in the medieval universities related to vocation, conceived of not simply as skill preparation but as preparation for a career, what one does with a life, a "calling."

(b)   Putting vocation or preparation for a career back as
the central aim of education, a number of things begin to
fall into perspective and some of the broad dichotomies
drawn in the past begin to disappear.

(c)   The recognition that the aim of education is vocation
suggests equal involvement in vocational or occupational
education whether one chooses the life of the secretary,
the classical scholar, the inhalation therapist, the auto
mechanic, the social worker, the medical doctor, the
lawyer, the electronics technician, the sociologist, the
engineer, or the philosopher. This does not invalidate
other aims of education such as personal enlightenment,
social development, exploration of the realms of knowledge, even adjustment to or search for identity, but does
give them point and direction. It does do away with the
pseudoelitism that separates white-collar workers from
blue-collar workers, the scholar or research scientist from
the businessman, the professional from the technician,
and recognizes that what all of us are or should be
engaged in is finding the most effective way to utilize and
develop our abilities in a changing society for our mutual
advantage.

(d)   Recognition of vocation or career as central does
away with invidious comparison among institutions and
programs. It calls for the kind of diversified educational
system which will in fact provide the range of opportunities commensurate with human interest and needs and
with societal demands. It means that the full range of
education is concerned with the vital business of societal
renewal and development.

(e)   The aim is to open doors—not to close them. In the
context of "vocation" the arts and sciences may be as
integral to the life of the dental technician as some
knowledge of mechanics may be to the budding philosopher.

Millard's observations, which I have quoted at length quite
deliberately, are all the more important for reasons of who he is
and what experiences and disciplines he brings to his task.
Basically a philosopher and former chairman of the Department
of Philosophy at Boston University, Dr. Millard has served as the
University's Dean of the College of Liberal Arts and Dean of the

Graduate School. He now occupies the very strategic post of Director of Higher Education Services in the Education Commission of the States.

These screenings of testimony from the past, fortified by contemporary observations by respected educators, offer a setting for a futurist statement by Nell Eurich. Writing in the present tense as of the year 2001, she says:

> Our society today could not conceive the restrictions formerly placed on the educative process. Young people do not automatically go on to college. Congress enacted a program financed from public and private funds that provided for work experience for all youth. They gain life experience in a variety of ways: they serve as aides to teachers, doctors, nurses, lawyers, engineers, architects, public officials, and professionals of many types. It was like a rebirth of the apprenticeship in the Medieval Ages.
>
> Both the students and the nation have gained from this program. Many youths find the work experience satisfying, and remain with it. They no longer feel the same pressure to go on to college immediately, and they know they can study at any time in their lives. Industry and business corporations provide many opportunities, some of our best learning materials, and the technical means for their use. *Career education—in which business cooperates with colleges and universities as well as communities —is the answer for many.*
>
> This has helped define the objectives for the liberal arts college. No one now expects that study in liberal arts will increase personal income or get you a better job. Instead, those studying in these fields realize that the purpose is thoughtful self-development, aesthetic pleasure, sensitivity toward others and man's goals, a greater understanding of institutions in society and how they work, and objective judgment developed to cope with crucial issues.[14]

As the ideas and the testing of ideas on the subject of career education went forward during 1971 and 1972, notably in several bureaus of the Office of Education, across town, quartered in the Old Executive Office Building, a different set of people with a different mission were at work. The President's Science Advisory

Committee, working under the authority of the Office of Science and Technology, was engaged in its very impressive work, *Youth: Transition to Adulthood*. The findings of the committee voice extraordinary, though fortuitous, compatibility with the career education concept. As is so often true in Washington, there was very limited exchange between the two agencies until late in the Committee's period of activity. Nonetheless, it is noteworthy that a high order of congruity prevails between the two efforts, particularly as we examine the issue of "growing up to work."

James S. Coleman, Chairman of the President's Science Advisory Committee, writes in his introduction to the report:

> So long as school was short, and merely a supplement to the main activities of growing up, this mattered little. But school has expanded to fill the time that other activities once occupied, without substituting for them. These activities of young persons included the opportunities for responsible action, situations in which he came to have authority over matters that affected other persons, occasions in which he experienced the consequences of his own actions, and was strengthened by facing them—in short, all that is implied by "becoming adult" in matters other than gaining cognitive skills.

> Nevertheless, as these activities outside the school dwindled, society's prescription for youth has been merely more of what was prescribed for them as children: more school. It appears reasonable now, however, to look a little more carefully at the task of becoming adult, to ask not the quantitative question, "How much more schooling?," but the qualitative one: "What are appropriate environments in which youth can best grow into adults?" It appears reasonable now, not merely to design new high schools and colleges, but to design environments that allow youth to be more than students. That these environments will include schooling does not lessen the difference of this task from that of creating more schooling. It is the task, no more, no less, of creating the opportunities for youth to become adults in all ways, not merely intellective ones.

> This panel has attempted to open the discourse which can inform attempts at such reconstruction of environments for youth. It asks both what attributes are necessary to

become an adult, and what institutions can fill these needs. It cannot provide final answers, but it asks urgently that we get started with better answers than increased schooling has so far provided.[15]

I have attempted to demonstrate that the American people want their schools and colleges to equip our young for occupations, as well as to equip them for cultivated, intellectual, and humane lives. The countervailing forces, of which there are many, have so isolated academic learning from occupational development, at *all* levels of instruction, that a major reform of the system is proposed. This reform now carries the name *career education*. The name is not important. Subsequent chapters will develop more precisely what we mean by the term. But it can be stated concisely that the total education system must, in addition to many other tasks, inescapably help young people "grow up to work."

5

Costs and Benefits

It would be a mistake to conclude from the preceding chapter that all is wrong with education, from kindergarten through the universities. The critics and observers I have cited are not antagonists hostile to our system. They are part of it, as I am. From Parsons to Dewey to Conant to Bailey to Millard to Coleman we see a constant voice of educational reform, spoken knowingly, constructively, and with passionate concern for orderly change. The change points up to a system that will provide occupational development; reality in the learning environment; humane consideration for the individual's right, knowing and well-informed, to shape his own destiny—and to provide these educational measures in harmony with formal academic learning.

Education has become the nation's largest enterprise. It now costs $96.3 billion a year, and by 1980 the price will exceed $115 billion. In 1974 this surpasses defense outlays, previously our largest expenditure, by some $15 billion. Of the gross national product, almost 8 percent is devoted to education. This is twice the share of the GNP that was afforded twenty years ago. There is no question about the value that Americans attach to education.

The cost of elementary and secondary education is about $61.6 billion annually to teach 51 million children. The per-pupil cost is $1200 a year, or about $14,000 to get each child through twelve years of schooling. College costs are now between $2000 and $4000 a year.

And what do parents and other taxpayers get for this very large investment?

In Galbraith's "Affluent Society," we in the United States, representing 6 percent of the world's population, consume between 30 percent and 40 percent of the world's production of goods and services. "Today, 98 percent of all households in the United States wired for electricity have a TV set. Not quite as many have flush toilets and bathtubs or showers. Four out of every 5 households own a car and have telephone service. Nearly all of the wired homes have a refrigerator, and 95 percent have a washing machine. In most of the countries of the world only the richest 2 percent or 3 percent of all households are able to own a car and refrigerator and TV set."[1]

It is not mere coincidence that the nation which dedicated itself long ago to a free public education for all its people should enjoy the economic benefits that education, along with other natural and human resources, has provided. "According to economist Edward F. Denison, improvements in the *quality* of the labor force contributed 23 percent of the total growth of national production during the period 1929–1957. This sizable contribution was the direct result of workers having more schooling than workers had before this period."[2] Denison projected that education would contribute almost the same proportion of economic growth during the period 1960–1980.

Most of us are familiar with the generalization which states that increased education has a direct correlation with increased earnings. While some very recent writers, Christopher Jencks for instance, have questioned this proposition, it remains a widely held and respected position by most economists. It is therefore useful to examine the present condition of completed education levels in relation to the work force. The Department of Labor has examined this relationship and projected it to 1980:

YEARS OF SCHOOLING COMPLETED BY CIVILIAN LABOR FORCE

Years of schooling completed	Average 1967–1969	Projected 1980
	% distribution	
ELEMENTARY		
Less than 8 years	10.3%	5.8%
8 years	11.0	6.1
HIGH SCHOOL		
1 to 3 years	17.6	16.8
4 years	36.4	42.4
COLLEGE		
1 to 3 years	11.0	12.0
4 years or more	13.7	16.9
TOTAL LABOR FORCE	100.0%	100.0%
SUMMARY		
Less than 4 years of high school	38.9	28.7
4 years high school or more	61.1	71.3
TOTAL LABOR FORCE	100.0%	100.0%

As a close companion to the foregoing table, let us examine the data, also from the Department of Labor, which reveal the correspondence between education and earnings. Separate tables cite the circumstances of men and women in the civilian labor force. While I am sure these tables reflect accurately the historic disparities in earnings among different levels of schooling, there is some current evidence that the gap between those with a college degree and those with only a high school diploma may be closing.

Considerable attention is being paid currently by business and industry to investment in *human* capital, as distinct from other capital investments. This means encouraging personal development of the work force through education and training. "Economists who have studied investment in schooling in the United

ESTIMATED LIFETIME EARNINGS, FOR MALES,
BY YEARS OF SCHOOLING COMPLETED

Years of Schooling Completed	Lifetime Earnings	Difference In Lifetime Earnings[a]	Earnings as % of H. S. Graduates
Less than 8 years	$189,000	–	55%
8 years	247,000	+$56,000	72
1 to 3 years of high school	284,000	+ 37,000	83
4 years of high school	341,000	+ 57,000	100
1 to 3 years of college	394,000	+ 53,000	115
4 years of college	508,000	+114,000	149
5 or more years of college	587,000	+ 79,000	172

Source: U.S. Bureau of the Census, *Current Population Reports,* Series P-60, No. 56, p. 9.

Note: Subjects range from 18 years to death; estimates are based on 1966 dollars.

[a]Compared with group listed immediately preceding.

ESTIMATED LIFETIME EARNINGS, FOR FEMALES,
BY YEARS OF SCHOOLING COMPLETED

Years of Schooling Completed	Lifetime Earnings	Difference In Lifetime Earnings	Earnings as % of H. S. Graduates
Less than 8 years	$167,000	–	67%
8 years	184,000	+$17,000	74
1 to 3 years of high school	213,000	+ 29,000	85
4 years of high school	249,000	+ 36,000	100
1 to 3 years of college	312,000	+ 63,000	125
4 years of college	326,000	+ 14,000	131
5 or more years of college	436,000	+110,000	175

Source: U.S. Bureau of Census as quoted in Herman P. Miller, *Rich Man, Poor Man,* 1971, p. 178.

Note: Lifetime earnings calculated from age 25 to death for year-round, full-time women workers. Estimates are based on 1966 dollars.

States estimate that the rates of return for the eighth year of school are about 30 percent—approximately 3 times as high as average returns on non-human capital. Rates of return on the fourth year of high school (leading to a diploma) are estimated to be about 15 percent. And rates of return on investments in the fourth year of college also are 15 percent. These rates of return, based on estimates as measured by earnings, suggest that in the future it might be wise to place more emphasis on investment in human resources than in machinery and equipment—exactly what many economists and manpower experts are recommending today. A word of caution—the estimates reported are still being checked and are subject to change. Nevertheless, the tentative judgment clearly is that investment in human capital is a wise use of economic resources promising big payoffs, both for the individual and for the economy as a whole."[3]

Clearly, one of the goals of career education is to insure that all persons leave the education system qualified both in skills and attitudes to enter the work force productively and happily. This leads us to the matter of unemployment as a national problem of continuing urgency. While career education was not conceived, as some have suggested, as a hasty political response to unemployment, it should have a significant long-term influence on reducing unemployment. But given the implicit inverse connection between schooling and unemployment, the following two tables[4] are illuminating, though not surprising.

This evidence of incompatibility between people and jobs, on the order of 5 or 6 percent of our work force, is bad enough. But even worse is the persistent disparity affecting minority employees. In better times, or worse times, it seems that the minority citizens are "twice as unemployed" as whites. While career education is not intended to respond specifically to the educational needs of Blacks, Chicanos, Puerto Ricans, and American Indians, it *is* intended to respond to the needs of *all* young people in all schools and colleges. It must follow that given an equal opportunity in the market place, minority youth will be qualified as never before, whether at subprofessional or professional level, to redress this dreadful record.

The graph on page 74 gives further meaning to that statement.

Occupational Groups	Actual 1970 Employment		Projected 1980 Employment		Percentage of Change 1970-1980
	No.	%	No.	%	%
WHITE-COLLAR WORKERS	37,997	48.3%	48,300	50.8%	+ 27%
Professional & technical	11,140	14.2	15,500	16.3	+ 40
Managers, officials & owners	8,289	10.5	9,500	10.0	+ 15
Clerical	13,714	17.4	17,300	18.2	+ 26
Sales	4,854	6.2	6,000	6.3	+ 22
BLUE-COLLAR WORKERS	27,791	35.3%	31,100	32.7%	+ 12%
Craftsmen & foremen	10,158	12.9	12,200	12.8	+ 20
Operatives	13,909	17.7	15,400	16.2	+ 11
Nonfarm laborers	3,724	4.7	3,500	3.7	− 5
SERVICE WORKERS	9,712	12.4%	13,100	13.8%	+ 35%
FARM WORKERS	3,126	4.0%	2,600	2.7%	− 16%
TOTALS, All Groups	78,627	100.0%	95,100	100.0%	+ 21%

U.S. EMPLOYMENT BY OCCUPATION, 1970, AND PROJECTED 1980 (Numbers in thousands)

Source: U.S. President and U.S. Department of Labor, *Manpower Report of the President 1972*, p. 259.

It is an unhappy fact that our schools have, until very recent years, taken the dropout for granted. He or she was not necessarily dull and not necessarily poor or Black or Mexican American. The dropout has often been the rather typical young person who simply was not finding meaning or worth in the time spent in school. I can recall with considerable shame, as late as the mid-sixties, the practice in a school system where I worked which

UNEMPLOYMENT RATES BY SEX AND COLOR, SELECTED YEARS, 1958–1971
(Percentage unemployed)

Year	Total[a]	Male[b]	Female[b]	White[c]	Negro and Other Nonwhite Races[c]
1958	6.8%	6.8%	6.8%	6.1%	12.6%
1961	6.7	6.4	7.2	6.0	12.4
1966	3.8	3.2	4.8	3.3	7.3
1967	3.8	3.1	5.2	3.4	7.4
1968	3.6	2.9	4.8	3.2	6.7
1969	3.5	2.8	4.7	3.1	6.4
1970	4.9	4.4	5.9	4.5	8.2
1971	5.9	5.3	6.9	5.4	9.9

Source: *Manpower Report of the President 1972*, p. 175.
[a] Unemployment rate for total labor force, including both sexes and all races.
[b] Includes all races.
[c] Includes both sexes.

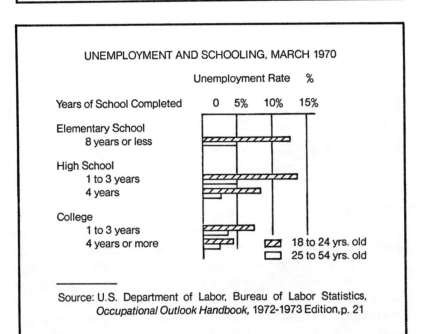

UNEMPLOYMENT AND SCHOOLING, MARCH 1970

Unemployment Rate %

Years of School Completed

Elementary School
8 years or less

High School
1 to 3 years
4 years

College
1 to 3 years
4 years or more

18 to 24 yrs. old
25 to 54 yrs. old

Source: U.S. Department of Labor, Bureau of Labor Statistics, *Occupational Outlook Handbook*, 1972-1973 Edition, p. 21

quite routinely and dispassionately calculated each year the number of dropouts to expect in our high schools. The task was performed not inhumanely, but as an administrative adjunct to calculating the needs of the system for classrooms, teachers, books, and floor wax. *We took the dropout for granted*, rather than change the schools in order to keep him or her productively involved! In recent years conscientious teachers, counselors, and administrators have turned earnestly and compassionately to efforts to salvage the dropout—and with modest success. But they have not yet gotten at the root of the problem. They have not yet turned the schools around to make them exciting, joyful, fulfilling places for *all* learners with all their varied capacities and hopes.

I have not calculated the real cost of unemployment as a professional researcher in economics would, but I can make a layman's guess. If we have about 80 million people in our work force, and unemployment rates range to 5 percent or more, we have 4 million people in serious personal and psychological distress. If we add their families to the number, say a spouse and two children, we have 16 million people undergoing the anguish, anxiety, and probable hardship of an economic and employment system that does not match their talents and interests. This comes under the human part of the cost-benefit appraisal. It seems wholly as important to me, as a consideration pushing us toward educational change, as does, conversely, the *happy* evidence of education's contribution to our affluent society.

If we count the 4 million unemployed as objects of nonproductive compensation-welfare benefits, let us roughly declare $6000 a year as subsistence level for a family. This rough calculation, quite apart from other welfare costs, comes to $24 billion. One would think we were creative enough as a people to turn these dollars into constructive education programs and employer-incentive programs that would bring full employment. Of at least equal importance would be the redress of despair—measurable only in unquantifiable, but enormous *human* terms.

For illustrative purposes, let us trace a young person through the education budget. It costs about $1000 a year to educate a child in elementary and secondary school. (This figure is low, but useful for quick arithmetic.) Let us, conservatively, use $3000 a year for college costs. This does not count foregone income, but includes "keep." We have been profligate in the expenditures of these sums, whether from the public treasury or from the family bank account. This is not to say that we should pay less for our schools and colleges. We should, and I believe will, pay more. But we have not gained the potential benefits consistent with that *cost* in terms of fulfilled human beings, or the economic outputs that should have accrued to both individuals and to our society.

Of 3.8 million young people leaving formal education in 1972–1973, an estimated 2.5 million lacked skills adequate to enter the labor force at a level commensurate with their academic and intellectual promise. Many left with no marketable skills whatsoever.

In 1973 nearly 900,000 students (of the 2.5 million) dropped out of elementary and secondary school. Assuming that, on the average, they left at the end of the tenth grade, at $12,000 per child for schooling that began in kindergarten or first grade, these dropouts represented an outlay of nearly $11 billion annually. As noted above, many of them are statistics in the unemployment tables.

Also in 1973, another 750,000 students graduated from the high school general curriculum that has traditionally been the never-never land for students who do not elect vocational training or plan to go to college. At $12,000 per graduating student, total cost to the country was about $9 billion.

Another 850,000 young people entered college but left without a degree or completion of an occupational program. If these students, on the average, left at the end of the second year ($12,000 plus $6000 invested in postsecondary education), they added $15 billion to education costs.

This all adds up to 2.5 million young people and expenditures of some $35 billion. This is not a one-time calculation. It is happening *every year* so long as our dismal data sustain the conditions of 1973. That is over one-third of the entire $90 billion cost of education for one year.

What we can't measure are the personal and psychological losses of these young people—their frustrations, their shattered hopes and dreams—their understandable anger and alienation. Nor can we calculate the contributions they might have made to our country's progress had their education been more responsive to their needs and aspirations.

Obviously it is not implied here that $35 billion in costs of education for "early leavers" was wasted. Some learning and growth took place, inescapably. But how much more we could have derived in personal-economic benefits had they *wanted* to stay!

Who are these young people and what will happen to them?

Department of Labor projections show that 100 million Americans will be working or seeking work by 1980. That's 15 million more people, mostly young, who will have to be accommodated in the labor force by 1980 than we had in 1970. If 2.5 million youngsters are now leaving our schools and colleges each year without adequate preparation, how many of those 15 million are apt to be unprepared for the demands of the 1980 labor market?

The other extreme, of course, is the overeducated young person, at least in terms of career opportunities consistent with his training and aspiration at the time he or she is ready to enter the labor market.

I had a painful conversation with a young graduate in physics from a first-rate university. His goal was first to teach high school physics and, he hoped, later to teach college physics as he advanced his degrees. He had applied to sixty high schools in the New York City area, as a beginning teacher candidate. Either no reply (understandable with the volume) or blue slips came from all but one. A suburban high school had an opening. He went for an interview. There were twenty-seven candidates, including a few Ph.D.s, for the position. This young man was bright, seemingly dedicated, eager to teach his science to the young. He did not get hired in the suburb. His only other job option was that of assistant ski instructor ("provided it snows") for two months this winter. It snowed, and he will work through the winter. Something is wrong, he feels. I do, too.

In some fields there are seven applicants for every teacher opening. And there are instances where highly qualified but also highly specialized engineers and skilled technicians, displaced in the aerospace and related industries, have turned in desperation to running hamburger drive-ins or tending bar.

The era of the 1960s, when job openings were waiting for

college graduates, is over. The crunch for the college graduate has come from both ends—diminishing job prospects for the college graduate and a growing number of students completing college. By 1980, for example, there will be nearly 650,000 more students awarded B.A.s than there were in 1960. And this will occur during a period when 80 percent of the new jobs available in the 1970s will require training and skills, but not necessarily a four-year degree.

Already we have begun to feel the pinch. One of every four young chemists in the United States as I write in 1974 is out of work. Law schools graduated 10,000 more men and women in 1973 than could find their place in legal work. Officers from the American Bar Association called upon me as Assistant Secretary for Education in 1973 to help lay out new federal job descriptions, apart from legal work, for this oversupply of bright and able men and women who wanted to practice their profession, but could find no places that needed them.

Trying to pinpoint responsibility for the imbalance between jobs and the market place is a fruitless exercise: there is more than enough blame to go around. But for many years now, most noticeably in the post-Sputnik period, educators, parents, industry, and government have been obsessed with the notion that a college education is a young person's only ticket to social worth, economic success, and emotional and intellectual wholeness. Yet I believe that fully 50 percent of these young people now in college have no real goals toward which to aim, and they have little information or professional help for establishing their goals or pursuing them systematically. K. Patricia Cross, writing in *The College Board Review*, declares, "Mounting pressures for college attendance have forced some reluctant learners into involuntary attendance . . . The Carnegie Commission has estimated that almost one-third of the undergraduates are less than fully committed."

One of the reasons for this is the tremendous increase in the number of young people in America. Notes *Youth: Transition to Adulthood*: "Between 1960 and 1970 the proportion of the population between 19 and 24 jumped from 15% to 20% after declining for over 50 years. In absolute numbers the youth population grew by 50% in the sixties (from 27 million in 1960 to 42 million in 1971)." This has presented an important new problem in the youth labor market. "These changes in the youth population, and the associated changes in the supply of youth labor, far dwarf any changes in industrial structure or technology that would alter . . . the demand for young people. . . . While there has been a significant increase in the youth labor force . . . the crest of the wave has only now begun to reach the full time education-completed labor market and will be inundating it in the years to come."[6]

We have provided good high school programs for the 50 percent or so of our high school population going on to higher education, if *only going on* is what we expect. We have provided adequate vocational training for the small percentage of students who were not college-bound and recognized the need for immediate job skills by enrolling in skill, craft, and trade programs in high school.

Anyone who has studied the Department of Labor projections for the 1970s and 1980s can understand the reasons for changing our education system now to stress the importance of relating learning to a career. For the majority of young people, the education for the 1970s and 1980s is not necessarily a four-year degree, though that is desirable for many; nor is it just a high school diploma without career content. The Department of Labor says that by the end of the decade four out of every five jobs will not require a four-year degree. The new technologies and service industries have created a new middle ground of job opportunities that require two years of training beyond high school but do not require a four-year college degree. As noted in an earlier chapter, this may point toward a revision of our value system, which values the college degree in and of itself but does not attach artificial economic absolutes to it.

The job market of the future will be geared for those individuals who have skills and developed intelligence, and who are able to cope with change, whatever level of formal education they possess. There may have been a time when we could afford the luxury of twelve or sixteen or more years of formal education without work-related purpose. But swiftly moving technological and social evolution no longer has a place for the skilled and unschooled, or the schooled and unskilled. It certainly has no place for the candidate lacking *both* schooling and skills.

It is important here to declare the enduring place of the liberal arts and sciences of our traditional college-preparatory curriculum in our high schools, and certainly in our colleges. The blending of the liberating learnings of language, history, economics, the arts, government, philosophy, the social and physical sciences are all essential to well-developed men and women. But these essential intellectual learnings are no more essential to the well-developed person than the acquisition of personally and socially useful techniques for *application* of his or her learnings in the world of work.

Small wonder so many drop out, not because they have failed, but because we have failed to make the curriculum real in terms of the learner.

Who would not, at the earliest convenient and legal moment, leave an environment that is neither satisfying, entertaining, nor productive in the eyes of the learner? We properly deplore the large numbers of young men and women who leave high school before graduation. But, in simple truth, for most of them, leaving an unhappy place is the most natural elective they can choose.

This economic, educational, and social situation has presented us with a set of problems that, perhaps, can best be summed up this way:

- Unemployment among teenagers is far in excess of the national average.

- A sizable number of young people have no clear idea or purpose as to their educational or career goals, yet many persevere in classrooms, secure for the moment, but ill-equipped to leave.

- Young people are not being afforded, in elementary and high school, an awareness of the world of work, nor are they afforded any systematic guidance in planning their lives. Those following the college-bound education custom are doing so, except for their own ingenuity, for reasons unrelated to occupational purposes.

- While in high school, a third of all students are taking a general curriculum that is neither fish nor fowl and leaves them unskilled, unschooled, and probably very despairing upon graduation.

- Taxpayers and college students given their options are no longer willing blindly to support education or to engage in it solely because it is good, in and of itself.

The evidence of high cost and high economic benefits of education are at best only relative. High costs as compared with what? We could make a case for greatly increasing costs, especially for the disadvantaged, the handicapped, and the minorities. And high economic benefits, as compared with what? The underdeveloped human beings our schools and society have passed by are not warmly touched by the affluence our system has produced. The 16 million men, women, and children comprising the families in the 5-percent-unemployment category are probably not impressed by the numbers of cars and television sets we enjoy as a people.

The total subject of welfare, with its clear implications for career education, has not been treated in our review of costs and benefits, but it clearly has large relationship with our subject. For example, one relatively fixed component of the welfare budget of HEW is $14 billion. This is for the social and rehabilitation service of HEW, for support and maintenance—public assistance, work incentives, and rehabilitation services. If we could, over time, turn this same sum of money over to the constructive investments of educational services to the same people, it would be a social reform of the highest order. Instead of simply *sustaining* families in poverty, it could give them the resources for putting poverty behind. "Give a man a fish, and he will eat for a day. Teach him to fish and he will never be hungry."

Taken altogether, the American people are investing more in education at all levels than in any other public or private category. They do expect our educational system, good as it is, and cost-beneficial as it is, to be better. The changing technologies, the changing work place, the changing manpower needs (slippery as they are to forecast) all call for corresponding change in our educational institutions. This is not a zero-sum game—put in career education and take something else out. This is a proposal to build upon the splendid record of two hundred years of American education by increasing its responsiveness through relating its teaching to the normal motivations and the informed occupational aspirations of all people.

Toward a Definition of Career Education

"By far the most significant reform strategy that attempts to provide a coherent philosophy and deal with the many limitations [of education] is the career education movement. It is an attempt to change the entire educational system, from kindergarten through postsecondary education, by diagnosing the shortcomings of both vocational and academic training in the context of their mutual isolation. . . . Part of the problem . . . is . . . it is broad in scope and ill-defined."[1]

Professor David Rogers, sociologist and member of the faculty of New York University's Graduate School of Business Administration, goes on to note in his very painstaking appraisal: "It is a little early to make any summary judgments until it becomes apparent how the career education programs work out. Far from being just another fad . . . the career education movement, as enunciated in the recent literature, synthesizes many of the best reform ideas of the past decade . . . and proposes to apply them in a systematic way, not just to vocational high schools, but to the entire system. . . . "

Earlier chapters noted the sequence of events at USOE leading to the determination in late 1970 to undertake a major strategy of educational reform and to give it the name "career education." From the early stages of this endeavor, I held that the concept needed much national debate, much research, much scientific analysis, much testing of assumptions in real schools and classrooms before it could be given a dependable definition. I have been both criticized and applauded for insisting that there should be no "approved definition" of career education by the federal government during the initial years of its conceptualization. But some people do like definitions.

There is a story about James Conant, who was often called upon to be the oracle on educational matters following his turn as President of Harvard and Ambassador to Germany. He was asked once to give his definition of a university. He thought a moment, then said, "Well, the literature is full of all kinds of definitions of a university—I guess I would just say *it's what happens in one.*"

One of the principal reasons that prompted me to shun an early attempt to define career education was based upon my understanding of how teachers and school systems operate. I cared very much about the large potential that career education, as I perceived it, held for the young people, the not-so-young people, and the educational institutions of the United States. I wanted very much to see it come into place as an evolutionary reform. But "evolutionary reform"—or indeed educational changes of any kind—do not come about as a result of proclamations from Washington. In America the ultimate determination of what happens in elementary and secondary classrooms rests with the classroom teacher. American teachers do not take kindly to being told to change. They *can* change, and *will* change, but only as they, individually and collectively, choose to do so.

This condition is even more fundamental in the colleges and universities. Faculties in all disciplines are not about to be directed by anyone, least of all the federal government, in matters pertaining to their teaching philosophy or to adaptations in the treatment of their academic disciplines that might be viewed as change. But they, too, are quite capable of change, if *they* decide upon the merits of the process. Hence, we declined to declare a definition.

Career education is a large idea, and the decision to array its parameters before the thoughtful educators of the nation for a full and continuing debate was, in my opinion, the right decision, and remains so.

But we did not turn away from *describing* what we were about. I suppose I gave at least fifty major speeches on the subject and wrote at least twenty-five journal articles during 1970–1973 that endeavored, with varying audiences, to speak to the relevance of career to the essential interests of that particular audience. Whether the secondary school principals, the National Chamber of Commerce, the guidance counselors, the Congress, the Black leaders in education, the deans of liberal arts, the presidents of the prestige universities, the community colleges, or many others, they heard the message of reform implicit in career education as it related to *their* jurisdiction. Most of them listened earnestly. Some of them were already in motion, and did not need the persuasion; others have moved; many remain unconvinced, or only partly convinced.

Describing the broad objectives of career education (as distinct from declaring a definition) took several forms in the process of developing the concept in the Washington offices. The later pages of this chapter will cite eleven descriptive criteria by Duane Mattheis, Deputy Commissioner of Education during this period.

Equally important were the contributions of Elizabeth Simpson, Robert Worthington, Michael Russo, Peter Muirhead, Joseph Cosand, Marie Martin, Harry Silberman, and many others in the Office of Education.

As the National Institute of Education came into being in the spring of 1973, additional intellectual resources were brought to bear on the furtherance of the descriptive process. Dr. Corinne Reider, leader of the Career Education Research Division of NIE, and Dr. Thomas Glennan, Director of NIE, with a working staff of young researchers, took seriously the objectives of the statute establishing NIE. Congress had specified career education as a theme to be addressed by the new Institute. It was one of the very few categorical charges in the statute.

By the system of management by objectives, first in OE and subsequently (November 1972) in the new Division of Education, we attached high priority to the work of further analysis, funding exemplary programs and giving technical assistance nationally to the initiative. The President, in his State of the Union message in 1972, had called for strong efforts by the schools and colleges of the land and by HEW to advance the thrust.

In government agencies there is always a sharp ear turned to the State of the Union message, hoping for favorable mention. The President devoted a special radio message that year to his education message. We had helped to draft the paper, which of course gave considerable attention to career education. For many months we had been struggling to clarify nationally the large differences between vocational education and career education. The President did well with the address, and came to the clinching passage on career education: "Now, I want to talk about one of the most promising educational initiatives of this administration—career education! *You know—vocational education.*" His well-intended ad lib on the air devastated the earnest staff members gathered in my office for the event. But it gave me a one-liner that I could use in speeches for months that helped more than ever to make our point.

In January 1973 Elliot Richardson left the post of Secretary of HEW to become Secretary of Defense and was succeeded by Caspar Weinberger. Secretary Weinberger, former Director of the Office of Management and Budget, was mindful of the general theme of career education, but had not been a part of its genesis as a federal priority as Secretary Richardson had been. During the early months of his administration in HEW, he asked for more information, not only from me but also quite properly from his immediate staff of planners. In June 1973, a new Assistant Secretary for Planning and Evaluation had been named by Weinberger, Dr. William Morill, and he in turn, as part of his very large responsibilities in shaping HEW programs across all agencies, wanted to know what we were up to in the Education Division— especially in career education. At that time, an internal HEW memo elucidating the career education concept was written for Assistant Secretary Morill and the Secretary by Martin Kramer, Morill's principal education officer. It should be noted here that, in the hierarchy of HEW, the line officers such as Assistant Secretary, Health, and Assistant Secretary, Education, report directly to the Secretary, and staff officers of equal stature as Assistant Secretaries do the same. The Assistant Secretary for Planning and Evaluation was such a staff officer and a very important one. Quite appropriately, the Secretary draws intimately upon the advice of staff officers in giving general direction and delegation of authority to the line officers, such as 1 was.

Martin Kramer's memorandum, dated June 13, 1973, was a staff paper developed for his immediate chief and the Secretary with detachment and objectivity (as distinct from my admitted advocacy) that makes it useful as a description of what we were about. (This document is offered as a useful instrument *at the time*. The career education priority as advanced by the Office of Education and endorsed by Secretary Richardson had been evolving for a little more than two years. Secretary Weinberger and his new planning expert, Bill Morill, wanted to know more before sustaining the Richardson priority, as they did with several other key initiatives across the Department.)

CAREER EDUCATION

[from an internal HEW memo by Dr. Martin Kramer,
Office of the Secretary, June 1973]

Career education means different things for different age groups as the individual's perspective on his life changes:
—For the young child it means envisioning a future in which learning will enable him to do the kinds of work he will wish to do when he grows up. It involves gaining an awareness that learning will enable him to have rewarding relationships with other people in which he will earn their respect along with material benefits. It means not feeling lost in a world where other people are doing a vast variety of jobs because he can appreciate their common goals.
—For the adolescent, career education means learning what all the choices he faces imply—the work demands others will place on him and the demands he can make of others. It is the process that turns fantasies into aspirations. Career education helps him get "down to earth," but it also makes the "earth" an exciting rather than a drab and alien place.
—For older people career education is an awareness of

second chances, of opportunities to learn how to be useful to other people in new ways and a sense that new options for the individual are created by technological and social change even when old options disappear.

The need for career education—in all of these aspects—is not new. It is one of the more clearly universal human needs. For a number of reasons, however, it now needs to be a major concern of public policy. Parents, educators and employers and students themselves are increasingly concerned that students are finding difficulty in articulating their motivation for learning in terms of clearly perceived facts about the adult world and realistic plans for participation in that world. Put another way, it is as though many students today do not perceive the problems for which learning is the solution. Various explanations can be offered:

—As education through high school begins to approach universality, the difference which schooling makes is less intensely perceived, even though schooling becomes more indispensable.

—Children see less of their parents' work.

—Advancing technology and increasing job differentiation cause the areas of work where learning makes a critical difference to become harder to talk to children about.

—Both technological and social change make parents reluctant to encourage their children to follow in their own footsteps.

This list of explanations is not, of course, exhaustive. There is much we do not understand. For example, the problem may be related to very fundamental changes in the American family.

Whatever the explanation, it is clear that more than job training is needed. The difference can be expressed in this way: a person's career education must be well launched *before* he is ready to pursue job training with an understanding of what the job will mean in his life and the lives of others. If career education is successful, specific job training can be provided by many kinds of institution—employers, proprietary schools and special training programs, as well as schools and colleges.

Schools and colleges will, of course, offer many types of job training, but what makes it career education is a concern that the student have a sense that he is on his way somewhere. This need is just as valid in the case of the college preparatory student as for the student who has chosen to concentrate on particular vocational skills.

The implication of this is that a school which offers vocational courses which are perceived as leading to "dead-end" occupations has failed to provide career education, however superbly the institution is equipped to provide specific vocational skills. Adequate programs of career education will seek to keep the student's options open. This means, for example, that skills which will be useful in a great variety of adult activities—however "academic," like mathematics—will continue to be pursued, even by students whose curriculum is predominantly vocational. Moreover, the kind of liberal arts background which will be useful in the part of his adult career which is spent away from the job will not be neglected.

If career education may not mean changes in the direction of a lower priority on academic and liberal arts subjects, what changes are implied? For one thing, it almost certainly should mean an end to the "general track" which gives the student no sense of being on his way anywhere—neither into an occupation which he understands and respects nor into college and a profession. For another, it means less preoccupation with the learning style of the academic profession. Social science, for example, would not be taught as a diluted version of the kind of inquiry conducted in a graduate seminar in sociology, or not at least in the case of the many students who do not see themselves as having careers in academic scholarship. In other words, some of the excesses of the post-Sputnik emphasis on the academic side of the academic disciplines would be corrected. Other styles of learning would be recognized as valid and even preferable when they tended to enchance the student's sense of motivation to do something with his life.

Not only will changes be made; we can expect to see the results of the changes and it will be possible to evaluate the success of our efforts. Evaluation criteria for career education are in need of much development work, but crude criteria can be stated now:

—The ability of young people to identify with the functional roles being played by adults around them and on the national scene should increase.

—The sense of helplessness measured by indices of alienation should be reduced.

—The kind of wandering in and out of jobs and training

> programs which is common among young people who do not go to college should be reduced, whether this wandering is seen as an undesirable consequence of inadequate career education, or whether it is seen as itself an informal kind of career education.
>
> —The tendency for many young people to drift on to college without being able to offer a considered and personal reason for being there should decrease.

I found Kramer's lucid paper even-handed, objective, and informative. A few little items here and there could be the object of minor debate, but it was and remains a good paper. The Secretary and Bill Morill sustained the program's high priority, and I was directed to keep the Secretary fully informed of progress.

The educational literature of 1972 and 1973 began to burgeon with career education articles reflecting theory, practice, experiments, curriculum development, criticism, and comment. Edwin Herr's synthesis of 1972 is an excellent distillation of the many descriptions of career education that had evolved not only from the Office of Education but from numerous other authorities during the preceding two years:

> In summary, the descriptions of career education . . . suggest that the term can mean, in relationship to different contexts and purposes, at least the following:
>
> 1. An effort to diminish the separateness of academic and vocational education.
>
> 2. An area of concern which has some operational implications for every educational level or grade from kindergarten through graduate school.
>
> 3. A process of insuring that every person exiting from the formal educational structure has job employability skills of some type.
>
> 4. A direct response to the importance of facilitating individual choice-making so that occupational preparation and the acquisition of basic academic skills can be coordinated with developing individual preference.
>
> 5. A way of increasing the relevance or meaningfulness

of education for greater numbers of students than is currently true.

6. A design to make education an open system in that school leavers, school dropouts, adults can reaffiliate with it when their personal circumstances or job requirements make this feasible.

7. A structure whose desired outcomes necessitate cooperation among all elements of education as well as among the school, industry, and community.

8. An enterprise requiring new technologies and materials of education (i.e., individualized programming, simulations).

9. A form of education for all students.[2]

I do not have anything against definitions. But career education is a very large and complex proposition, carrying various levels of abstraction according to the setting. It has a definition for, say, a state department of education, a different level of detail for a fourth-grade teacher or a dean of the faculty at a university. It is not important, furthermore, that any one individual, whether a government official or not, declare a definition intended to serve all situations. On the other hand, *descriptions* of what career education is intended to *do*, what implications for *educational change* it carries, and what *goals it seeks to realize* are more useful. Accordingly, I accept Herr's descriptions cited above as wholly adequate to the present state of this "evolutionary reform," and suggest they be used by those who *for their own purposes*, and *within the scope of their jurisdictions* choose to develop their own definitions.

There is no lack of definitions for career education. Scholars, school administrators, state legislators, teachers, professional associations, and other worthy sources have developed a multitude of definitions during the last three or four years. All that I have seen are useful. They are adequate for the immediate situation, provided the individuals who will bear the responsibilities for implementation of the programs had a hand in the construction of the definition. And that is precisely what was intended by our decision to leave definition-building, within broad descriptive parameters, to those who were close to the instruction that should follow.

In September 1972, Dr. Sidney C. High, Jr., Chief, Exemplary Program Branch of our Office of Education, collected all the official definitions of career education adopted to that point by action of state boards of education and certain other authorities he found noteworthy. Dr. High found nineteen "official" state definitions; that number, I'm sure, has grown. Other definitions have appeared, coming from educators who over these last few years have begun to refine the concept of career education. Dr. Kenneth Hoyt, at the invitation of the Office of Education, then assembled and clarified the definitions. They were subsequently published in the 1973 American Vocational Association *Yearbook*.

Here are some of these definitions, some adapted because of their length, from Dr. Hoyt's review.[3]

SELECTED CURRENT DEFINITIONS
OF CAREER EDUCATION

Definitions from State Educational Agencies

Arizona (from a speech made by Dr. Weldon P. Shofstall, State Superintendent of Public Instruction, November 1971):
"In Arizona, we have defined career education as combining the academic world with the world of work. It must be available at all levels of education. . . . Career education is not an add-on . . . it is a blending of the vocational, the general, and the college preparatory education. . . . Synonymous with 'all education,' 'career education' must become the term. When we say 'education,' we must mean 'career education.' "

California (from a statement of the California State Department of Education Career Education Task Force, May 4, 1972):
"Through . . . career education, each student will develop positive attitudes about himself and others, make sound decisions regarding alternative and changing careers, acquire skills leading to employment, and pursue a life style which provides self-fulfillment and contributes to the society in which he lives."

Maine (from a State Department of Education bulletin entitled "Career Development in the Elementary Schools," September 1972):
"Career education . . . signifies a concerted effort to educate youth as early as kindergarten in exploring careers and acquiring the skills necessary for transition to a job. Career education is a melding of diverse curriculum efforts into a unified whole that requires the academic, vocational and guidance specialists to plan integrated learning events. In summary, it is a planned, sequential, orderly curriculum effort."

Minnesota (adopted by State Board of Education, May 2, 1972):
"Career education is an integral part of education. It provides purposefully planned and meaningfully taught experiences for all persons, which contribute to self-development as it relates to various career patterns. Career education takes place at . . . [all] . . . levels of education. Emphasis is placed on career awareness, orientation and exploration of the world of work, decision making relative to additional education, preparation for career proficiency . . . and understanding the interrelationships between a career and one's life style."

Nevada (adopted by State Board of Education, July 1972):
"Career education is a comprehensive education program focused on careers and an educational process where people gain knowledge, attitudes, awareness, and skills necessary for success in the world of work (career success)."

New Hampshire (draft presented to State Board of Education, October 1972):
"Career education is a concept of relevant and accountable education centered on the individual which provides the opportunities for educational experiences, curriculum, instructions, and counseling leading to preparation for economic independence. The development of this concept is a lifelong process which involves a series of experiences, decisions and interactions that provide the means through which one's self-understanding can be implemented, both vocationally and avocationally."

New Jersey (from "Answers to Five Basic Questions About Career Education" by Patrick Doherty, Director of Career Development, New Jersey State Department of Education):
"Career education is an integral dimension of the nursery through adult curriculum which provides for all students a sequential continuum of experiences through which each individual may develop a more realistic perception of his capabilities and which prepares him for entry and re-entry into employment and/or continuing education."

North Dakota (from Dr. Larry Selland, Assistant State Director of Vocational Education, North Dakota State Department of Education):
"Career education is an integral part of education. It is a concept that includes as its main thrust the preparation of all students for a successful life of work by increasing their options for occupational choice and attainment of job skills, and by enhancing learning achievement in all subject matter areas . . . a total effort of the home, school, and community to help all individuals become familiar with the values of a work-oriented society, to integrate these values in their lives in a way that work becomes useful, meaningful, and satisfying."

Tennessee (prepared January 1972 by State Staff of Vocational Technical Education, State Department of Education):
"Career education is all the learning experiences through which a student progresses in an educational program regardless of the length of the program . . . not an additional or separate phase of the educational program . . . a comprehensive, dynamic, programmatic, and integrative educational program . . . it must utilize the common and unique contributions of all educators and the resources of home, school, and community."

Texas (Texas Education Agency, April 1972):
"Career education is coordinated instruction, integrated into the entire curriculum, K–12, and designed to assist students in: (a) understanding both the world of work and attitudes toward it; (b) understanding the relationships which exist between education and career opportunity; (c) understanding the economic and

social structures of our society and how they influence the ways people support themselves; (d) making informed decisions concerning how they will earn a living and taking responsibility for making those decisions; and (e) acquiring marketable skills as preparation for earning a living."

Utah (adopted by State Board of Education, May 12, 1972):
"Career education is defined as a comprehensive, correlated educational system . . . focused on individual career needs . . . begins in grade one or earlier and continues through the adult years . . . is not separate and apart from total life education . . . calls for a united effort of the school and community to help all individuals become familiar with the values of a work-oriented society; to integrate these values into their lives; and to implement them in such a way that work becomes useful, meaningful, and satisfying."

Washington (statement of Dr. Dean P. Talagan, Department of Education):
"Career education is one of the key purposes of education. It is a concept through which we instill a sense of self-identity and self-awareness within each student. It is individualized and geared to the 168-hour living week, not just the 40-hour work week. This concept motivates children to want to learn and makes them capable of economically supporting themselves and their families."

Other commonly quoted definitions, some fragmentary, and serving more as descriptors than definitions:

Bureau of Adult Vocational and Technical Education, U.S. Office of Education (from "Career Education: A Model for Implementation," May 1971):
"Career education is a comprehensive educational program focused on careers, which begins in Grade 1 or earlier and continues through the adult years."

American Vocational Association (from "Task Force Report on Education," AVA *Journal*, January 1972):
"Career education is needed by and intended for all people. . . .
It is a lifelong process which extends from early childhood

through adulthood . . . based upon the premise that all honest work and purposeful study is respectable . . . provides the means by which the educational system can focus on career development . . . provides a unifying core for the total educational enterprise with intensive occupational preparation as a significant aspect . . . it will be necessary to utilize the common and unique contributions of all educators and the resources of home, school and community. . . . "

Keith Goldhammer and Robert E. Taylor (in *Career Education: Perspective and Promise* [Columbus, Ohio: C. E. Merrill Publishing Company, 1972]):
"Specifically, career education is designed to capacitate individuals for their several life roles: economic, community, home, avocational, religious, and aesthetic. . . . Designed for all students, career education should be viewed as lifelong and pervasive . . . career education is a systematic attempt to *increase* the career options available to individuals and to facilitate more rational and valid career planning and preparation. Through a wide range of school- and community-based resources, young people's career horizons should be broadened. Their self-awareness should be enhanced."

Kenneth Hoyt (in *Career Education: What It Is and How to Do It* [Salt Lake City: Olympus Publishing Company, 1972]):
"Career education is the total effort of public education and the community aimed at helping all individuals to become familiar with the values of a work-oriented society, to integrate these values into their personal value systems, and to implement these values into their lives in such a way that work becomes possible, meaningful, and satisfying to each individual." (Kenneth Hoyt and Rupert Evans appear to have agreed upon the foregoing definition, since both use it in their writings. Both are very substantial educational leaders.)

Wesley Smith (Director of Vocational Education, California State Department of Education):
"Career education is a comprehensive, systematic, and cohesive plan of learning organized in such a manner that youth at all grade levels in the public schools will have continuous and

abundant opportunity to acquire useful information about the occupational structure of the economy, the alternatives of career choice, the obligations of individual and productive involvement in the total work force, the intelligent determination of personal capabilities and aspirations, the requisites of all occupations, and opportunities to prepare for gainful employment. . . . It is a priority objective of public education, with achievement measured by employability in occupations, both gainful and useful, that are a reasonable match of both talent and the ambition of every citizen."

John Costar (Director, Center for Occupational Education, North Carolina State University):
"Career education has as its mission the attainment of an optimum level of work proficiency for each individual within the context of the social, individual, and work systems. Career education (1) facilitates the acquisition and processing and integration of information by the individual; (2) enhances the decision-making process; (3) provides alternatives for action through programs that are designed to equip the individual with salable skills to start his/her career; and (4) provides for continuous recycling of information, decision making, and action through retraining and upgrading of skills."

Sterling M. McMurrin (Philosopher and former U.S. Commissioner of Education):
"In determining the meaning of career education the task of locating the differentia is especially difficult. For while 'career' is apparently a differentiating term, just what it means and how it sets career education apart from other education and thereby provides it with specific intention is not obvious. I have come to the tentative conclusion that 'career' should not function as a defining term, but should be considered explicative in character; i.e., career education is properly synonymous in meaning with education. Or to put it differently all education, in addition to whatever else it may be, should be career education."

National Institute of Education (Extracted from NIE's Forward Plan for Career Education Research and Development):
"More specifically, career education is defined as the develop-

ment of knowledge and of special and general abilities to help individuals and groups interact with the economic sector. Economic and psychological incomes from employment comprise the long term outcomes which are proper questions for research and development."

From these definitions, Hoyt has pointed out there is general agreement among state agencies and educators about career education. There is a consensus that career education begins at the earliest levels of education, no later than grade one; that career education is for all students, not just some; and that the emphasis of the education is preparation for work. There is also agreement that vocational education, as we traditionally know it, becomes a part of the total career education structure.

Nearly all statements describing career education take pains to point out that career education is different from vocational education. These authorities also agree that career education is not something "added on" to curriculum as a new subject, a new body of knowledge. Rather, career education is to be a new integrative force, engaging the total educational program.

There is, as one might expect, some disagreement among those who have begun to define career education. Dr. Hoyt sees three areas of diverse judgment: (1) the reason for the career education concept; (2) the long-range goals of career education; and (3) whether career education should be an effort only of the schools and colleges or whether it should involve the home and community as well.

Reasons for Career Education

The controversy here, according to Hoyt, "centers around whether the career education movement was born because of a need to restructure American education, because of a need to improve the quality of transition from school to employment, or because of a need to restore work as a vital and viable personal value among our citizens."

Hoyt feels that it is necessary to resolve this controversy because "until and unless it can be resolved, we will continue to find the case for career education, and so the nature of career education itself, made and operating in quite different ways." These positions are, nevertheless, not in opposition to one another, and all contribute to the development of the concept, thereby giving it diversity and variety as the work progresses. I happen to feel that all three of the reasons underlying the need for reform through career education are valid and sensible, and are contributing to its advancement.

Long-Range Goals

Current scholars and practitioners, including Hoyt, find several areas of disagreement among the statements of purpose. There are, for example, those who would "limit the long-range goals of career education to post-educational job experience of former students."

Other career education definitions use such terminology as "total life education," "total life style," and "economic, community, home, avocational, religious, and aesthetic life roles." These "definers" seek a broadly based definition of career education.

Then there are others who declare the goal of career education is to make work *possible, meaningful,* and *satisfying* to everyone. They would also include nonpaid work in their career education concept. These writers are "concerned about ways in which a person can increase his feelings of self-worth, self-identity, and accomplishments through work he performs—whether or not that work is in the form of a paid job."

Hoyt is correct in calling for more clarity and consensus on the long-range goals of career education. His own scholarly application to the subject gives promise of generalizations that will gain broad adoption.

Career Education in the School, Home, or Community

Seven of the twenty-one definitions of career education, as analyzed by Hoyt, include the home and community in their statements. Nine define career education as an effort of the educational institution alone, and the remaining five are unclear as to whether the home and community are part of the educational environment. There is an area of disagreement, therefore, in both the scope and the locus of career education. As the dialogue continues, these differences, I believe, will be narrowed, and still sustain appropriate distinctions from one jurisdiction to another. Nonetheless, I find it very difficult to exclude the home, the community, and the realistic working environment from any meaningful design for career education.

It is essential to remember that career education will really be defined by the individuals themselves, who are designing programs, and by the intrinsic teaching and experiential activities of communities and schools across the country. Definitions invented by the participants are much more important than those pronounced in books. The Office of Education and NIE, in keeping with this strategy, are assisting schools that are committed to developing comprehensive career education programs by allocating funds for demonstrations; disseminating the products of research and development deriving from such institutions as the Ohio State Center for Vocational and Technical Education and other federally funded agencies; and providing technical assistance to other educational agencies.

The Center at Ohio State has developed a Comprehensive Career Education Matrix, for example, as a resource to educational planners engaged in the subject. The Matrix identifies eight broad elements, each stated in terms of student activities and student outcomes, which, taken together, serve as one *operational* means of defining career education. The complete Comprehensive Career Education Matrix (CCEM), involving 32 subordinate themes, 1500 goals, and 3000 general performance objectives associated with these eight elements, stands as the most comprehensive operational definition of career education yet developed.

The eight broad elements of the Comprehensive Career Education Matrix as they translate to the learning of individual students follows (some adaptations have been made by the author for brevity and continuity):

Career Education Elements	Element Outcomes
1. **Career Awareness**—knowledge of the total spectrum of careers	1. **Career Identity** — personalized future role or roles within the world of work; options remain open for the individual to move among occupations
2. **Self-Awareness** — knowledge of the components that make up self	2. **Self-Identity**—know himself; consistent value system; ability to make decisions based on values held by individual
3. **Appreciations, Attitudes**—life roles; feelings towards self and others in respect to society and economics	3. **Self-Social Fulfillment**—active work role; satisfying work role; responsibility beyond self to civic and individual needs
4. **Decision-Making Skills**—applying information to rational processes to reach decisions	4. **Career Decisions**—career directions; has a plan for career development; bases decisions on information as distinct from fantasy
5. **Economic Awareness**—perception of processes in production, distribution, and consumption	5. **Economic Understanding**—solve personal and social problems of an economic environment; relate values to compensation, security, growth and related economic measures
6. **Skill Awareness and Beginning Competence**—skills in ways in which man extends his behavior	6. **Employment Skills**—competence in performance of job-related tasks; varies from unsophisticated to very sophisticated skills depending upon learner

Career Education Elements	Element Outcomes
7. **Employability Skills**—social and communication skills appropriate to career placement	7. **Career Placement**—employed in line with career development plan; affective behavior such as attitudes, coping, self-discipline, integrity are parallel attributes to the specific skill or skills
8. **Educational Awareness**—perception of relationship between education and life roles	8. **Educational Identity**—ability to select educational avenues to develop career plans; decision-making as to postsecondary options, including immediate work, or further education, or both. Awareness of in-and-out options for continuing education through adulthood

This CCEM model is a way of defining career education through expected student outcomes, all of them being cast in behavioral terms.

Another way of defining career education in operational terms was presented by Duane J. Mattheis, Deputy Commissioner for School Systems in the Office of Education, in an address to chief state school officers in 1972, a year after our first presentation of the idea. These eleven operational objectives for career education as stated by Mattheis offer a different approach to a "definition." It should be noted that Mr. Mattheis served as the principal deputy in the Office of Education concerned with elementary and secondary education, and with vocational education at the time of this statement. (Although Mattheis was Deputy Commissioner to me, these are his words, not mine. We did not have time to check out our speeches with each other, but we were all working on the same wavelength.):

1. Provide students with a more unifying, relevant curriculum;

infuse academic and general curriculum course offerings with career relevance; end channeling of students into tracks.

2. Provide educational experiences to give students increasing knowledge of occupational alternatives and the world of work. This experience should begin in elementary school and continue as long as needed.

3. Provide nonacademic career options (at secondary, post-secondary, and adult levels) which have equal status with academic career options. The unfairly discriminating distinctions between the academic track and the vocational track must be eliminated.

4. Provide students with a comprehensive and flexible program of career-qualifying opportunities—one that will allow students to progress at their own pace and yet will not lock them into a particular curricular track. It should increase the options available at the secondary and postsecondary levels through greater breadth of course offerings, more meaningful content (jobs with a future), and availability of different types of learning modes.

5. Provide for greater involvement of employers in the educational experience of all students. Employers can make an important contribution through work-study and cooperative education programs, involvement in occupational guidance, career orientation, and placement activities, and in employer-conducted alternatives to the "in school house" education.

6. Provide students with career counseling that begins early in the educational program and follows through to job placement or further education. While the system should be built on the principle of maximizing individual choice, students should be provided with options that are realistically related to labor market conditions. A job placement function should be located in the schools.

7. Provide opportunity for counseling, for reentry, and retraining for those who have exited the system—both for those who have failed to gain employment and for those in the world of work. Individuals whose skills are no longer marketable, those in

dead-end jobs, and those who want a career change for personal happiness should be able to reenter the system.

8. Provide its graduates from the secondary level and each level thereafter with either the skills to enter the world of work or to embark on additional education. Many career options will require education beyond the secondary level, and the system should provide this experience. The criterion should be that at the exit point for each career option the student is qualified to enter that career.

9. Provide students with some notion of what is wrong with the world of work, particularly the way jobs are structured. Simply preparing students to accept the occupational system is insufficient. (Mattheis was, I am sure, mindful here of the new evidence of worker frustrations developed by O'Keefe and others in *Work in America*.)

10. Provide the consumers of career education with a role in its design and implementation. If individuals are to gain greater self-autonomy and control over their destiny, it is important they by involved in the planning and development of career education.

11. Provide students with credentials that overcome discriminating distinctions both in school and in the society at large. Give credits for vocational courses that are of equal value to those given for college preparatory courses. For those whose work performance qualifies them, give credentials of competitive value for academic or occupational options. This will require an active role in seeking to change the credentialing procedures for entry into the world of work.

These eleven operational goals as conceived by Duane Mattheis are inclusive enough to indicate what a comprehensive program of career education is all about, but they do not limit a school system in providing the additional programs that are required because of a particular regional or local circumstance, job market, location, or community needs. As Kenneth Hoyt has said so well, "In the long run, of course, 'career education,' like any other educational concept, will be defined by individual school systems and communities across the nation. . . . The real leadership in the career education movement has come from those local communities throughout the country who have undertaken to define career education in terms of the action programs they run."[4]

Like Hoyt, we know that the final definition of career education—if it ever assumes a permanent form—will be constructed not in Washington but in the states and communities and in the colleges and universities, and by the scholars and practitioners closely related to the implementation of this instrument for educational reform.

A significant move toward consensus in the definition of career education is unfolding during the summer of 1974. The Chief State School Officers, assembled in Washington on June 13, 1974, accepted a report from its Committee for Career Education in which the following statement was ratified, including the tentative definition:

A Definition

The Committee is cognizant of the need for operational definitions of Career Education to be developed within and by the individual states. The Committee is of the opinion, however, that the Council should adopt, as a base, some type of functional definition into which state definitions might fit.

It is therefore recommended that the Council adopt, or indicate its agreement with, the following tentative definition of Career Education.

Career Education is essentially an *instructional* strategy, aimed at improving educational outcomes by relating teaching and learning activities to the concept of career development. Career Education extends the academic world to the world of work. In scope, Career Education encompasses educational experiences beginning with early childhood and continuing throughout the individual's productive life. A complete program of Career Education includes *awareness of self* and the *world of work, broad orientation to occupations* (professional and non-professional),

in-depth *exploration* of selected *clusters*, career preparation, an *understanding of the economic system* of
which jobs are a part, and placement for all students.

The Critics, Bless Them

"The great campaign against the . . . school has now reached the stage of overkill. It is impossible to believe that anything new can be added to the attacks already delivered . . . the critics are repeating themselves." (Robert M. Hutchins, February 1973)

There are at least two kinds of critics who relate to education—those who would like to help and those whose criticism is either nonconstructive or based on faulty data. For our purposes here, I do not plan to treat the former, the constructive critics of career education, in any detail. I count myself among them. For example, one of my distinguished predecessors in the post of U.S. Commissioner of Education, Harold Howe, II, has been described as lining up on the other side. I think not. In May 1972 Mr. Howe addressed a conference on the subject sponsored by Educational Testing Service:

> As I see it, the concept of career education should be supported by the professional educational establishment of this country . . . it holds the hope of helping to make their educational experience more useful for more young people [and] . . . could bring about very useful institutional reforms. . . .

As an informed critic, Howe continues:

> In some of the statements I have read, I find disturbing
> suggestions that it may be a panacea. I am reasonably sure
> it is not.

To say that Howe and all other critics of career education are altogether opposed to the concept would be to count Paul Tillich as opposed to religion, or Vincent Canby as opposed to motion pictures. So I will quickly agree with Howe's admonition, and pass on to the more negative and possibly ill-informed critics.

The absence of any kind of noticeable criticism to the career education idea during its first year or two of development in the Office of Education (1971–1972) gave me serious concern. At that time the concept received such unqualified endorsement from all observable quarters that I knew something was wrong. The unanimity of response, at first, was like a time of quiet in military combat—more to be suspected than enjoyed.

One reason I attach to the lack of opposition in the first two years was that potential opponents thought it a passing notion that would soon go away, and not without reason, for such is the destiny of most educational ideas leading to reform. But another serious condition seemed to set in, dampening the clash of debate. Many who first examined the concept of career education saw it as a Rorschach design; they read it as they saw it, and they saw it as something they wanted to believe in. But they may have misread it.

In due course, the silence was broken, and opposing views began to surface along in mid-1972. I was relieved, for, without the discipline of debate and the clarifying effect it would have on our purposes, I felt career education would drift into a catch phrase for justifying nearly any educational design that individuals wanted to attempt. That condition is not resolved yet, and there is still a Rorschach effect in many quarters. But the confrontation of criticism, both positive (as in Howe) and negative, is essential to the advancement of understanding.

The negative criticisms fall into several general categories, and derive from several general types of individuals or institutions.

The general categories of disagreement, as I perceive them, are as follows:

1. Career education is anti-intellectual.

2. The concept is too fuzzy and ill-defined.

3. Blacks and other minorities are threatened by what might become "tracking."

4. Young children are not ready to "decide" about their careers.

5. Career education is solely concerned with getting jobs and filling manpower needs in a capitalist system.

6. The colleges and universities are already threatened with a lowering or a leveling-off of enrollments—career education may aggravate this problem.

7. Career education programs are "taking money away" from vocational education programs.

8. The unpredictability of the manpower needs of this country makes career education a "futile exercise."

9. Career education is a device for perpetuating a "corporate social order," reinforcing big business and productivity, as distinct from values related to human services.

10. The concept appears to perpetuate the stereotyping of occupations by sex, and gives insufficient attention to women in all occupations.

One of the first systematic expressions of disagreement with the career education concept occurred in October 1972, when the Council for Basic Education asked me to meet with their board of directors and "enter a conversation on the record" with James Koerner, former Council executive and now an officer of the Sloan Foundation. Other individuals and groups have taken positions similar to those expressed by Mr. Koerner. Their general message is: *"Career education is anti-intellectual."*

I greatly enjoyed my "confrontation" with the Directors of the Council for Basic Education. It was useful to me as the first encounter with earnest critics, and I hope it prompted some enlightenment to the members. As the three-hour discussion drew to a close, Clifton Fadiman, member of their Board of Directors and distinguished author and critic, observed: "Commissioner, you and I are nearer to each other than I thought."[1]

We Americans seem to have a disposition to assume that, if someone is *for* something, he is *against* something else; in this case to be *for* occupational training suggests that it follows that one must be against academic development. Not so. Broadly, this is the basis, I believe, of the "anti-intellectual" misperception. While I doubt that I could convince all the members of the board of the Council that this is a faulty assessment, I believe it is. Intellectual development and all that it implies for academic excellence, cultural and aesthetic growth, and the liberalizing of the mind and spirit are basic and unequivocal objectives of education at all levels. The career education theory asks that the development of the intellect not be isolated from other worthy goals for education. I hold, with considerable feeling, that for many of our young people much of our formal academic and cultural education will be enhanced and enriched by articulating such learning with an individual's personal goals. We ask for the humanizing and individualizing of formal teaching in our schools and colleges through consciously relating academic teaching to the vast array of useful purposes to which it can be put. The center of instructional focus shifts from the *content* to the *learner*, but in no way diminishes the learning to be acquired. It should enhance it. James Spradley, anthropologist at Macalester College, notes: "The goal of career education is to enable every person to make informed choices as he develops his own career. The objective is to give a person a greater command over his own life. . . . I suggest . . . that this be . . . its primary goal."[2]

The State of Arizona was one of the first, under the leadership of Weldon P. Shafstall, State Superintendent, and a legislative committee of the State's General Assembly, to formalize career education in state law. This occurred in the 1971 legislative session. A publication for general circulation growing out of the new law states:

Career education *combines* the academic world with the world of work. It must be available at all levels of education from kindergarten through the university.

Another extract from the Arizona statement quotes F. R. Vihel of the state Advisory Council on Career Education:

We certainly don't want to discard the basics—the three r's are more important than ever, but our educational system must relate them to the world in which we live—to the world of work, and the world of leisure.

An Arizona fifth-grade teacher, James Leader, notes:

Career education is a good vehicle for the average teacher in that it provides motivation for the lesson. [Careers] can easily be related to specific lessons in any subject. . . . Career education is self-motivating and a natural for the teacher.

In 1970, Yale's President Kingman Brewster brought to the campus Philip F. Nelson, musicologist, to head the Yale School of Music. Dr. Nelson observes: "Not one music school in the country is really a professional training ground. Nobody has faced up to exactly what it is that they're training their students to do—and to help them find their way into the profession."[3] Part of Dr. Nelson's mission was to "shake Yale music out of its Ivy League isolation . . . to bring Yale closer to the practical side of music." In addition to attracting "distinguished musical artists," the school is involving union officials, recording company executives, and concert managers. It will come as no surprise that some "restiveness" prevails, according to Dr. Nelson, "among those who have been here a long time."

I cannot believe that bringing purposefulness and reality to music at Yale can be truthfully described as "anti-intellectual." As with younger learners, I believe it will enrich the quality of teaching and learning in the formal curriculum.

It is hoped that those who mistrust career education as being anti-intellectual will take the trouble to weigh other facets of this book. I believe that, like many quick appraisers, they have confused career education with vocational education. If they have, their judgment is correct—it would be an anti-intellectual exercise.

The second issue raised quite generally by critics is that *The concept is too fuzzy and ill-defined.*

In a very scholarly critique and analysis of the topic, David Rogers observes that career education is a "most significant reform strategy" but, he continues:

> The movement has, not unexpectedly, many critics who argue that it is in reality just the most recent fad; that it is old wine with a new label; that it remains a well-kept secret in Washington, not having been articulated or spelled out to any degree. . . . [4]

Professor Rogers' statement is quite valid, as he *reports* the impressions of others. He appears not to support all of their criticisms himself, but "fad," "old wine," and "well-kept secret" are comments I have heard regularly. Rather than simply respond with my own rhetoric, it may be useful to hear others. Keith Goldhammer of Michigan State University notes:

> It is argued . . . that Career Education constitutes a new, vitalizing thrust in education. There are, of course, those who will say that it is just another passing fancy and, if we don't pay too much attention to it, it will go away and leave us undisturbed. The evidence mounts daily that this is not the general reaction. The increasing public and legislative reaction to Career Education is one of hope that a new paradigm for educational operations has finally been found which will not only provide a basic social return consistent with the anticipated human and financial inputs, but a relevance for youth which will help them find their social identifications and secure a sense of mission and destiny as participating members of society. . . .

Returning to Rogers, in the critique cited above he addresses the fuzziness of the meaning of career education:

> Perhaps a major error in strategy has been to apply the

label so fully, without at the same time explicating to interested parties how and why particular programs exemplify it and how they are to be implemented. Social movements often tend to over-simplify and adopt slogans to develop a following, and career education may be no exception. On the other hand, if excessive use of the term produces increasing cynicism it should be dropped and some other language used. What is important is not the word magic attached to the slogan "career education," but the substantive program ideas that go along with it.

Whatever may be perceived by the critics, we did not choose *career education* as a slogan. Rogers may well be right in raising the faulty perception, held by some. I would quickly agree that it should be set aside if found to be a hollow catch phrase. We chose the name, as noted in an earlier chapter, as a brief and hopefully meaningful descriptive term. Chapter 5 explains in some detail our reasons for shunning an official federal definition. This may, indeed, as Rogers notes, have been a strategic error. If so, I take personal responsibility for the fault. Having viewed the unfolding of the idea, however, over the past four years, I am certain that, given the chance to start again, I would still have avoided the convention of an early definition. I believe there would not have followed the vigorous, creative, and enterprising initiatives by state and local school systems and universities nor would there have been the constructive debate that has ensued. The "fuzziness" is a product of many responsible people taking earnest measures to act upon the general criteria of career education, and quite expectedly in Vermont producing different conceptions from those in Oregon or Alabama. At this stage of development, if there is "fuzziness" (translated "inexactness"), I believe it is good. It is also consistent with the pervasive discipline in Washington that places primary responsibility for education in the states and assiduously avoids anything that smacks of federal prescription.

On the matter of "old wine with new labels," the critics are probably falling into the trap of viewing career education as vocational education with a new name. While we have endeavored from the start to make the distinction clear, there are those who run too swiftly as they read to comprehend the difference.

One of our country's most competent authorities in the field of vocational education, Lowell Burkett, Executive Officer of the prestigious American Vocational Association, treats the "old wine, new labels" issue:

> In some quarters, vocational-technical education is syn-
> onymous with career education, and nothing could be
> further from the truth. While vocational-technical educa-
> tion is an important part of career education, it is only a
> part of the total career education system.[5]

As long as the concept continues to flourish, with reasonable differences in definition evolving, it remains a lively instrument for reform. If Washington was indeed viewed as "keeping a secret," it was not keeping silent on research initiatives, alloca-tion of funds to states and cities, declarations of high-priority federal goals, and Presidential messages. Something unsecretive was happening, and still is.

The next issue to be examined is less simple to express, or to debate: *Blacks and other minorities are threatened by what might become "tracking."*

While it is simple to state very bluntly that the reverse is true, the fact remains if minority observers believe it is so, we have failed adequately to convey the message. Black and Chicano educators have had a significant part in helping to shape the concept of career education, and I find these colleagues warmly supportive of its intent. But it is no world-shaking news to note that not all Blacks and all Chicanos speak for each other any more than whites do.

Sally Barber Spitzer, speaking for the National Urban League's Educational Policy Information Center, writes:

> [Career education] may be used as a weapon of oppres-
> sion against the community of non-Whites in this country,
> trapping them into an occupational fiefdom of servitude to
> a privileged professional class.

One could argue that the absolute opposite direction is intended by those of us who helped to advance the theory. The unhappy record of our society's ineffectiveness in elevating minority people to a position of equity in employment is well known. It is a disgrace. If we treat the subject of employment alone (and career education addresses many other topics) we must face the fact that unemployment rates for Blacks are twice those of the total population at about 11 percent, and for Black females it is worse.

The hasty reader of our career education philosophy fails to take account of our hope that elementary and secondary education will, finally, be meaningful and useful to those who now are finding it irrelevant. They leave the system in large numbers, without pride or purpose or salable skills. This condition is not, by any means, limited to minority young people, but it affects them in more than ordinary degree. Career education, while in no way focused especially toward the minority student, has particular meaning. It seeks to give a sense of *control* over the ultimate personal goals for its learner with corresponding expectations for motivation in basic studies, and it asks that every learner be equipped upon leaving the system to enter productive work. Both of these conditions of career education have immediate and affirmative values for the minority student, including the implications for more promising access to postsecondary education.

Whereas "tracking" and all that the term implies is viewed as a threat to minorities, career education asks that *all* tracking be eliminated—the general curriculum, the vocational curriculum, and the heretofore exclusive college curriculum. All students learn in a sequence of their own choosing. Tracking is *not* accommodated in the career education concept.

Lawrence Davenport, Vice President for Development at Tuskegee Institute, a Black, has written:

> The concept of career education holds greater promise for Black students to attain a good education and preparation for interesting and constructive careers than any of the civil rights acts [or] Supreme Court decisions. . . . Career Education is *not* a tracking system that puts the sheep on one path and the goats on another. All students will

receive both academic and occupational training, and their interest in one area will not preclude their switching to another if they change their minds. . . . The choices involved will be made by students, not teachers or administrators.[6]

Edmund Gordon, a Black professor at Columbia long before Black professors were commonplace, has stated:

Career education does not involve a separate emphasis on one's education or natural development, but a comprehensive concern with career development, in which "career" is defined as the course by which one develops and lives a responsible and satisfying life.[7]

Representative Shirley Chisholm has had some good things to say about career education. She has also expressed concern. She is especially sensitive about another "put-on" for minorities. She has seen educational programs come and go, with presumed attention to the needs of minority young people. She is understandably cautious.

So am I.

George R. Quarles is the chief administrator of the Office of Career Education in New York City's Board of Education. He is Black. He reports to Associate Superintendent Edyth Gaines, who is also Black. Quarles is the author of New York City's policy statement on Career Education:

Career education is derived from the logical assumption that the education process should help the student to develop the capacity and skill to achieve self-fulfillment and economic independence. . . . Career education concerns itself as much with the academic backbone which supports skills training as with skills training itself. . . . [It] acknowledges and recognizes the inevitable interdependence between the humanities and the tool skills. . . . Career education is as vital to the academically successful student as it is to the disaffected and the marginal achiever.[8]

These Black educators—who have thought deeply about career

education and are contributing to its advancement—are clearly not worried about tracking in the elementary and secondary schools.

Addressing the subject at the postsecondary level, Robert C. Weaver, distinguished Professor of Urban Affairs at Hunter College, has written:

> The most challenging aspect [of the urban university's] mission lies in the imperative to provide high quality educational opportunities for the newer groups admitted into the institution. . . . it cannot be ignored either in our thinking or in the university's performance. It calls for dedication, innovation, experimentation, and commitment of resources. Related to it is . . . the growing emphasis upon career training in urban universities.[9]

At the suggestion of a number of minority leaders in education, the Office of Education in February 1973 shared the sponsorship of a conference devoted solely to the minority student and career education. Other sponsors were the Council of Chief State School Officers, the National Advisory Council on Vocational Education, and the State Higher Education Executive Officers. The registration for the three-day conference included 161 Black Americans, 83 white Americans, 29 Mexican Americans, 20 American Indians, 20 Chinese Americans, 12 Japanese Americans, 7 Puerto Ricans, and 1 Philippine American.

The conference, after extensive deliberation, with several formal addresses by minority educators as well as by government officials, including me, submitted some twenty recommendations concerning the further development of career education.[10] While neither endorsing nor taking a position against career education, the conference presented caucus reports from the several ethnic bodies represented, along with resolutions guiding further policy development. Congresswoman Chisholm, in addressing the conference, voiced the spirit of the assembly: "The first point I want to make is that seeing representatives of minority groups getting together *before* a new educational concept is put into practice rather than *after* the damage, if any, has been done is very important."[11]

The full thrust of the conference was distilled in a discerning paper by Alfredo G. de los Santos, Jr., President of El Paso Community College, who wrote:

> There is an old *dicho*—a saying or proverb—in Spanish that says that a cat which has been burned with hot milk will even blow at cottage cheese. This is my position with career education. We in the Chicano community have been so burned by hot milk—not only vocational education, but the whole of the educational system—that we wish to blow on the cottage cheese—career education—before we partake of it.
>
> I am not saying that I as an interested Chicano educator do not accept the concept of career education. I have been involved in community/junior college education all my life and I have been working to develop curricular patterns and educational systems that incorporate most of the ideas upon with career education is based.
>
> So . . . it is not the concept of career education about which I have questions. It is with the implementation of the concept that I am concerned about. It is with the many, many safeguards that need to be taken to insure that the Chicanitos receive from the educational system the services they deserve. The many sins of omission and commission have the possibility of doing more harm to the Chicanitos than has been done to date. It is some of these questions that I hope to discuss in this paper, particularly as they relate to the problems of the Chicanitos in higher education, beginning with the pre-admission counseling, through upward mobility, through job placement.

The next issue to be addressed is the fairly frequent expression of misunderstanding about career education in the elementary schools: *Young children are not ready to "decide" about their careers.* This issue should be readily dismissed if the questioner puts the question in context. Since it derives from a faulty perception, I will not treat it in detail. Career education does not in any way seek to address career decisions in the elementary schools. The brief expression of the goal for elementary schools is "career awareness." Earlier chapters have dealt with the need for helping children become more familiar with work as a basic and respectable and necessary part of living. The elementary schools in the career education philosophy seek to restore what was once commonplace in our society in simpler times.

A mother from Tucson, Arizona, where career education has been introduced in the elementary schools, offers the following counsel:

> I have a child in kindergarten, and I am in favor of career education beginning at this level, as I can see a great interest in my child as to the workers around us and their function in society. . . . What better way is there to prove to the children that there is a need for [learning]. I have a great deal of confidence in the career education program.

Let us now examine another issue, as stated by some critics: *Career education is solely concerned with getting jobs and filling manpower needs.* This issue relates closely with the anti-intellectual issue, and calls for similar responses. Those of us who helped to conceptualize career education had no such thought in mind as a *primary* goal of career education. On the other hand, there is nothing wrong with getting jobs and meeting manpower needs. The critic here fails to comprehend the wholeness of career education as a proposition that blends the academic, cultural, and humanistic parts of education with the ultimate utilitarian parts, now often scorned by teachers and professors.

Our purposes in advancing career education in a fashion which would refute this criticism is offered by Cas Heilman and Keith Goldhammer, professor and dean, respectively, at the College of Education, Michigan State University:

> The schools [of the past] were only accountable for ensuring the adequate preparation of the select few. The success of the schools was noted in the large numbers of students who graduated and entered universities in the sciences and engineering. The failures of the school were noted in the dropouts and "push-outs" who constitute the foundation for the almost invisible social pathologies of the day.

Today, a new era is upon us. The general public, while not aware of the historical perspectives, are demanding an accountability which supersedes all others. This accountability is manifesting itself in the public's demand that the schools provide the same opportunity for all individuals which existed for the few in the 1960's and before. As we witness the growth in the human and social pathologies—crime, unemployability, the drug culture, the failure of individuals to cope with reality, the growth of custodial and welfare populations—the demand increases for the schools to do something to provide both the preventive and corrective measures.

The solution lies in the educational system's ability to help every child become a self-fulfilled, participating, and contributing citizen; to help all individuals acquire the competencies necessary to gain economic independence, social awareness, self- and social identity, and social status. This is the thrust and purpose of career education.[12]

Another quite different concern toward career education arises from the four-year colleges and universities: *The colleges and universities are already threatened with lowering or leveling of enrollment—career education may aggravate this problem.* This is a reasonable and fair appraisal. But the question to be raised is whether the colleges and universities should indeed engage the numbers of young people that they now engage, and whether all the young people who have enrolled in colleges and universities over recent years belonged there. During the 1960s, the higher-education institutions enjoyed a dramatic growth, a comfortable economic condition and a swiftly rising proportion of the age-population enrolled.

The emergence of career education has not contributed to the lowering or leveling off of college enrollment. Career education is, hopefully, a part of the solution—not the problem. When the long-awaited cessation of military obligations abroad occurred in 1972, many young people no longer had a reason for the shelter of the campus. More important, I feel, many young people had begun to find the conventional prescriptions of college and university curricula not suited to their purposes. For the first time, in 1973–1974, the percentage of white students entering college fell off, and this shook some college presidents and admissions officers and faculty. While the drop was a *percentage* drop only, and the total enrollment in absolute numbers continued to grow about 3.9 percent in 1973, the fall-off was seen as a disquieting straw in the wind.

But another force has entered the picture, apart from the disenchantment of some students. The Congress had, in its Education Amendments of 1972, acknowledged the presence of other institutions beyond high school which were embraced under the term "postsecondary education." This opened up a new access and respectability for community colleges and other two-year institutions: proprietary schools with very strictly limited occupational orientation; and the more flexible external degree programs and nontraditional studies within conventional colleges and universities. These are pragmatic learning resources, and they have begun to attract a pragmatic student population. I do not have a position yet as to whether this is altogether good or altogether bad. But I do believe that the career education philosophy is hospitable to the free choice of individuals in pursuing postsecondary education, and that the stereotype of the essentiality of the bachelor's degree for respectability is diminishing. Its eminence was a product of many things, including school superintendents like myself, who a few years ago saw college entrance as the simple symbol of "success" and accordingly pushed the children, the teachers, the counselors, and the principals as well as parents to go that way.

A statement from the Carnegie Commission on Higher Education, dated October 1, 1973, treats this topic:

> An expanded concern for postsecondary education that includes, but is not limited to colleges and universities is urged in a new report of the . . . Commission. . . . Colleges are not for everybody . . . the Commission urges young people and their parents to consider more carefully alternative channels to life, work, leisure. Because of their concentration on college education they have tended to ignore all other channels. . . . Academic degree-credit instruction for full-time students is an absolutely essential part of the whole, but is by no means the sum total of the formal education of Americans beyond the high school.[13]

More will be said of career education's relationship to higher education in a subsequent chapter.

Another frequently heard criticism is recorded as follows: *Career education programs are taking money away from vocational education*. This message most often comes from the state directors of vocational education, who have become accustomed to the *separateness* of vocational education from other parts of the education spectrum, especially at the secondary-school level. The issue begs the question. The fact of *separateness* has been the curse of vocational education from the beginning, as noted in earlier chapters. The earmarking of federal funds, starting with the Smith–Hughes Act of 1917, has created a fraternity of *different* programs, *different* teachers, and *different* money. The goals of career education are no different than the goals of vocational education, except that they reach all the young people and afford them a more complete educational experience. To claim that vocational moneys are to be used only for serving the small percentage of students who are enrolled is to claim that moneys appropriated by the local district for, let us say, English are "taken away" from music or any other budget item that must be drawn upon to serve a given need for a given student population.

Recalling the decisions made by chief state school officers in the summer of 1971 (Chapter 1) to commit Vocational Educational Act funds to career education model-building, it must be noted that the action was not an arbitrary ruling from Washington. Further, as a later chapter will describe, the federal funds for career education were drawn from many relevant authorizations, and were not limited to vocational funds. It is true that those funds established in law as discretionary resources for disposition by the Commissioner of Education were, by agreement with states, targeted on career education model-building, of which vocational education is an essential part. While traditional vocational education administrators and teachers may see this as a misdirection of "their" money, it is fair to say that nothing more supportive of vocational education has happened in the fifty-seven years since Smith–Hughes. As one vocational education state director put it, "We've suddenly become big-league."

The most sobering criticism of the career education concept is the fundamental question of future employment opportunities. With much validity the question is raised by those who see career education as overpromising the future: *The unpredictability of the manpower needs of the country makes career education a futile exercise.* Of the several declarations of doubt cast toward career education, the one I find most compelling is this one. The case is stated with exceptional clarity and scholarly analysis by T. H. Fitzgerald, writing in the University of Chicago's *School Review* for November 1973:

> Career education suggests an essentially futile exercise because most people simply cannot plan how they will spend their years. . . . Training youths in job skills will simply not produce more jobs (except for instructors). . . . The level of [occupational] choice is greatly reduced when there is high unemployment, while the wider availability of choices in full employment is bought at the cost of inflation.

Fitzgerald goes on to express distress over excessive "credentialism" in the work force, and the corresponding unrealistic hiring standards of many employers. "Career education opens up the whole question of institutional gatekeeping in a society which not only wants to be free and equal, but also wants to be efficient."

In short, those who take this position question the responsiveness of our economic society to the capacities and hopes of the young. I share this concern. Eli Ginzberg, who should know, told me that the art and science of manpower forecasting is still operating at a very low level of reliability. (Note the surplus of teachers, aerospace engineers, lawyers and chemists.) He also sees little hope in the short run for improvement. (Dr. Ginzberg has served as chairman of the National Manpower Committee since 1962 and holds the directorship of the Columbia University project on the Conservation of Human Resources.)

Yet, the concept of career education is not as restricted in its purposes as Fitzgerald would imply, nor is it as dependent upon the predictable and specific manpower needs that Ginzberg admits are difficult to foresee.

As noted by Howe in a citation earlier in this book, career education is not offered as a panacea. Those of us who are essentially educators do not claim to have the answers to the future economic and manpower circumstances of our society. We are mindful of their uncertainty and the precariousness of prediction. It is for this very reason, along with others, that we urge against specific and narrowly conceived job preparation or professional development. We make the assumption that most people will need to work and will want to work in the following generations. We hold that readiness in attitude, values, versatility, and comprehension of work options are necessary ingredients of an educational program designed to help young people enter the work force. We declare one of the goals of career education to be the readying of young people for coping with change. But we are not saying that bricklayers, or computer programmers, or cosmetologists or physicians will, in the future, perform their tasks, if their tasks persist, as they are performed today. Coping with uncertainties and having the developed capacities to make good decisions is part of career education's offering for the young.

Willard Wirtz, President of the Manpower Institute and former Secretary of Labor, reaches beyond the anxieties of Fitzgerald and asks for a higher order of articulation between education and work than our limited view now provides:

> What seems to be important in the relationship between education [policy] and manpower policy can be reduced to three propositions:
>
> 1. These are both concepts in quest of themselves. In the case of education, it is a mature pursuit, while manpower policy is a foundling looking for its birthright.
>
> 2. Part of the answer to each of their seekings lies in a fuller recognition of their interrelatedness.
>
> 3. There is neither an ultimate educational nor ultimate work ethic which is meaningful apart from a rational life ethic. . . . The real quest must be for the relationship of learning *and* work to an ultimate purpose lying beyond either of them.[14]

Wirtz continues: "The reason a lot of those 4 million 16 to 19 year-olds will be delayed too long moving from education to employment is that they will have ended their education without ever even being exposed to what work—employment—means."

I have not, even with Wirtz's help, wholly responded to the dilemma of the unpredictability of manpower needs. This is not education's business, but we do not wash our hands of the issue. Educators and employers along with labor must forge a much more fruitful alliance than we now have to help resolve this predicament. But even that is not enough, for today's vice president for personnel can only tell us what the needs of his corporation are a year or two hence. We have to have better signals in education for what the needs will be a decade or two ahead. Career education as now conceived will not *depend* upon this new wisdom, but it would help if we had it.

On the other hand, lacking a knowledge of the future, we *could* sit on our hands and worry. It would be easier. We must intensify the systematic forecasting of manpower needs. This is probably a Department of Labor responsibility, but it is a problem to be addressed by all levels of government and by the private sector.

Two thoughtful writers have expressed misgivings about what they see as an insidious alliance between big business and career education. Writing in the *Kappan* in February 1973, Robert J. Nash and Russell M. Agne, professors of education, state to the following effect: *Career education is a device for perpetrating a "corporate social order" reinforcing big business and productivity as distinct from values related to human services.* Joining Nash and Agne for other reasons would be some voices from organized labor, such as John A. Sessions of the AFL–CIO Department of Education.

These observers suspect a collusion between education and the business world that would constrain young people to enter conventional employment meekly, without considering alternative work themes. Sessions particularly mistrusts the implications of work experience for young learners as a threat in the form of "what might be done to relax the minimum wage laws and child labor laws."

As far as I know, career education has no sinister alliance with big business. It has enjoyed enthusiastic support from some businessmen and from the U.S. Chamber of Commerce, as well as from some distinguished labor leaders. Yet it does attempt to address, for purposes of acquainting students with the world of work, real situations in which industrialized America is moving toward ever-enlarging corporate institutions with the danger of corresponding reductions of individuality. This is a fact, not something that education encourages. We also note that Nash and Agne mistrust education's implicit acceptance of "high productivity; spiraling wages; automation; increasing economic growth; acceleration . . . social change; systematic administration; complex, long-scale organizations; and a technical approach to the resolution of human problems."

If these attitudes and conditions are, indeed, a part of our present economic system, I say young people should be mindful of them. But no one engaged seriously in career education says that young people are all obliged to enter the big corporate system. Our early clusters of occupational options took note of the artists, musicians, poets, and players as worthy career models as well as those who more directly serve society in the humanistic tasks of social worker, nurse, city planner, teacher, and clergyman. We have noted over the past three years that some young people may not choose careers relating to economic gains or goals. Some have, in the Peace Corps spirit, showed evidence of shunning traditional, economically oriented employment for work that they feel is of a higher order of human service. And more power to them; they may have discovered an ethic better than those of their elders. But the facts of career education still hold; if the idealistic young volunteer wants to serve without significant material reward, he would be well advised to have a useful skill or a developed talent that will turn his idealism to meaningful ends, such as building dams, or raising poultry, or ameliorating disease.

The final criticism did have validity: *The concept appears to perpetrate the strengthening of occupations by sex, and gives insufficient attention to women in all occupations.* During the early year or two of career education's development, we tended to fall into the trap of stereotyping work opportunities by sex, though not deliberately.

Among those who challenge the career education concept insofar as equality for women is concerned is Professor Edna Mitchell of Smith College. She, quite aptly in my judgment, declares that career education has failed to recognize "the seriousness of the vocational misdirection of girls." She believes the "sexist prejudices still pervade the entire curriculum and are subtly reflected in the attitudes of school personnel." Pressing for corrective measures in the elementary schools, Professor Mitchell argues that "attitudes limiting women's career opportunities are rooted deep in early childhood."

Harold Howe has served again as a constructive critic. "I have seen precious little in the literature about career education on this . . . problem [of job stereotyping for females]. But if the schools mean business about it, they will have to start in the elementary schools to change the image of women's roles. . . . Career education in schools will have to decide how to deal with these new aspirations."

Admitting inadequate attention to the subject of women in occupations during the beginning years of career education's emergence, there seem now to be affirmative measures afoot. The Office of Education in 1973 made clear to all grantees receiving federal funds that true equality of opportunity would be required in access to all career education programs, without regard to sex.

Of more importance as a fundamental force in moving to affirmative action is the research of the National Institute of Education. The NIE priorities give emphasis to the place of women in the work force. The following statements are extracted from research and development plans for NIE dated December 3, 1973:

> . . . problem areas have been identified for research and development: These are . . . *B1.* to increase career opportunities for women and minorities.

Under the subhead Access to Careers, the NIE plan states:

> . . . Stereotyping of occupational opportunities, es-
> pecially on the basis of sex, occurs at an early age and is
> not changed by usual school experiences.
>
> Materials designed to assist in the development of career
> awareness often limit an individual's horizon, or channel
> his/her development on the basis of sex rather than
> abilities and interests.

More will be said later on the work of NIE, but, under the
current direction of Dr. Corinne Reider, I am certain that career
education's research and development arm will give a full accounting to the place of women.

Nearly all those who have negative views toward career education express a "well, it has its good points, but . . ." In response
I can say with earnestness that they, too, have their good points.
They will, hopefully, bring a steadily increasing meaning and
effectiveness to career education through honest inquiry and
debate.

In preparing this chapter I have drawn heavily upon a 1974
special report of the National School Public relations Association,
*Career Education: Current Trends in School Policies and Pro-
grams*. After a very lucid and even-handed examination of career
education, including full attention to the critics, the report
concludes:

> But in spite of the pitfalls, the criticisms and the continu-
> ing dialogue about how to define the concept and imple-
> ment it, the evidence all points to a strong possibility that
> career education is the major redirection of the entire
> educational system.

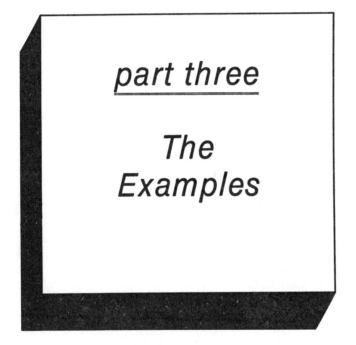

part three

The
Examples

Career Education
in Georgia

Georgia's initiatives in what has now come to be called career education trace back to the 1960s, when some basic decisions affecting the direction of education in that state were made under the leadership of Dr. Jack P. Nix. Dr. Nix has since become the State Superintendent of Schools. At the time, as director of Georgia's vocational education program, Nix began to guide the state toward an early career education model, first by adding the function of career guidance to the vocational education division. Then he began to push toward a statewide network of comprehensive high schools, gaining the full commitment of both the State Board of Education and the Georgia legislature in this effort.

I have chosen to describe in considerable detail in this chapter the work going on in Georgia. While the terms may have been different in the early stages, the public elementary and secondary schools of Georgia have been undergoing major educational reform for about ten years. The central theme of that reform is the articulation of occupational learning with academic learning. Both as director of vocational education and later as the chief state school officer Jack Nix has brought vision, continuity, and powerful professional leadership to the educational institutions of his state. Other states which seek to move in the direction of career education would do well to examine Georgia's program, and profit from their trail-breaking.

In 1966, during his first year as state school superintendent, Dr. Nix set fifteen goals for education in Georgia for the next decade—and one of these was the establishment of exploratory vocational programs for elementary and junior high students. In 1968, Department of Education staff, under Director of Vocational Education George Mulling, began to design these exploratory programs, starting with revamping the prevocational curriculum in industrial arts, agriculture, business education, and home economics. To meet the need to acquaint junior high students with career opportunities and the process and effects of career decision-making, PECE (Programs of Education and Career Exploration) was approved for pilot implementation in 1969. Since then it has grown to offer career exploration opportunities to more than 27,300 students in 112 Georgia programs.

Today, the entire Georgia Department of Education is committed to the concept of career education. At the end of Fiscal Year 1973, the Department reported 6000 students in 114 programs of Coordinated Academic and Vocational Education, 9720 students in 54 elementary career education programs, 11,505 students in mini-prevocational programs, 860 students in 74 ACTION programs, 3360 students in 84 World of Construction and World of Manufacturing programs, and 54 job placement programs around the state. Georgia had 347 high schools offering some vocational programs at the end of FY 73, 61 of them comprehensive high schools offering a wide range of career development options. The state is opening 17 more comprehensive high schools in 1974, as implementation of the statewide plan and objectives goes forward.

Georgia's continued leadership in the development of a career education program has come about under the guidance of Associate Superintendent of Schools Dr. H. Titus Singletary, Jr., Instructional Services; Assistant Superintendent Dr. Russell Clark, Vocational and Adult Education; George Mulling, Director of the Division of Planning and Development; and Dr. Gene

Bottoms, Director of the Division of Program and Staff Development.

Dr. Bottoms and other Georgia educators such as Debera Sharpe, Don Hogan, Raymond S. Ginn, Paul Scott, Dr. Fred Otte, Vick Bullock, Dr. George L. O'Kelley, and Dr. H. R. Cheshire, have actually put the career education concept into operation.

Their program is comprehensive, detailed, and successful. Early data—fragmentary at this stage—have indicated that the career education program is resulting in more positive attitudes on the part of young people toward schools and toward themselves. There has been a reduction of school dropouts, a growth in academic achievement, and an increase in student motivation.[1] Much of the remainder of this chapter draws heavily upon interviews with Georgia educators and upon their official publications, paraphrased and condensed here and their, but not excessively footnoted.

In Georgia, according to Dr. Bottoms, "Career education is viewed as an approach, a concept of education that cuts across all program areas and has considerable potential for achieving our often stated educational objectives."

They began by defining terms. Dr. Bottoms regards "career" as meaning "a purposeful life pattern which an individual possesses." It means more than pursuing an occupating, being employed, or holding a job. The term "career" in the Georgia context is described as follows:

1. A career is what one lives to do, rather than what one does to live.

2. A career is that mission in life which serves as an integrative factor to other arenas of one's life.

3. A career may or may not be a paid activity; it could represent voluntary work.

4. A career does not imply a given educational level; a career may require considerable preparation and skill or may require little training and skill.

5. A career should take into account the continued choices an

individual has to make throughout his life regarding education, employment, or voluntary work; it sould provide for relating individual decisions to existing, intermediate, and future choices.[2]

If "career " connotes a "purposeful life pattern," according to Dr. Bottoms, "career education is a range of educational processes that focuses upon facilitating the individual's achievement of his own life planning and fulfillment. It is the process through which each individual discovers himself, achieves a self-determined life goal, and acquires competencies necessary for achieving his self-fulfillment."

But this was career education in broad idealistic terms, and the Georgia Department of Education acknowledged the need to refine and pin down the definitions. "It's one thing," said Dr. Bottoms, "to define career education in generalized terms and concepts; it is another to agree on what it is operationally." The educational leaders in this state realized that anything new or innovative, such as career education, would be defined by other educators, students, and the community in terms of their own experience and expertise. They also knew that many of the definitions would vary from each other. They anticipated what different authorities would construct, and fashioned a set of issues and answers:

1.   To some vocational educators, career education is a new word for the traditional programs of skill development.

Certainly job skills are a *part* of any comprehensive career program, but career education also includes personal and social adaptive skills necessary to direct one's own career life in the midst of rapid change.

2.   General educators may interpret it to mean a special unit or course on career orientation taught by the social studies teacher.

Yes, career education involves career content, but it is also infusing into *each curriculum area at all educational levels* career oriented activities designed to accomplish career development tasks and objectives, as well as other educational objectives.

3. A counselor may interpret it to mean career day, an occupational library, an interest inventory, a unit on how to apply for a job.

Such activities can and do add to the overall career education effort, but students should also know, observe and imitate a wide range of workers, gaining "real life" experiences from which they can continually clarify and define their own career identities.

4. An industrial arts specialist may see career education as the teaching of technology.

Understanding the nature of our technological society is certainly important. But career education is also self-understanding in relation to that society. Such understanding comes from students having had the opportunity to "try themselves out," to test their hypothetical career self-images through real experiences in the broad work areas that make up our technological society.

5. The scheduling committee may think career education is for students who are failing Georgia history and freshman literature.

Career education does add a new dimension of relevance to the academic skills as well as the opportunity to acquire entry level job skills and an identity for future work roles. But career education is for all students, all teachers, and all curriculum areas; it assists in developing the personal, academic, and occupational skills needed by all individuals, regardless of their chosen careers.

6. To some educators, career education means a chance to explore the real world of work, to get "hands-on" experiences.

Without this aspect, career education is a hollow exercise in rhetoric, another program "telling" the students what it's like to be adults. But, in addition to "hands-on" experiences, career education should also assist students, through structured group or individual activities, to personalize and interpret such experiences in terms of their own career self-images. It is constant practice in the decision-making process so that when the big decisions must be faced, the student has had realistic practice on which to draw.

7. A curriculum specialist may think of career education as a rebirth of the old core curriculum idea.

Indeed, career education has some points in common with previous curriculum innovations, but it varies in several important ways, among the most important being that career education is a blend of instructional and guidance techniques grounded in the reality of the adult working world and geared to the student's individual interests, aptitudes, and, when appropriate, his own career objectives.

8. The businessman may view career education as the school's effort to get students ready to go to work.

Yes, it is the school's way of meeting, in part, its responsibility to prepare students for a smooth transition to the adult world. But career education may fail without the active support and participation of the home and community, which are learning laboratories for the skills of living in the adult world. The school must be ready to give equal recognition and credit to learning experiences in all three settings. The community must make learning experiences in business, home, agriculture, and industry available to students for orientation, exploration, and skill development.

9. The elementary teacher may see career education as a concept appropriate to the senior high school.

Career education is important for the student exiting from the security of the high school, but development of values, interests, self-concepts, and aptitudes cannot wait until the tenth grade. Such ideas begin forming very early in life and continually undergo growth and revision. Career education, therefore, is a development concept, extending over the entire life span of the individual, affecting all levels of education.[3]

To make career education operational at any school level without great financial outlay, the Georgia Department of Education, according to Debera Sharpe, decided to "use much of what teachers already knew and were doing." The strategies developed were characterized as follows:

1. The fusing of career activities into the ongoing curriculum

2. The interlocking of related subject areas around a core curriculum

3. Exploratory, prevocational and vocational curriculum, grades seven–twelve

4. Guidance

5. Job placement and follow-through[4]

Fusing is the process by which any teacher may bring related career content, activities, and resources into the ongoing curriculum in order to accomplish the following career development tasks and goals with the students:

1. Career planning and decision-making

2. Self-evaluation and clarification

3. Skills in relating to others

4. Career exploration and job preparation

5. Achieving work habits and attitudes appropriate to the individual

6. Educational and occupational information experiences

7. Development of skills needed in seeking employment

Of course, the degree to which these goals may be attained varies at different grade levels, but fusing career content and objectives into the curriculum is both useful and appropriate at all grade levels. In terms of structure, fusing is applicable in teaching plans for any curriculum area or self-contained classroom, enhancing student motivation and mastery of academic skills and concepts. Fusing enables students not only to see the relationship of each subject area to the world of work, but also to assess their own abilities and interests in terms of careers related to that field.

More specifically, not only would a student know about careers, say in chemistry, and his own preferences and abilities in the area, but he would also understand how chemistry is useful in a broad variety of occupations, how new discoveries in chemistry can affect the occupational structure of the economy by creating new industries and making old products obsolete, how—through pollutants, sanitation control, etc.—chemistry can affect the total working and living environment. Not only would he learn about careers in government at all levels from his civics teacher and have had experience "trying on" some of these roles, but he would also understand how governmental decisions at all levels affect the structure of a working economy as well as specific career areas and industries. For a student talented in English, the information and individual experiences relating to careers in the field should be coupled with illustrations of how communications skills are practiced by workers in a wide variety of occupations.

The elementary child learning to read or multiply would practice the use of that skill in connection with a unit on a specific career area, putting into practice John Dewey's theories that "no arrangement of facts exists for purely abstract ends" and that "knowledge [centering] around occupational activities is vital because it has reference to needs."

"What concepts am I teaching this quarter? Who uses these concepts in their work? How can I arrange similar experiences for my students so they may use the concepts I want them to master to solve problems they may face in a related career area? How is a knowledge of what I teach useful to all persons who work?" In very simplified terms, these are questions a teacher fusing career education into the subject matter might ask. They illustrate the kinds of teaching methods implied by the fusing strategy.

It is interesting to note the Education Amendments of 1972; in establishing new legal authority consistent with career education, the new law gives strong emphasis to the term "fusion." Georgia educators were using the term some years earlier.

Interlocking academic and vocational education, in the Georgia design, encompasses the same student goals as fusing, but differs in several important ways. Interlocking is the correlation of academic and applied learning. Basically, it means that a team of teachers meets together to develop all of the student's learning activities, in all of his junior high or secondary classes, around his career objective. For example, if the student is excited about a possible career using skills learned in the construction cluster, then the English, math, science, and social studies teachers would meet with the construction instructor to plan to teach the concepts of their disciplines as they apply to persons employed in various phases of the construction field. The intent of this instructional technique is not to limit the student's learning experiences to one specific set of skills, but to begin to develop academic skills in relation to his interests and successes. (This bears upon the motivational force of career education noted in earlier chapters.) As the student progresses, the content of the subject area may take on more abstract learning, but until he is on firm ground with basic concepts, he cannot grasp more sophisticated levels of the curriculum. This approach lays a firm foundation for the student who learns best from concrete examples related to activity-centered learning.

Interlocking involves a degree of curriculum change, maintaining the basic concepts of the subject area but turning content and teaching methods to focus on the individuals' specific career interests and alternatives. Fusing, by contrast, focuses on the existing curriculum and incorporates career content and objectives into the ongoing lesson plans. Fusing, generally speaking, is a technique appropriate to all students in all grade levels, while interlocking meets the needs of a specific group of students involved in one phase of the curriculum.

Interlocking involves structural changes, a team planning period, and block scheduling, while one teacher can successfully fuse career-oriented activities into any given subject area. Interlocking produces a unified learning program for students who are working toward a specific career goal, while fusing strategies can be useful to students pursuing a variety of goals or for students who are still in the process of exploring careers.

Exploratory, prevocational, vocational curriculum, 7–12, presented here and shown in the pages which follow, is a model used by Georgia in the junior high schools and in the comprehensive high schools and postsecondary vocational-technical schools to insure adequate preparation for students pursuing career options through these educational avenues.

(Junior High) At the junior high level, a three-year curriculum enables some students to progress toward a tentative choice of an occupational family and gives others an overall look at the structure of the world of work, stimulating further exploration and understanding of their economic environment. The first year includes orientation to several occupational categories classified according to the personal characteristics of workers. Students are placed in business, industrial, and agricultural settings in the local community to observe workers and work processes. Organized group sessions then encourage students to articulate their experiences with their formal learning, clarifying their own self-concepts in terms of the many dimensions of the world of work.

During the second year, students may elect to explore several occupational families by enrolling in mini-prevocational exploratory courses six to twelve weeks in length. In these courses, students perform simple tasks in a simulated work environment where they use the tools, materials, processes, and products peculiar to a given work setting.

During the third year, students may select a single occupational family for in-depth, "hands-on" experience in performing organizational, creative, operative, maintenance, and motivational tasks.

After each concrete experience of observing work first-hand or participating in a simulated work role, students look at that experience in terms of these types of questions: How did I feel about myself while involved in the work role? What are other jobs in our society that might provide similar satisfaction? What are the different decisions I would have to make to enter this kind of work? What kind of schooling would prepare me for it?

(Senior High) During grades ten through twelve, students may choose from several in-depth occupational clusters to develop job-entry preparation. In the eleventh or twelfth grade, students may specialize in an occupation by enrolling in a cooperative program or by applying for advanced placement in a postsecondary vocational school. Some students may prefer to enroll in a twelfth-year vocational course in preparation for further study at the postsecondary level.

(Postsecondary and Adult) At the postsecondary and adult levels, students may select from several institutions and from several specific occupational offerings. These offerings cover occupations requiring highly developed skills as well as those of a short-term and more specialized nature.

Guidance, in the context of career education, is broader than traditional interpretations. To accomplish the career development objectives outlined earlier, the entire school staff adopts guidance goals, with the counseling staff serving in a coordinating role. The counseling department's role continues with individuals and groups of students in personalizing their own career experiences, developing personal and decision-making skills, and planning for the future. But the guidance staff, as a part of the coordinating function of career guidance, also directs a team effort with teachers, parents, businessmen, and others to assist in matching career objectives to appropriate activities and resources.

Job placement and follow-through are the functions of assisting youth and adults to enter, to adjust, and to progress satisfactorily in a job. How does this look in practice? Consider the record of this north Georgia high school: One hundred nineteen graduating seniors, 26 school-leavers, and 63 high school students seeking summer work earned a total of $25,000 during the summer of 1972. These working young people paid over $4500 in state and federal taxes, gained valuable work experience, and made successful exploratory transitions from school to the adult world. In hard figures, this report represents a valuable accountability tool for the school and its job placement team.

Throughout the state, vocational teachers with community contacts and counselors have teamed together to help students find employment most suited to their individual interests and abilities. Extended-year contracts make possible concentrated summer efforts to find and develop job openings, to help students decide how and where to begin, and to follow through to see that the individual makes a satisfactory adjustment to his new employment setting, usually until he acquires job-seeking skills and acceptable work habits.

Job placement is a logical component in a career education effort designed to help each student prepare for his next step.

As well designed and thought-out as the Georgia plan for career education is, weaknesses are apparent. "My observation," says Dr. Bottoms, "leads me to believe that there are many reasons for these weaknesses, all of which are within our power to change without an outlay of dollars." The areas of weakness exist mainly at the secondary level, and Dr. Bottoms believes the obstacles revolve around these issues:

1. Why does the school exist?

2. Does the school serve all or just some students?

3. Is the curriculum adaptable to the individual needs of the students?

4. How can we combat general isolation and lack of interdepartmental communication?[5]

The continued advance of career education in Georgia will depend upon continued state leadership from all educators and the extent to which the secondary schools can be reformed through incorporating the principles and approaches of career education.

A promise of success is held out in Dr. Bottoms' reply to a teacher who asked, "I've seen so many things come and go in education. How do I know that this isn't just another fad?"

Dr. Bottoms replied, "Education must answer the challenge of a complex, rapidly changing society with creative ways of making the school experience meaningful and personally rewarding for *all* students in their preparation for successful entry into some adult role. . . . Career education is a step toward meeting that task. The name may change, but the survival of education as an organized institution within our society may very well depend upon the lasting adaptation of the goals, purposes, and strategies of career education."

Georgia, in my judgment, offers a good example of what can happen favorably under strong professional leadership committed to reform. This detailed accounting of Georgia's career education program is not offered as an explicit model for other states because each state should construct its own. However, the Georgia system has been emerging for nearly ten years; it can save other states much trial and error.

Career Education
In California

The fifty chief state school officers agreed in June 1971 to proceed
with the development of career education models. This agreement pertained to the uses of discretionary federal funds which
were under my jurisdiction as Commissioner of Education. California, under the leadership of State Superintendent Dr. Wilson
Riles, wasted no time in setting about its task. The U.S. Office of
Education, in tandem with Dr. Riles, identified Los Angeles as a
site for one of the national models.

On October 28, 1971, the Board of Education of the Los Angeles
Unified School District unanimously adopted the following position regarding career education:

> We believe that it should be the policy of our school
> district to provide career education for all youth and
> adults of the district to the end that . . .
>
> - no student drops out of school who is not prepared to
>   enter the world of work.
>
> - no student graduates who does not have salable skills
>   for productive work or college education.

- no adult is denied an educational opportunity to become properly employable.[1]

From this statement the district administration developed an operational definition of comprehensive career education:

> Comprehensive career education is a total program which interrelates content and delivery systems to provide cognitive, affective and psychomotor learning experiences appropriate to the developmental stages of students. Its purpose is to assist *each* individual to acquire a functional understanding of occupations and careers in both the contemporary and future worlds of work. It further serves to provide experiences both within and beyond the existing educational environments for the continuing accomplishment of an individual's career goals. Its [curricular] focus is the examination of human and non-human *resources, institutions* and *technology* as these interact to affect our social, political and economic way of life.[2]

This operational definition declares the system-wide policy of the Los Angeles Unified School District to implement the comprehensive career education concept at all grade levels. Los Angeles school leaders and the board of education consider career education a framework for the entire educational program, functioning as the *essential* articulating force within a broad-based curriculum. Their policy statement continues:

> [We] believe that this comprehensive position embraces an ethic broader than the work ethic. Discussion and debate of this issue have led us through the work and service ethics to the *ethic of intent*. [We] believe the ethic of intent is more congruent with and appropriate to the present and future needs of both individuals and society. This ethic assumes that each man is responsible for the effects of his own actions and that each individual must become a more potent force in shaping his own destiny and that of society.
> [We] further recognize that certain individuals have been excluded from practicing the ethic of intent. The idea that man reacts to the forces of society is, in our opinion, giving way to the notion that society must be continuously

regenerated by man. We view a comprehensive career education system as a facilitating process through which all individuals may better accomplish this emerging notion.

It is our belief that a comprehensive career education program which provides options and opportunities for *each* individual to experience the effects of his actions and thus to exercise the ethic of intent offers students a more realistic opportunity for full development.

The programmatic and organizational implications of our operational definition suggest a unifying and stimulating way to organize our educational programs. Our District is committed to the development of a balanced program in which guidance and its related pupil personnel services perform a complementary role to that of instruction.

We are further committed to a comprehensive involvement process at all major points at which schools contact other segments of our society. That is, we believe that honest articulation must occur between the education community and
• the lay public
• the business and industrial sectors
• the labor sector
• the governmental sectors.
  Equally important is the need to recognize the essential nature of an internal articulation within and among sectors of the educational community, such as:
• teachers
• counselors
• administrators
• university level colleagues.[3]

The comprehensive career education program is one of the five new goals established by Superintendent William J. Johnston and the Board of Education and designed for the "renewal" and revitalization of their public education system.

In September 1972, the Los Angeles City Schools were invited by the Office of Education to join five other school districts to form working models of career education within the existing school structure. The Center for Vocational and Technical Education at Ohio State University served as contractor for the Office of Education to coordinate this national developmental project.

The Los Angeles model was initially developed at Belmont High School and at three of the junior high schools and six of the elementary schools which fed into it. This pattern of clustering a sector of a school district, embracing K–12 or K–14, is fairly typical for the introduction of career education. The teachers and staffs of these ten elementary and secondary schools cooperated in the task of refocusing the instructional program, participating actively in the planning and design.

The Belmont subdistrict serves about 12,000 students, of whom more than one-half are Mexican-American or have Spanish surnames. Nearly 20 percent are Anglo and 10 percent are Oriental. Almost two-thirds of the junior high and senior high school students were enrolled in the general curriculum; one-fifth were enrolled in academic/college-preparatory programs. These data lead us to conclude that a very small fraction were engaged in conventional vocational education programs. The large percentage (two-thirds) enrolled in the general curriculum is regrettably typical of most large cities, especially those serving concentrations of disadvantaged children. Career education, as noted earlier, would eliminate the general curriculum.

"The installation of career education," according to Mr. Robert A. Sampieri, Director of the Los Angeles Comprehensive Career Education Model, "can only be originated from an understanding and an acceptance that a major role of education is to have every young person leaving our schools be capable of pursuing further formal education or entering useful and rewarding employment. Now the question is: Should the world of work be the school's concern? Our project's position is that the school should accept this role and begin early to provide experiences for *all* youngsters appropriate to achieving this goal."

Los Angeles' decision to adopt the career education concept was not an attempt to solve all the problems facing education. "It was, however," said Mr. Sampieri, "an attempt to make the process of education more relevant to the world of work and leisure by broadening each student's awareness of his capabilities and assisting him in learning the means of achieving his personal goals."

In developing their comprehensive program, Los Angeles' total educational sequence—K–12—focused on four major phases as described below.[4] These *phases* are consistent with the general guidelines developed by the U.S. Office of Education. Some states and districts have modified them or expanded them.

Phase I: Career Awareness Phase I is concerned with the K–6 level. The goal is to develop in students an awareness of the personal and social significance of work. Each student will be helped to become more aware of himself, of his personal aspirations and abilities, and of the spectrum of careers available to him. At the K–3 level, children will develop a degree of career awareness consistent with their maturity. Two career clusters will be employed to cover the entire world of work: goods and services. Opportunities for developing awareness will be woven into existing curricular activities with stress laid upon recognizing the total life style of workers.

In grades 4–6, an increased sophistication of the student population will allow a clustering of occupations into five areas: (1) industry, (2) commerce, (3) social science, (4) services, and (5) arts. Students will explore all five clusters through curricular experiences. The building of career awareness will emphasize the nature and the interrelationships among occupations, the function of personal interests and aptitudes in career choices, and the continuing examination of value systems involved in the world of work, including affective learnings and decision-making.

Phase II: Career Exploration Emphasis in grades 7–8 focuses on career exploration, a series of highly detailed studies in twelve career areas: (1) natural resources, (2) construction, (3) manufacturing, (4) transportation and communication, (5) trade and finance, (6) government, (7) education, (8) health and welfare, (9) personal services, (10) product services, (11) arts and humanities, and (12) recreation and entertainment. These clusters have been developed and expanded from the five used at the 4–6 grade level, and are adaptations of the suggested fifteen clusters developed by the U.S. Office of Education.

This step in exploration will offer the student an opportunity to focus upon a more concentrated study of selected clusters, perhaps three or four. This exploration will include field trips and "hands-on" experiences as well as simulated experiences.

The objective is to provide exploration-observation experiences for all students in evaluating their interests, abilities, values, and needs in relation to their career and life aspirations. Such an evaluation could then guide the student toward his gradual selection of fewer career areas for the deeper exploration and career orientation of Phase III.

Phase III: *Career Orientation* Phase III is primarily concerned with grades 9–10. More in-depth exploration and beginning of the development of some skill competences in selected careers and career areas is the focus of this phase. Additional counseling and guidance activities are being designed to assist students in selecting career specialties for further development in grades 11–12. It is at this point that many students begin to tire of formal education, or at least to "vote with their feet" and drop out. Career education offers two responses to this problem: (1) It is hoped that the reality and satisfactions of the career curriculum will be sufficiently attractive to persuade the student to continue his studies, and (2) If he still chooses to leave at the legal age, he will have acquired a job-entry skill which suits him.

Phase IV: *Acquisition of Specific Career Competences* For the final high school grades, the goal will be to provide intensive preparation in a career objective of the student's choice. Curricular provisions are available to the student for meeting higher education entry requirements, if such a goal were to be the student's choice. Guidance and counseling will be intensified at these levels to assist in job placement, continuation of formal career training, or continuation into higher education with tentative career objectives clearly in mind. It is planned that guidance services will provide a continuous follow-up for all students leaving high school. This service is intended to afford a longitudinal information system which will be drawn upon by the staff for further program refinements over time.

Once the conceptualization of the program was decided upon, Los Angeles began to build the curriculum. This started with the setting of the parameters of the task, moved through construction of course-of-study units, validation, in-service training, and then delivery.

"A task force of thirty-three people, thirty of whom were teachers," explained Mr. Sampieri, "were assigned to set the limits of the program. Each person was relieved from regular duties so that he or she could devote full time to the curriculum." The task forces were guided by the criteria for curriculum construction established by the Center for Vocational and Technical Education at Ohio State University. These criteria include the following eight elements of career education as defined by the Center: (1) career awareness, (2) self-awareness, (3) appreciations and attitudes, (4) decision-making skills, (5) economic awareness, (6) skill awareness and beginning competence, (7) employability skills, and (8) educational awareness.

The task force worked under no other restrictions and was empowered to develop as many goals for the curriculum as it wished. Members of the task force were equally divided by grade levels, covering the full range of all subject areas. The goals that the Los Angeles task force developed were forwarded to the Ohio Center—as were the curriculum goals developed by the other six school districts engaged in designing career education models. Thousands of goals were submitted to the Center and about 150 course-of-study units were selected. Los Angeles in turn received the U.S. Office of Education contract to refine and develop thirty-five units under the Ohio State University agreement. According to Mr. Sampieri, "Curriculum building efforts have been standardized to a great extent, with all participants agreeing to a rather stringent set of guidelines." Following the guidelines closely assures the possibility for transportability of the units to other schools in the city and in the United States.

Los Angeles was also concerned about guidance. "The guidance components, or values," said Mr. Sampieri, "are to be fused into the curriculum. It is hoped that it will be difficult to decide where instruction leaves off and guidance begins." Through a planned set of experiences, every child in the comprehensive career model now under development will explore his interests, abilities, and achievements as they develop. "Rather than occasional meetings with counselors," explained Mr. Sampieri, "classroom teachers will help children to evaluate where they are, where they are going and methods for getting there."

Career education faculty and staff are able to get support for the changes implicit in the program by involving parents in the educational process. Mr. Tony Calvo, of the Los Angeles career education staff, says that "by getting parents involved in curriculum planning you get relevance. These people have real work experiences that none of us has." Parents of these schools, according to Mr. Calvo, are involved for the first time in curriculum development. "They are developing programs, talking about guidance, making the traditional curriculum more relevant."

Parents have, in fact, been involved with the development of career education at every step, as has the community in general, particularly the business sector. In the statement by the Board of Education defining the role of career education for the Los Angeles City District, the Board declared:

> We acknowledge the obvious limitation that a purely school-based program faces in attempting to deliver a comprehensive career education system. It is this limitation that has motivated us to seek a formal relationship with our business, industrial and labor sectors. This program is being developed primarily through a consortium of approximately 85 corporations and companies which had identified itself as "The Los Angeles Community Alliance for Career Education."
>
> It is our opinion that through such consortia and other organizational configurations which combine schools business, government, labor and other community-based organizations, we will be better able to deliver comprehensive career education to all our students.

The Los Angeles City Schools are given further community support by the surrounding Los Angeles County community. In the Los Angeles County area, top executive officers representing a hundred leading employers are now participating in the development and implementation of the six major programs which make up the thrust of Project 70's—Los Angeles Alliance for Career Education. Project 70's is a community partnership of business, government, labor, and education; it exists to provide more effective career education opportunities for all junior and senior high school students (including high school students in adult education programs) throughout Los Angeles County. "In contrast to other community-wide efforts," their report states, Project 70's is a "bold new action organization" focusing the resources of education, government, labor, and industry in a sustained attack on a single serious community problem— preparing students for more effective career choices.

The Los Angeles Unified School District (the city schools) is aggressively working with Project 70's and its six major programs which make up the thrust of the volunteer assistance offered by employers. These six programs focus upon: Work Experience and Exploration, Career Information, Tutoring, Teacher and Counselor Training, coordination of eight Industry/Education Councils, and management aid to school administrators. These programs are being coordinated through the techniques of managment by objectives to insure effective performance.

The following extract from the descriptive materials illustrates the range of competences in the citizen leaders surrounding the career education activities in the Los Angeles area:

> Our high level of community commitment and support for this alliance is demonstrated by outstanding community leaders who have agreed to serve as senior advisers. They include: Messrs. Sigmund Arywitz, Executive Secretary, Los Angeles County Federation of Labor, AFL–CIO; Daniel P. Bryant, Chairman of the Board, The Bekins Company; Gordon R. Elliott, Director, Federal Executive Board; Charles F. Horne, President, Industry-Education Councils of America; James E. Kenney, Vice President, Southern California Pacific Telephone Company, and Drs. Richard M. Clowes, Superintendent, Los Angeles County Schools, William J. Johnston, Superintendent, Los Angeles City Unified School District; and John A. Greenlee, President, California State University at Los Angeles. Mr. Victor Carter is Chairman of the Advisory Council and Dr. Kent Lloyd is General Chairman. Wayne M. Burnette, Pacific Telephone, is volunteer Executive Director.

In addition to the research and development effort in establishing the initial program, carried out with the Ohio State Center, the Los Angeles City Unified School District was also engaged by contract to do additional research for the state through the California Career Education Task Force. They were asked by the state education office to undertake four tasks.[5]

The first task was to investigate the feasibility of expanding career guidance capabilities. This task involved four simultaneous phases: (1) equipping each secondary school with a career resource center; (2) conducting a workshop for guidance personnel in the operation and maintenance of such a facility; (3) developing and publishing a resource for eighth-grade guidance classes; and (4) developing and publishing a career reference resource for use in the elementary grades.

The second task was to develop a computer-based prototype for a student information system which would be compatible with other data-gathering and display techniques and present system capabilities in various school districts. A summative assessment of the values and capabilities of such a system was also to be undertaken.

The third task would investigate the feasibility of a career awareness culminating experience for elementary children. The experience would involve travel beyond the district for observation of occupational roles beyond those more commonly available for inspection. An instructional guide to such an experience would be prepared.

The fourth task called for a study of the feasibility of training and utilizing paraprofessionals at the college level as counselor aides. This study is currently in operation with the aid of a local college and is being monitored by California Career Education college and school personnel.

The Los Angeles City Unified School District is one of ten sites in California that is doing the research and development in the field of career education. This initial work in Los Angeles—and the other sites—will serve as the experimental models for the master plan for implementation of career education throughout California.

The goal for California career education was developed at a workshop in Sacramento in April, 1972. It reads:

Through a comprehensive program of career education, each student will develop positive attitudes about himself and others, make sound decisions regarding alternative and changing careers, acquire skills leading to employment, and pursue a life style which provides self-fulfillment and contributes to the society in which he lives. Students of different ethnic origin, sex and socio-economic strata will be provided equal opportunities for successful achievement of these goals.[6]

Additionally, the following ten goals were developed for California's statewide program of career education:

1. *Career Awareness.*—Students wil demonstrate early and continuing awareness of career opportunities and relate them to their aptitudes, interests, and abilities.

2. *Self-Awareness.*—Students will develop a positive attitude toward self and others, a sense of self-worth and dignity, and motivation to accomplish personal goals.

3. *Attitude Development.*—Students will develop a positive attitude toward work and appreciate its contribution to self-fulfillment and to the welfare and productivity of their family, community, the nation and the world.

4. *Educational Awareness.*—Students will recognize that their educational experiences are a part of their total career preparation and development.

5. *Economic Awareness.*—Students will understand the economic systems of our society and become aware of the relationship of productive work to the economy, and their own economic well being.

6. *Consumer Competences.*—Students will achieve sufficient economic understanding and consumer competences to make wise decisions in the use of their resources.

7. *Career Planning and Decision-Making Skill Development.*—Students will engage in their own career-making development process. Students will increase their self-knowledge and

their knowledge of the world of work and of the society that affects it, and accept responsibility for a series of choices that carries them along the career development continuum.

8. *Career Orientation.*—Students will gain career orientation that will increase exposure of the options available to them in the world of work.

9. *Career Exploration.*—Students will plan and participate in a program of career exploration which will contribute to personal and career satisfaction.

10. *Career Preparation.*—Students will acquire skills leading to entry-level employment in one or more careers with provision for advance training and continuing education.[7]

The job of making career education a reality in the schools of California has been delegated to Paul N. Peters, Chairman of the Career Education Task Force. This Task Force is a component of the office of the California Superintendent of Public Instruction.

The Task Force and the Superintendent's office realize that career education will not work if imposed from the top down. "Change," says Mr. Peters, "comes from the bottom up. We will not get career education in California until the teachers are willing to change."

"It is easier," according to Mr. Peters, "to make the changes in the fifth, sixth, and seventh grades," for "elementary teachers have a wider view of education than the subject teachers in high school and college, while the students in the higher grades have a greater sense of career awareness than students in lower grades. What needs to be done throughout the school system is to shift the teaching emphasis and create 'learning managers' as well as teachers. This kind of emphasis places the student at the center of the learning process, not the teacher of the subject matter."

But making career education work in California will not be easy. There is resistance from parents and teachers and from minority populations, black and brown. The biggest problem appears to be the feeling that career education is just another form of tracking. "But career education," says Mr. Peters, "gets rid of tracking, especially in the secondary schools, by doing away with the general education curriculum which is the dumping ground for so many students."

California has earned the respect of educators for generations in its willingness to take major initiatives in educational reform at all levels. It is not surprising that under the skillful and enlightened leadership of Dr. Wilson Riles, State Superintendent of Public Instruction, the state is moving vigorously to implement career education.

Career Education In Oregon

The introduction of career education in most states, as an initiative of the State Department of Education, has been largely confined to the public elementary and secondary schools. Oregon has been exceptional, creating an overarching system of services that bridges across the public school system into postsecondary education and other institutions. While this chapter will deal largely with the elementary and secondary schools, it is noteworthy that the *total* educational structure, linked closely with the community, expresses Oregon's response to the career education opportunities.

As early as 1970 the Oregon State Board of Education established career education as one of its top priorities. Steady growth and reform of all levels of education have followed during the ensuing years. A recent development is the Career Information System which illustrates the comprehensive and interagency scope of the Oregon plan.

Supported in part through a grant from the Fund for Improvement of Postsecondary Education (Division of Education, HEW), the Career Information System has been designed to provide career counseling resources, realistic occupational choices, and hands-on training opportunities. A statewide interagency consortium made up of the state's Department of Education, the Oregon Employment Division, Community Colleges, local school districts, and the Oregon State System of Higher Education, the structure offers a new instrument for assembling up-to-date labor-market information in usable form by students and institutions as a component of career education.

The leadership of Dale Parnell, until recently State Superintendent of Public Instruction, is clearly visible in the major reform of education now going forward in Oregon. He was at work in the career education philosophy well before the theme became a priority of the U.S. Office of Education.

The Oregon Legislature has been in the vanguard of progressive lawmaking, removing many of the stultifying regulatory constraints affecting education "standards." New laws encourage flexible student scheduling, allowing credit-by-examination for graduation, off-campus study, and recognition of performance criteria as distinct from "time served." An early product of the liberalized laws is the recognition of the Career Education Military Cluster, affording accreditation of the learnings and competences gained in the state's National Guard program.

This chapter examines in some detail the implementation of career education as a statewide force, differing from the more specific school-district illustrations drawn from Texas and California. Dr. Parnell has been an effective national voice in the field as well as in Oregon. He has stated: "School life is too often separated from real life, work and community service. Young people have become bored, restless and disenchanted with schooling because it is not related to their experience."

Career education in Oregon is part of a comprehensive reorganization of statewide goals and planning for public schools and colleges. This reorganization focuses on the development of school programs that will prepare students for the actual life roles they will be expected to fulfill as adults. The Oregon Board of Education identifies six life roles as a framework for a contemporary elementary and secondary curriculum. "Students should learn to function effectively in the roles of: learner, individual, producer, citizen, consumer, and family member. A comprehensive learning system, continuously providing insight, exploration and preparation in these life roles at the appropriate interest and comprehension level of each learner, is the ultimate aim of the state reorganization."

The third life role, that of producer, is specifically related to occupational development. In preparation for the role of producer, "each individual will learn of the variety of occupations; will learn to appreciate the dignity and value of work and the mutual responsibilites of employees and employers; and will learn to identify personal talents and interests, make appropriate career choices, and develop career skills."[1] According to Dr. Parnell, "Preparation for an occupation is a strong motive in American culture. The challenge for schools is to use the student's occupational goals to motivate learning that will lead to self-fulfillment." This feature of the career education design, the implicit motivating force for all learning, all learners is not yet widely comprehended. Oregon appears to have caught the meaning quite well.

In another statewide effort to relate schooling to the real life needs of students, the Oregon Board of Education, as noted earlier, adopted new minimum requirements for high school graduation in September 1972.[2] The old standards of 1932 were primarily requirements for college preparation and attendance. The new requirements focus on competence-based instruction. Diplomas for the 1978 graduating class will certify that students have learned and demonstrated minimum "survival" competences, providing for effective performance in the six life roles identified by the Board of Education. Instruction in survival competences is only a part of the total school experience; local school districts are encouraged to expand their programs beyond the basic knowledge and skills required of all students in the state.

The new minimum requirements for high school graduation specify that each student will complete one unit of study in career education, which may incorporate some independent study, work experience, and/or research. In career development education, the basic survival competences fall into the following areas: (1) good work habits; (2) positive attitudes toward work; (3) ability to maintain good interpersonal relationships; (4) ability to make appropriate career decisions; and (5) entry-level skills for a chosen career field. Curriculum goals and student performance indicators, providing measurement of the development and demonstration of these competences, are currently being formulated throughout the state.

The installation of the comprehensive career education program in Oregon derived its impetus from the Oregon Board of Education goals and minimum high school graduation requirements as they have been described. The career education program is based on two premises: the first is that secondary schools should be preparatory institutions for all students. In the words of a state-level staff officer in Oregon, "For years, most high school students have been told,'You must take these specific courses if you want to go to college.' Consequently, most of the high school curriculum has been structured as if all students anticipate a four-year college education. High schools have generally failed to structure their counseling or curricula to assist students entering careers that require less than a baccalaureate."[3]

The second premise of the Oregon program is that the secondary curriculum should relate to the occupational goals of students, so that they are motivated in school and equipped to make good career choices when they leave—whether for on-the-job training, apprenticeship, community college, proprietary schools, or a four-year college.

The model for career education in Oregon articulates a continuous curriculum design at the elementary, middle school, secondary, and post-high school levels. This design is presented in the chart on page 161. Guidance and counseling is emphasized in each phase of the program, based on the premise that public schools should prepare students for the type of work they will do in life without encouraging value distinctions that elevate some occupations and disparage others.

CAREER EDUCATION

Career education uses the occupational role as the focal point for curriculum and program development. Such a curriculum and program may be organized to include knowledge and skill which a person uses in all related life roles.

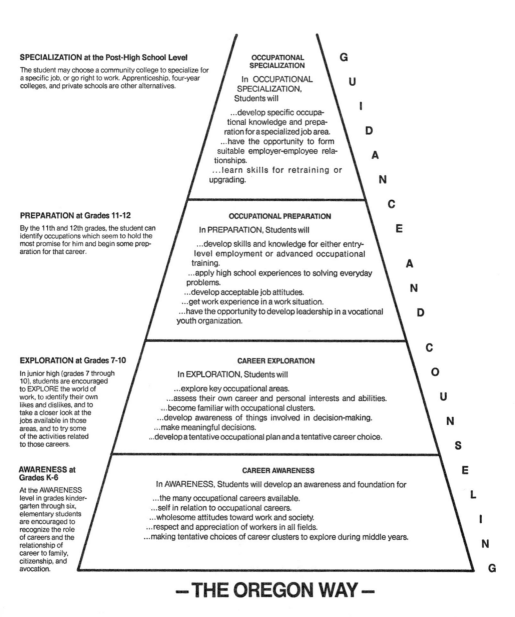

SPECIALIZATION at the Post-High School Level

The student may choose a community college to specialize for a specific job, or go right to work. Apprenticeship, four-year colleges, and private schools are other alternatives.

OCCUPATIONAL SPECIALIZATION

In OCCUPATIONAL SPECIALIZATION, Students will

...develop specific occupational knowledge and preparation for a specialized job area.
...have the opportunity to form suitable employer-employee relationships.
...learn skills for retraining or upgrading.

PREPARATION at Grades 11-12

By the 11th and 12th grades, the student can identify occupations which seem to hold the most promise for him and begin some preparation for that career.

OCCUPATIONAL PREPARATION

In PREPARATION, Students will

...develop skills and knowledge for either entry-level employment or advanced occupational training.
...apply high school experiences to solving everyday problems.
...develop acceptable job attitudes.
...get work experience in a work situation.
...have the opportunity to develop leadership in a vocational youth organization.

EXPLORATION at Grades 7-10

In junior high (grades 7 through 10), students are encouraged to EXPLORE the world of work, to identify their own likes and dislikes, and to take a closer look at the jobs available in those areas, and to try some of the activities related to those careers.

CAREER EXPLORATION

In EXPLORATION, Students will

...explore key occupational areas.
...assess their own career and personal interests and abilities.
...become familiar with occupational clusters.
...develop awareness of things involved in decision-making.
...make meaningful decisions.
...develop a tentative occupational plan and a tentative career choice.

AWARENESS at Grades K-6

At the AWARENESS level in grades kindergarten through six, elementary students are encouraged to recognize the role of careers and the relationship of career to family, citizenship, and avocation.

CAREER AWARENESS

In AWARENESS, Students will develop an awareness and foundation for

...the many occupational careers available.
...self in relation to occupational careers.
...wholesome attitudes toward work and society.
...respect and appreciation of workers in all fields.
...making tentative choices of career clusters to explore during middle years.

GUIDANCE AND COUNSELING

— THE OREGON WAY —

The following notations amplify the chart, starting in the early grades:

Career awareness at the elementary level. In the elementary grades, instructional programs stress developing career awareness by relating basic skill curriculum to a framework of career information; i.e., what people do for a living and how they live. Parents, the doctor, pilot, butcher, baker, carpenter, and others become subjects for reading lessons, writing exercises, geography and history lessons. Adequate career awareness programs in grades K–6 provide the student with opportunities to:

1.   Develop foundations for wholesome attitudes toward work and society.

2.   Develop attitudes of respect and appreciation toward workers in all fields.

3.   Develop an awareness of the many careers available.

4.   Develop an awareness of self in relation to occupational roles.

5.   Make tentative choices of career areas to explore in greater depth during midschool years.

Career exploration at middle school level. Students in grades 7 through 10 begin more concentrated career exploration of the knowledge, skills, technical requirements, working conditions, political/social environments, and responsibilities of each career field that interests them. Emphasis is also placed on understanding one's interests, aptitudes, and abilities as a basis for tentative career choices. A complete exploratory program provides opportunities for the student to:

1.   Understand relevant factors and gain decision-making experience pertaining to career selection.

2.   Continue to explore concepts and skills in preparation for career choices.

3.   Become familiar with occupational classifications and clusters.

4. Explore key occupational areas in relationship to personal interests and abilities.

5. Explore, select, and enroll in junior high courses that are relevant to career interests and aptitudes.

6. Arrive at tentative career choices and develop appropriate occupational plans.

Some instructional programs that provide these opportunities are: extended development of basic skills through the academic curriculum (reading, writing, math, science, etc.); classes in some vocational areas (industrial arts, homemaking, business); laboratory experience and field trips at work sites; programs such as Self-Understanding Through Occupational Exploration (SUTOE); and application of basic concepts to career areas in all general study.

Career preparation at the high school level. In grades 11 and 12, Oregon students have the opportunity to acquire knowledge and skills for entry-level employment or other postsecondary alternatives, including, of course, college. This career preparation is based on the occupational "cluster" concept. A career cluster is a group of occupations that include identical or similar knowledge and skill requirements. Curriculum guides are developed that present the knowledge and skills common to the key occupations within a cluster. For example, the *Construction Cluster Curriculum Guide* presents the knowledge and skills that are common requirements for trowel trades, pipe trades, carpentry, painting, roofing, floor covering, and ironwork. (Other states or school systems have different topics in the Construction Cluster: e.g., architectural drafting, electricity, sheet metal. Consistency among states in this type of detail is not important.)

The occupational cluster curriculum allows the student to gain basic skills and knowledge related to broad occupational areas rather than to a single job; this broad experience is more appropriate to the changing occupational demands and advancing technology of our present society. It helps to respond to the question "How do we know what jobs will exist ten years from now?" In addition, the career cluster organization provides for more effective career education programs, grouping about 25,000 current occupations into fifteen to twenty manageable units for preparatory training. Oregon has developed career cluster curriculum guides in the following areas of occupations:

> industrial mechanics
> electricity/electronics
> metals
> marketing
> agriculture
> food services
> steno/secretarial
> clerical occupations
> health occupations
> service occupations
> accounting/bookkeeping
> forest products
> building construction

These clusters as adopted by Oregon educators differ somewhat from the original clusters identified by the Office of Education in 1971. That is as it should be, again recognizing the need for creativity and individuality by state and communities. Career cluster curriculum guides are available in all of the listed areas at low cost from the Documents Clerk, Oregon State Department of Education.

Oregon's career cluster curriculum allows each high school student to:

1. Acquire occupational skills and knowledge for entry-level employment and/or advanced occupational training.

2. Relate high school experiences to general career goals, including postsecondary education.

3. Participate in cooperative work experience and vocational youth organizations.

It is obviously impractical for every high school to offer complete programs in all of the eighteen career families. Most Oregon high schools try to develop at least seven of the clusters, based on local occupational demands and surveys of the career choices of former students. Using state and regional planning, students who so elect are placed in programs not offered at their school, but available at other high schools, community colleges, or in business and industry.

Specialized career training at the post-high school level. At post-high school and adult levels, students may continue their career preparation through community colleges, apprenticeship programs, private vocational schools, four-year colleges and universities, or business and industry. The State Department of Education has begun an extensive program to integrate secondary programs with specialized post-high school training, providing for student exchanges, joint use of facilities, integrated guidance and counseling, cooperative advanced placement, and the sharing of instructional staff.

In order to achieve a comprehensive design for career education, the Oregon Department of Education has asked Oregon school districts to make the following basic changes in their instructional programs:

1. Change the present curricular tracking systems, which use such terms as "advanced college prep," "terminal-general," or "remedial-basic" to career cluster tracking systems.

2. Rebuild high school curriculums around the concept of minimum survival competences and career cluster preparation.

3. Include plentiful illustrations about careers and related life styles in general education programs.

4. Acknowledge the responsibility of training students for a specific job in post-high school institutions—community colleges, apprenticeship programs, on-the-job training, or private vocational schools and four-year institutions.

5. Improve and integrate the guidance and counseling programs at elementary, secondary, and community college levels.

The Oregon design differs from most state plans in that a much closer interdependence and articulation with postsecondary institutions is required. It is noteworthy that the above listing of reforms in high schools does not declare that the high school must equip the graduate for immediate job entry (see number 4).

According to Dr. Parnell, the Oregon policy on career education is that the total school curriculum, through guidance and counseling, be "tailor-made" to complement each student's career goals. While such an approach may not solve all the educational problems of any one student, it does provide a practical application for school experience that is related to real life concerns. "Our objective," says Parnell, "is the development of flexible advancement procedures that will enable every student to move throughout his lifetime between 'education' and the world of work, learning at his own rate, earning wages while he learns, and taking his place in the mainstream of a vigorous, viable society."[4]

Career education is a working reality in the David Douglas School District, located in the Portland metropolitan area. In 1967, the district reevaluated its educational programs. According to Dr. Howard F. Horner, Superintendent of the David Douglas Schools, "We wanted to build a comprehensive program for all students attending schools in the district." Parents, teachers, counselors, and administrators participated in developing the David Douglas Plan.

A detailed proposal entitled "Project VIGOR" was submitted to the U.S. Office of Education, requesting funds to support a three-year pilot program; it was approved and began operation in July 1970.

Workshops and in-service and other programs helped teachers establish career education programs in grades one through twelve. Teachers were challenged to increase educational experiences outside of the classrooms, to increase the use of local business and industry resources, and to develop strong lines of vertical communication and coordination between all instructional levels.

Primary children in the district learn about the world of work through classroom activities. Special courses for seventh- and eighth-graders focus on self-understanding. Cluster programs are available to all eleventh- and twelfth-graders. The courses are designed to help all students—those bound for immediate employment after graduation and those continuing formal education beyond high school.

Planned work-experience programs and post-high school placement assistance are available to all high school students who wish to participate. A follow-up program is planned for graduating students who have been involved in the cluster programs.

The goals and activities of the VIGOR program are explained as follows, giving illustrative accounts of actual teaching-learning practices:

Career Awareness: Grades K–6

Goal

Every student will explore the world of work as a part of developing his basic skills and an understanding of the world around him.

Activity

Several elementary schools prepared annual "Career Days." Speakers were invited from many walks of life to discuss specific jobs as well as broad career opportunities. In addition, films, books, and discussion groups were used to develop greater awareness of the world of work.

Each elementary school made an inventory of classroom activities at each grade level. Activities ranged from a student-stockholder-owned-and-operated business to a simulated television station. Skills in reading, math, science, and technical arts were applied to career-oriented activities.

"A Teacher's Guide for Career Awareness," developed through the cooperative effort of many elementary teachers, is a handy resource for classroom activities.

Goal

Every student will become aware of the many opportunities available in broad career categories and will, through the awareness process, prepare to enter the "exploratory" phase of his education.

Activity

"Careers in Action" at one elementary school helped students understand the relationship of learning to work. In another school, students "went to work" with a parent, seeing what their fathers or mothers did for a living and observing related occupations. Following this experience, each student presented impressions about his visit to his classmates.

Goal

Every student will increase his awareness of personal abilities and interests, and his relationship to the world around him.

Activity

Several elementary schools are developing additional career-oriented guidance services. Career Interest Centers and Learning Centers are being established for all elementary students.

Career Exploration: Grades 7–10

Goal

Every student will be able to use basic occupational information sources to increase his understanding of the requirements and opportunities of his career interest area.

Activity

All middle-school students have participated in a program called "Self-Understanding Through Occupational Exploration" (SUTOE). In order to help students relate their self-knowledge to various career requirements, SUTOE provides the groundwork for field trips or individual career exploration.

Goal

The use of community resources that support the career education learning process will be increased.

Activity

Both SUTOE and Guidance in Occupational Activities for Learning (GOAL) rely upon a variety of community resources to add meaning to their programs. Local merchants provide short-term exploratory work experience for these programs.

Project GOAL, a summer-school activity, provided an opportunity for the community to participate in the students' education. Eighth-grade students spent three weeks in on-the-job exploration. Following this period, students shared their experiences with the class in discussions and presentations, developing communications skills and learning about other job alternatives.

The middle schools will continue to offer this kind of experience for their students. In addition to GOAL and SUTOE, coordinators of career resources and experiences have been assigned to each building.

Goal

Every student will plan and make decisions based upon experiences related to his or her goals, interests, and abilities.

Activity

In 1972, the CRUISE program was initiated as a bridge between the middle-school exploratory program and the senior high preparation program. CRUISE was designed to introduce freshman students to the career programs that would be available to them during their junior and senior years. CRUISE provides information in three broad areas of cluster training:

1. Business: Accounting, Clerical, and Secretarial

2. Services: Child Services, Food Services, Health Services and Horticulture

3. Trade and Industrial: Construction, Industrial, Electronics, Industrial Mechanics, and Industrial Metals.

Career Preparation: Grades 11–12

Goal

Every student will be able to select a combination of program offerings which will enhance his post-high school plans and prepare him for a future career area.

Activity

With the advent of VIGOR, eleven new areas of occupational training were added to eleventh- and twelfth-grade programs. A program called "Diversified Occupations" was also added, providing a broad range of training experiences for students who are interested in several areas of employment. The resources of the community are this program's greatest asset, since most of the learning is done "on the job," in cooperation with local business and industry.

Postsecondary Options

Goal

All students will be provided with the training, information, and support required to make a meaningful transition from high school to the postsecondary goals of their choice.

Activity

Information is provided through the Career Information Center in broad areas of postsecondary employment and training. The information includes, but is not limited to: (1) four-year institutions, (2) community colleges, (3) apprenticeships, (4) military training, (5) private vocational and business training, and (6) immediate employment and on-the-job training opportunities. Personnel from all the areas provide students with the most current guidance materials available. Community college and high school personnel cooperate to coordinate materials and course offerings, evaluate training practices, and update programs when changes are needed.

In describing the success of Project VIGOR, Dr. Horner says, "Every concept that is taught in the classroom has a practical application. Take music for example: this experience includes learning in communication, listening, group participation, rhythm and social participation. By teaching with practical applications, you open up the classroom and make more learning possible." In addition to adjusting the curriculum and persuading teachers to orient their instruction to practical uses, Project VIGOR also involves the community. According to Dr. Horner, "Key community people need to be involved and observe other career education sites. It is always the people and not the program that makes success."

The David Douglas Schools have not had trouble getting the students to accept career education. According to Dr. Omer McCaleb of the Oregon system, "Career education has become something real, important, and memorable to them. Career education is the *why* to every other aspect of learning." For Dr. McCaleb, career education is not merely skill training. "Vocational education is preparation for a job. Career education is preparing a student to make choices and apply his education during his entire life."

The Oregon demonstration in this Portland-area school system, starting in 1967, has given us a model in motion for over six years. There are many success stories for students and staff in the David Douglas Schools. They have seen and experienced change in educational priorities, affirmative change in attitudes toward teachers, and affirmative change in the meaning of school. These changes support the concept of education for life, not merely for its own ends. As they say in the David Douglas school system and increasingly throughout Oregon, "We believe in careers by choice, not chance; by intent, not by accident."

11

Career Education in Texas

One of the most dramatic and innovative expressions of the career education concept taking place in America today is the Skyline Career Development Center of Dallas, Texas. It is a $21.5-million technological-age high school, one of the largest and most comprehensive secondary education facilities in the United States. While the State Department of Education in Texas is heavily committed to career education for statewide reform, this chapter takes a detailed look at one site in Dallas. This facility, built on an eighty-acre campus and housed in air-conditioned buildings that cover thirteen acres, is equipped with $5 million worth of technological and scientific equipment, including a 30,000-square-foot airplane hangar for aviation classes, a computer center which serves as the terminal for seventeen other Dallas high schools, a complete color television studio with a 250-room network within the complex, and a 1600-square-foot greenhouse for horticulture classes.

The Center is open to students from any high school in the Dallas Independent School District; students are selected for "their intellectual potential, their emotional maturity, and their ability for self-discipline." This is a school for the highly motivated—in thinking, in performance, and in ambition. While at this time Skyline is necessarily selective, being the only school of its kind in the district, it is a prototype of what all high schools might be in the comprehensive career education mode. Selectivity is not compatible with present perceptions of career education.

This extraordinary school might not have come about except for the leadership of Dr. Nolan Estes, General Superintendent of Schools, the Board of Education of Dallas, who designated career education as one of the seven priority goals of the district, the Texas Education Agency, and the Dallas Chamber of Commerce. It was these men and women and organizations, plus some experienced educational administrators and teachers like Bill Stamps, who now directs the Skyline operation, that have made the career education concept a reality for 1000 students, beginning in 1972.

Career education as an idea found its early starting point in Dallas in 1965 when the Board of Education made a commitment to develop a large, comprehensively equipped *vocational education* facility to serve students from all areas of the district. But by 1967, when a local bond issue was passed to finance the Center, new superintendent Nolan Estes and the Dallas Board of Education began to see that a "vocational school" was too limiting for what was needed for Dallas.

According to Stamps, who developed much of the early philosophy of career education for the Center, "We needed a school for all children so that the Center wouldn't become the place for those students *not* going to college." What developed was three schools in one.

The central core of Skyline Center is the Skyline High School with a principal as head. The Center for Career Development, the portion of the school with special occupational courses, has its own manager; and the third component is the Center for Community Services, an adult education school. The focus of all three schools of Skyline is on career development, using the career cluster approach.

Skyline has arranged its curriculum into twenty-seven clusters. "We think in terms of closely related interests," explained Dr.

Paul Harris, Director of Curriculum. "Each cluster encompasses several families of careers. These families, in turn, are made up of many specific career options. Thus, if a student is interested in any area of the arts, humanities, sciences or technology, he or she has the opportunity of exploring an entire galaxy of careers that are related to his or her area of interest. For example, within the clusters involving visual communications there are several families of careers—graphics, writing, product development, fine arts, television. Within each of these families are an even larger number of more specific career options." (See the New Jersey Manufacturing Cluster in Chapter 12.)

Following is the array of career clusters offered at Skyline:

Business and Management Technology   Facilities and equipment match those in any modern business office. Students here specialize in clerical, accounting, secretarial, or data-processing fields.

The Study of Man and His Environment   Opportunities for learning here are focused upon the individual approach. Students may elect to do research in a particular subject, using resources available to them in the school, or with businesses or professions related to the topic they select. These topics may range from welfare, rehabilitation, and legal aid to conservation, gerontology, and ecology. Students may also pursue studies related to the nature and ideas of man, such as philosophy, comparative religion, anthropology, and psychology.

Computer Technology   Students in this cluster operate and maintain the computer, do systems analysis and programming. They learn to use the computer as a means of communication, and to do inventory and personnel accounting.

World Languages   Students here have the chance to study advanced courses in classical or modern languages to any depth they desire. Specialized studies are offered for those who want to extend language studies beyond the usual high school limits.

Horticulture   In the horticulture cluster, students learn commercial techniques for growing and grooming flowers and plants. They also learn the fundamentals of flower-shop management and develop expertise in landscaping and gardening.

Higher Sciences   Courses here are coordinated with the student's work in his field of interest. This is college-level instruction in broad areas of science, including extended studies related to recent advances in the physical and biological sciences.

Higher Mathematics Talented students of mathematics come to Skyline to study in a concentrated way a chosen topic in mathematics. This is student-centered learning, highly individualized in approach, and suggesting a professional career related to the application of mathematical competences.

Metal Technology A student in this cluster may progress from simple metal-working machines through the most complicated and advanced equipment. The family of careers is designed around welding, industrial technology, and machine-tool operation.

World of Construction This cluster is used to enhance the experience of those who are planning to continue related construction studies in college. Or they can graduate directly from Skyline into careers as carpenters, bricklayers, structural iron-workers, and cement masons. They could also have careers as plumbers, pipefitters, or electricians. Subject to labor union policies and practices, it may be necessary for graduates to enter the trades through apprenticeship protocols.

Electronic Sciences Courses in this cluster are designed to prepare students for careers as construction and commercial electricians. These courses are also major preparation for students wanting to continue their studies at the college level.

Advanced English, Speech, and Journalism Students in this cluster are most likely preparing for careers in teaching, business, journalism and writing, acting, government service, law, or the ministry. This program is broadly and flexibly structured to provide unlimited opportunities for students to pursue personal interests in any reasonable area of advanced study.

Climate Control Technology Courses in this cluster include study of everything from the portable home window air-conditioner to large commercial refrigeration and climate-control installations. Students learn how to test, service, and install modern refrigerators, heaters, freezers, and coolers.

Aeronautics Comprehensive instruction in this cluster prepares students to take the FAA license examination for airframe mechanic, power plant mechanic, or a combination of the two. The school provides a helicopter pad and hangar for visitors and for the development of students in airport management techniques.

Transportation Services This cluster includes courses ranging from the simple tune-up of an automobile engine to large-scale studies of diesel engines, high-performance engine diagnosis, and work on large commercial power plants. Students are prepared for a variety of career opportunities in the automotive industry from mechanics to management.

Plastics Technology Students in this cluster explore two basic areas of plastics technology. In the fabrication and design areas, they learn how plastics are put together and how products are formed. In the making and using of molds, they learn all the major types of production methods used in the plastics industry today.

Aesthetics Students explore a variety of courses in the commercial and fine art fields. They can devote the majority of their time to whatever interests them most—oil or watercolor painting, sketching; ceramics or metal sculpture; general arts and crafts.

Dramatic Arts Advanced studies are available for students serious about drama or theater in various career-related offerings. It is possible for them to utilize the unique staging, recording and videotaping facilities of Skyline, and also to draw on the resources of several related clusters such as the arts and television clusters.

Photographic Arts Students have available to them a new 16mm color-movie film-developing unit, completely equipped darkrooms, modern enlargers, printers, and a variety of types cameras. Courses of study involve the major branches of photographic work and related career opportunities. Students can prepare for careers in either industrial or commercial photography. They could become press or public-relations photographers, portrait, illustrative, or advertising photographers. The experience, like many career education products, may also lead to avocational and recreational interests.

Graphics Technologies Students work with an array of advanced typesetting and printing equipment, study new kinds of lithography, learn bindery operations and press reproduction, photomechanical preparation, and the use of production materials. They also study production planning and control, estimating, production costs, and customer service. They may work in a single graphics area or explore the total industry.

Advanced Music Students in this cluster may specialize in specific instruments or in voice, but at a level considerably beyond the normal high school. This cluster prepares students for further study in schools of music and universities in three broad areas: performance, composition, or teaching.

Television Arts Part of the very contemporary facilities of the television arts cluster at Skyline is a professionally designed sound studio and control booth. Here, students gain practical experience in operating all kinds of audio and video equipment and prepare for the FCC licensing examinations. Courses are offered in the art of video photography, stage management, and associated dramatic arts and speech.

World of Fashion Students in this cluster are prepared for careers from designing to dressmaking. This array includes everything from the sample stitchers to machine operators and pressers and fabric specialists. Today, more than one million people are employed in this industry, and careers for men and women continue to grow.

Beauty Culture In this cluster, students are taught the range of cosmetology from hair styling to pedicure to prepare them for state board examinations and licensing upon graduation. Skyline has two extensive laboratories for training students in all phases of beauty culture and cosmetology.

Food Management Students operate their own in-school dining room and are prepared for careers in commercial cooking, baking, and meat preparation. Emphasis is placed on selective buying and handling of food supplies, on instruction in all aspects of food service and distribution, and in all areas of restaurant management. (I had the pleasure of eating a very delicious luncheon prepared and served by the boys and girls in this cluster; I would match the quality of food, service, and environment with any first-class restaurant or hotel dining room.)

Child- and Youth-Related Professions Skyline has a large and fully equipped Child Development Laboratory that is used as a modern day care center for preschool children. By providing a classroom for students to learn the care, guidance, and understanding of children through actual study and observation, it prepares them for careers at day care centers, nursery schools, hospitals, and private homes as well as for careers in early childhood education as teachers. In related clusters of study, these students may point toward careers in diatetics, home furnishings, food demonstration, appliance demonstration, and in textiles and food testing. Completely equipped kitchens and other facilities are available for those whose major interests lie in the fields pertaining to home economics as well as child care.

Health, Medical, and Dental Technologies Students in this cluster can select training as dental laboratory technicians, dental assistants, medical laboratory assistants, or licensed practical nurses. Students receive special assistance in preparing for any licensing examination in their selected field. The program also serves as the beginning of careers for physicians and other advanced practitioners in medical fields.

The Center's purpose, says Dr. Estes, is "to provide every student enrolled in its programs a balance of academic and occupational education that will put him or her well on the way toward a successful career." It guarantees the graduate these things: (1) a high school diploma; (2) preparation for entering the most exacting university, college, junior college, or advanced technical school; and/or (3) a salable skill that can mean immediate employment. The objectives are central to the meaning of the career education concept.

Skyline began to plan its clusters and philosophy of education in 1971 when a team of a hundred curriculum writers spent the summer developing career-related courses of study. For each cluster, career competences and behavioral objectives were written to serve as guides for the course and to provide a basis of evaluation. According to Ralph Burke, Director of Teachers at Skyline, "A student progresses through his individual course of study by completing tasks—behavioral objectives—of varying length and difficulty. He is evaluated on his degree of competency in completing these and not with the traditional grading." The career competences were defined and elaborated by the Skyline Advisory Board representing a broad array of industrial, business, and professional interests from the Dallas area.

A student's time at the Center is flexible and adjustable to individual needs. A student may spend part of the day in a selected field of interest and the remainder in academic studies, either at the Center or at a home school. A student may transfer from a home high school for full- or part-time attendance. He or she may transfer for a specific program, but stay in a home school for regular subjects and extracurricular activities. The choice is the student's.

Twelve clusters were developed in the academic areas as distinct from occupational fields. These were written by the teachers from the school district. To write the industrial and technological clusters, the school district engaged the RCA educational system over a period of a year or more to work in companionship with the faculty. The school district also contracted with the Educational Testing Service to design systems for measuring the performance of students. This was all completed within three years, but, as anyone at Skyline will say, it wasn't easy.

The biggest problem, according to Dallas administrators, was to take the stigma off skills training. At the Center, it wasn't just the vocational training with a new name. "To us," said Bill Stamps, "a vocational school trains a student in a single skill for immediate entry into a job. Here at the Center the primary focus is all-around education that will increase the employment options of the students."

Skyline began to enroll its students by being selective. The leaders and faculty said they didn't want students who couldn't make it elsewhere, but they did not want to select only the most able. The recruitment campaign started in March 1971 with a month-long information and identification effort. The goal was to locate young people who could most profit from Skyline's concept. The target was 2500 applications.

"The approach," said Bill Stamps, "was individual presentations and counseling sessions with all the ninth, tenth, and eleventh graders, tours of the facility by all 13,000 ninth graders, and extensive contact with principals and counselors in all Dallas secondary schools. In addition, the facility was opened two nights a week and Sunday afternoons for family tours and counseling sessions at which time both parents and students were oriented in the career education program."

Skyline wanted to get the better students, the best students in Dallas. They let it be known that students who couldn't make the grade in the regular high schools wouldn't be eligible for Skyline. They did not want predictable dropouts; Skyline was not going to be the dumping ground for those who couldn't make it academically in the conventional system. As an editorial aside, the exclusive flavor of the Skyline admissions process is not consistent with the concept of career education advanced by the Office of Education. The Dallas approach, necessarily limited to one school serving the entire city, was probably influenced by the need to overcome the stereotype of vocational education by insisting on the selection of very promising students. *Since career education theory has urged from the start that all students be engaged in the offerings, it is hoped that Dallas will extend the successful Skyline demonstration to all secondary schools.*

The school district also developed a professionally arranged public information program to attract students (and parents) to the new and unconventional institution. But even with all this the initial responses from students were not spectacular. The graphics-printing cluster, with room for 86 students, attracted just six; electronics had space for 288 and drew only 57; construction and drafting could handle 580 and enrolled only 64. Yet other area clusters were oversubscribed. There were more applications for the dental and medical professions and aeronautics than could be accepted.

Most of these problems were temporary, and course offerings were reevaluated prior to registration in 1972. Skyline began to understand what the students wanted in the way of career education and began to adapt the curriculum to jobs available in the Dallas area.

They were helped immensely by the Skyline Advisory Board and by Jack Andrus, the executive director. Extensive and innovative community involvement has come with this Skyline Advisory

Board, which is a joint undertaking of the Dallas Independent School District and the Dallas Chamber of Commerce.

The Board consists of committees representing each of Skyline's career clusters. Each committee meets regularly with Skyline teachers, administrators, and support personnel to advise, criticize, and give valuable input to insure that the curriculum not only fits the students' needs but is also compatible with the needs of the Dallas community.

The members of the Chamber of Commerce, besides giving advice and counseling students, help Skyline in other, very direct ways. Free plant materials, for example, are sent by the Dallas floral industry to Skyline's horticulture cluster for "laboratory" supplies, apart from those grown in the school's greenhouse. Companies have given printing presses, airplanes, computers, and dictating machines to the school. All of the companies believe deeply in the school and in helping individual students find appropriate careers, whether or not in a specific participating industry.

By treating the students as customers and having a wide range of career possibilities available for them, Skyline has been able to graduate a varied and productive student body. Some examples:

- Linda Lamb graduated in 1972 after one year in the business cluster. She wants to be a personal secretary, but started work as a typist and clerk. Her education at Skyline included a period of training in a simulated office setup. Her "performance sheet," indicating the machines she could operate and her level of efficiency on each, helped get her a job.

- Mike Hinton plans to be an architectural draftsman, and is going on to the community college to complete his education in that field. He won the statewide Vocational Industrial Clubs of America competition in architectural design. The model house planned and built in his class helped him win.

- Bob Parks entered Stanford University after graduating from Skyline. He took his fifth year of French language at Skyline and wants (he thinks at this point in his career) to become a diplomatic interpreter. Since he wasn't quite sure of what exact career he

wanted, he spent the afternoons of his year at Skyline
working with a lawyer in the community, looking at
law as a social science and weighing whether or not
he was interested enough to study law.

One great advantage of the school, says Skyline principal Frank
Guizick, is that "students are able to explore career fields never
before offered in an ordinary high school." There is also "hands-
on" experience instead of purely theoretical learning. Students in
the aeronautics cluster have six airworthy planes to work with.
Students in the construction cluster—along with classmates in
drafting, architecture, interior design, and horticulture—have
built a $35,000 house near the campus. Other students are trained
for jobs as carpenters, ironworkers, cement and brick masons,
plumbers, pipefitters, and electricians. The Federal Communications Commission grants a license in communications to graduates of the Skyline's TV arts clusters. These are skills that they can
take to the job market immediately upon graduation.

Students are not, however, "locked in" at a particular level of
competence. "The uniqueness of career education," according
to Marvin Berkeley, school board member, "is that it takes any
skill and elevates it to the state any student is capable of taking it.
That includes pre-med, pre-dental, pre-nursing. Or a student can
suspend his development at the technician level and become, for
example, a TV maintenance operator."

Such progression is possible because of the behavioral-
objective goals established for each cluster. The student is graded
against his achievement success by units and according to the
percentage of each unit he has completed. It is, says Bob Duncan,
a graduate of the horticulture cluster, like "stepping stones to a
higher learning goal. Each step is like a miniature course."

In horticulture, for example, students are given a list of
objectives, which may cover the range of skills from trimming
shrubbery to flower-arranging or how to manage a greenhouse or
a flower shop. Each student decides which objectives he wants to
complete and then proceeds on his own, at his own pace.

"Teachers give guidelines," adds former student Duncan, "but
we proceed on our own. If we have questions they may tell us the
answer, but often they help us find the answer for ourselves by

sending us to reference books." Students also learn by visiting other horticulture locations, doing summer and part-time work with flower shops, and receiving in-school instruction and counseling by businessmen.

Teaching in this manner presented Skyline with new kinds of problems. What were needed were men and women in the faculty who believed in the concept of the teacher as a "director of learning." Skyline was able to attract people who were flexible and willing to experiment, for the average high school teacher's training and the normal teaching arrangements were not sufficient to achieve Skyline's objectives.

RCA Corporation's Dick Bobbitt assisted in the selection of the new occupational instructors, and nearly all of them came from industrial and technological backgrounds rather than conventional educational settings. In-service training sessions were held, and these "new" teachers were granted special certificates while they took education courses at night and on weekends to qualify for professional certification.

These teachers were further assisted with the development of Skyline by "concept statements" which were used to "guide planning for the infusion of [occupational] education into the existing academic curriculum and to guide implementation through the teaching methods and activities to be used with students." The statements were used as the structure or organization of career education, not only for Skyline but for all of the schools in the Dallas Independent School District.

To explain this systemwide curricular reform, a chart was developed, reproduced on page 184. The column on the left represents the steps which an individual must take to make a viable career decision. These steps are a sequence that might be repeated many times during an individual's lifelong career development. Each step is taught to some degree at every grade level.

The middle column is a listing of some of the career concepts which are involved in each step. This is not a complete listing of all career education concepts; rather, the concept statements listed simply serve to clarify each step. Those concept statements marked with an asterisk (*) indicate the need for a student's going through that particular step.

CONCEPTUAL FRAMEWORK FOR CAREER EDUCATION DEVELOPMENT

Steps of career education	Concepts involved (•) and justification for step (*)	Process to implement step
Understanding and acceptance of self	• All individuals have worth. • Honesty of self is essential to acceptance of self. • Each individual is responsible for his own behavior. * An understanding and acceptance of self enables an individual to realize full potential, thus gaining personal satisfaction as a contributing member of society.	An acceptance of self is internalized through a positive interaction process which focuses on the individual.
Awareness of self and awareness of careers	• Individuals differ in their interests, abilities, and values. * Awareness of self is necessary to make one's interests, abilities, attitudes, and values. * Knowledge of a wide variety of careers is necessary to provide options for career choices.	An awareness of self and careers is maximized by a person's ability to retrieve and structure the data from available resources.
Exploring careers in light of self	• Occupations and life styles are interrelated. • Specialization leads to interdependency between people. • Individuals work to meet personal and social needs. * Relating personal characteristics compatibly with job characteristics increases probability of career success and satisfaction.	Exploration of careers in light of self is achieved by comparing and contrasting affective reactions, as well as cognitive and skill abilities to those reactions and abilities required in the jobs selected for investigation within chosen career areas.
Decision-making	• Each individual is responsible for his own decisions. • Occupational supply and demand have an impact on career planning. • Job selection is a compromise between personal needs and societal needs. * Career development involves a continuous, sequential series of choices.	Wise decisions are made in conformance with one's psychological and physiological needs and with the needs of society.
Preparation (Dallas Independent School District)	• Education and work are interrelated. • Individuals must be flexible in response to changing job characteristics caused by societal change. * Career preparation that enables the individual to accomplish effectively job responsibilities results in self-satisfaction and feelings of worth.	Preparation that focuses on understanding the relationship between the fundamental ideas of a discipline facilitates the independent transfer of skills and provides a stable base for continuous learning.

The purpose of the third column is to communicate the type of training programs and materials to be used with teachers to enable them to teach career education. It suggests the teaching methodology necessary to accomplish each step.

In Dallas, the Board of Education and the administration and faculty are committed to "making every kid a winner." Recognizing that the vocational education and the academic programs had not been meeting the needs of the students and that "many youth were leaving the schools even at graduation with no marketable job skills, limited knowledge of their real career interests, and little awareness of occupations available to them," they decided on career education.

This required a basic shift in philosophy for the Dallas Schools and a belief that career education represents a system of education "that students will enjoy because of its realism, educators will advocate because of its relevance, communities and school patrons will approve and espouse because of its congruence with societal needs and business and employers will aggressively support because of its practicality and efficiency."

To achieve this kind of career education, programs were developed to infuse and integrate career education into the entire curriculum, early childhood through adulthood. The intent was to provide a sequence of options and to assist each student through an array of planned programs in:

- developing a positive self-image.

- developing an understanding of the economic and social structures of our society.

- developing and expanding occupational awareness.

- defining and developing personal goals for self/career identity through a continuing process of decision-making based on a knowledge of self and career opportunities.

- developing positive attitudes toward work, toward the dignity of man in work, and toward the society in which man lives.

- developing an understanding of the value of education relative to meeting the responsibilities of the anticipated goal.

- acquiring marketable skills as preparation for becoming a self-sustaining citizen.

The Dallas Independent School District's commitment to career education, as indicated by the Skyline Career Development Center and the District's integrated program of career education throughout the system, is an example of the philosophy of the District that the public schools are responsible for the education of *every* child in the community. In assuming this responsibility, declares a Board publication, "the district has sought to provide all young persons with learning opportunities that will assist them to discover and to use optimally their individual interests, aptitudes, and abilities."

When Skyline was first envisioned, the term *career education* had not come into usage in its present meaning. Indeed, as noted earlier, the school was first intended to be a fine vocational school. By the fortuitous combination of people, such as Estes, Stamps, and Andrus, together with the committed construction funds on a large scale, at a time when the philosophy underlying career education was beginning to be felt not only by educators but also by the public, a significant and enduring breakthrough may have occurred here for American high schools altogether. One never really knows a breakthrough until history has declared it such, and it is a little early to make absolute claims for Skyline. But history, as well as contemporary educators, should look closely at this extraordinary institution, assuming that it redresses soon its policy of selective enrollment.

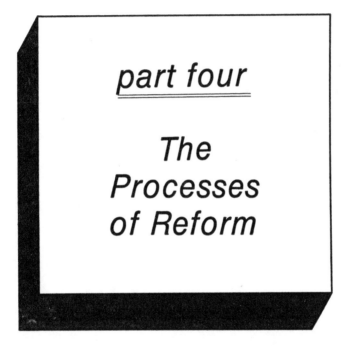

part four

The
Processes
of Reform

12

The Teachers and the Counselors

It will be the classroom teacher who ultimately will determine whether career education will become a reality. Counselors have a large and crucial role to play. And "the successful installation of a comprehensive career education system," says Bruce Reinhart of Rutgers, "requires all teachers and supporting personnel to assimilate new knowledge, new skills and new attitudes which must result in new professional behaviors."[1] This is no easy task, and to prepare staff for the implementation of career education in the classrooms of our schools and colleges will first call for changes in the traditional teacher-training institution for elementary and secondary teachers, and changes in teaching philosophy on the part of many professors of higher education.

According to Dr. Keith Goldhammer, former Dean of the School of Education at Oregon State University and now Dean, College of Education of Michigan State University career education "calls upon schools of education to develop new educational paradigms, new instructional strategies which put emphasis upon what individuals can do, how they can perform as result of their educational experiences, not just what they happen to know."[2]

This chapter is concerned primarily with the increased responsibilities of elementary school and secondary school teachers and
counselors. The postsecondary design for career education and
its implicit reforms will be treated in a separate chapter. But
"reform" is the message of career education, which, translated,
means *change*. Rationally designed change is not offensive to
teachers, provided they have a fair hand in its conception. This is
especially true of the experienced teachers and counselors now
on the job and upon whom the proposed reform will depend
almost totally. Teachers do not change simply because they are
told to. They change or share in the reform of their school
system, when the procedures and objectives make sense. Most
teachers I have observed engaged in the career education process these past three years are enthusiastic about its potential. Not
the least of their satisfaction derives from perceived motivation
for all learning, especially the academic subjects, in the career
mode.

Dr. Elizabeth Jane Simpson, of the Bureau of Adult and Vocational-Technical Education of the Office of Education, has identified three basic requirements in any teacher-education program
for career education:

1.   All teachers will need to be involved—those in the traditional
academic areas, those in vocational education, and those in the
arts. Teachers for all educational levels have a role in implementing the concept of career education in educational practice.
Hence, for teacher education, first attention must be given the
development of awareness and understanding of the concept of
career educaion. Teachers will need to be regrouped in new
configurations for exploration and preparing to use the expanding educational materials of career education.

2.   Teachers will need meaningful personal experiences in the
real world of work if the goal of "correlation of academic subject
content with occupational opportunities and real life situations"
is to be truly realized in educational practice.

3.   Teachers will need to explore their own fields for the variety
of dimensions of career-relevant content and methodology.

Teacher education must aid in the process. The exploration must be a continuing one that takes into account technological and social changes and their implications for the world of work and career education content.[3]

Apart from the suggested changes in the schools of education where *newly* developed teachers are educated, equally important in-service development of *current* elementary and secondary teachers at the local school level is needed. The Center for Vocational and Technical Education at the Ohio State University has developed a model for such in-service staff training. There are five distinct steps in the Ohio State plan:

1.   An orientation to the philosophy and basic concepts of career education. All staff should have a common understanding of the goals of career education, as well as an acquaintance with the content and strategies recommended for each level and discipline.

2.   An orientation into all the curriculum that will be installed. The elements, themes, and goals in the units; the grade levels for which they are designed; and the discipline areas.

3.   An initial, individual-needs assessment of all staff members. This is to be directed to specific unit-related needs as well as role-related needs.

4.   A homogeneous grouping of staff personnel—teachers, counselors, subject area personnel, etc.—for their specific roles. Teachers and other staff directly responsible for unit delivery should also receive an in-depth orientation to the specific units for which they are responsible.

5.   The organization of in-service sessions based on the needs identified in step four. This will include sessions prior to unit installation and follow-up sessions.

These five steps are not to be considered discrete, according to the Ohio design. Orientation sessions would be repeated as new personnel join the system, and as needed to maintain key concepts and motivation. The needs assessments are ongoing;

the unit-related sessions coincide with unit installation schedules, and special sessions are held whenever necessary.[4]

In-service training will be the way that the majority of teachers become aware of career education and confident of its effectiveness. According to Hoyt, "in-service [development] has become career education's most articulate spokesman. . . . The ambiguity once associated with the educator's self-examination has been transformed into a purposeful investigation of an institutional and personal capacity for change."[5] In the excellent book *Career Education and the Elementary School Teacher*, Kenneth B. Hoyt *et al.* describe several in-service patterns that are already operating in one or more states[6]:

The Working Sabbatical Approach

Hoyt offers a design for releasing key teachers in all levels and subject areas for a period of time to develop curricular materials consistent with the system's career education goals, from kindergarten through grade twelve. He is mindful of the reality of teacher behavior that calls for genuine involvement of the faculty in any activity that calls for change. He offers a format for the task: *The charge*: to survey both the literature on, and the live example of career education in practice—thus to create curricula linking each subject matter area to an operational definition of its application to a worker's life style. *The test*: to concurrently select a pilot system, K–12, in which to test developed curriculum, and another, closely matched system which could serve as a control. *The implementation*: to move certain members of the researching team into the pilot setting to serve as resource to staff while training them in the use of the new materials and approaches.

Hoyt's foregoing design proposes, in addition to the curriculum development, the in-service exposure of teachers to actual working conditions outside the school. Most teachers have little firsthand experience in business or industry. It is intended that, given experience outside of schools, teachers will generalize more effectively their articulation of academic teaching with occupational relationships. Hoyt continues:

The Planned Summer Work Experience Approach

A pilot school continuum, K–12, contracts with a number of local businesses representing nine broad career areas (environmental, agribusiness, health, real estate/banking/finance, personal services, public services, communications, manufacturing, construction, and transportation) to provide up to eight weeks of full-time employment for two teachers from each grade level (total, 26) during the summer months. Employers assign one worker to each teacher as an "advocate." The school district bears all costs in year one by extending ten-month salaries into a twelve-month category. The state education departments arrange with a local college or university to bear the cost of tuition "credit" for worker advocates, while working teachers pay the usual tuition fees to obtain graduate credit for their paid summer experience.

In each succeeding year, increasing numbers of teachers have this exposure with a proportionate increase in the employer's financial contribution (and a proportionate decrease in the school district's subsidy) issuing from the employer's perception of the program's value and the teachers' work performance. The college or university continues to award credit, or to provide "rain checks" for course work in guidance to those advocated assigned to teachers.

Hoyt's array of models for teacher development in career education include additional approaches:

The Intensive Summer Workshop

This model declares a state leadership area for the intensive statewide development of cadres of teacher trainees in career education. Either in affiliation with a college or university, or directly under the institutional responsibility of state education department personnel, teachers, counselors, subject supervisors, principals, and curriculum directors are assembled. All costs are borne by the state; varying forms of course credit or other compensation are afforded the participants, including the alternative of regular salary recognition for particiapnts.

The cadres return to their school districts with formulations of curriculum designs for further development, and prepare to conduct counterpart workshops for the district faculty and staff.

Released Time

In this model, Hoyt describes the more customary design for in-service faculty development. Teachers are scheduled in groups for perhaps two hours a week, with substitutes provided during school hours, to participate in training programs and curriculum construction, under central staff leadership. The process includes field trips and other opportunities for exposure to varied work experiences for articulation with the curriculum, according to grade level.

Industry Visitation

In this model Hoyt describes a year-long arrangement for planned experiences by teachers in work settings in business and industry. Either on released time, or apart from school hours, teachers observe closely a wide variety of occupational settings, under the planned and systematic management of the employers involved. Interviews with workers and managers are a part of the plan. Graduate credit for the activity is granted by participating colleges and universities.

Resource Staff Added

This model departs markedly from conventional in-service staff development patterns. Individuals with meaningful occupational competences are drawn from the community and employed by the schools as adjuncts to the faculty. Alternatively, regular teachers with discrete occupational experience apart from teaching are given added responsibilities beyond the school day to share in the instruction of their colleagues, not only in career education curriculum development, but in advancing the perceptions of their colleagues as the subject of jobs. Hoyt includes retired workers and former high school dropouts as potential sources for these "added resources."

State Leadership

In this model, under the leadership of the governor, the state engages the business and labor community, the legislature and the professional leadership in the education department. Formal resolutions or legislation establish a basic policy affecting the installation of career education and the corresponding statutory authorities and procedures for teacher training. Exemplary practices or sites are identified as models responding to the state's policy and are offered for statewide replication, presumably allowing for individual faculty participation by districts in meeting local needs.

This model suggests state funding in company with enabling legislation. It proposes state, regional, and local advisory councils consisting of laymen and educators capable of guiding the advancement of career education through the appropriate governing bodies.

Hoyt concludes his array of models with what he calls "The Project or Interdisciplinary" approach. Here the individual school, following general systemwide developmental work in concept design and curriculum, establishes an interdisciplinary (multisubject, multigrade) task force or team to carry forward the career education installation according to the immediate perceived needs of the students and community affected.

Much of the development of in-service training and the introduction of career education to new teachers depends on schools of education, for the aim is not to train special "career education teachers" in any reorganization. Rather, the aim is to train new teachers in a completely different way. "The undergraduate teacher education programs must be invested with a career education emphasis. Such an emphasis is now almost completely lacking."[7]

These new teachers in their preservice preparatory programs should have, first and foremost, an understanding of the world in which their students will be living and earning a living. Schoolteachers and college professors quite naturally have developed their own careers around teaching and have correspondingly had little opportunity for engaging in other forms of work. Narrowly viewed, the teacher's own path to intellectual fulfillment and career is the only path he knows well and therefore views his subject field as quite adequate in *itself* as the course for others to follow. "The fact that most academic teachers in elementary and secondary education today would violently deny that they hold such attitudes makes it even more imperative that some systematic attention be devoted to helping teachers understand and have an opportunity to embrace the attitudes and philosophical premises on which career education is based."[8] This calls for teachers at all levels to climb outside their own academic field in order to scrutinize the usefulness of their teaching in the social, cultural, and economic setting in which it is to be enjoyed or applied.

It is also necessary that teachers have an understanding of the wide range of possibilities of work. Some practical knowledge is required. Too many teachers have never worked outside of their profession. Work experience other than teaching should become a part of the preparation of teachers.

Because of the implicit reforms of the processes of learning through career education, Goldhammer declares that schools of education will need to place the "primary emphasis in the preparation of teachers . . . upon their acquiring knowledge and competence to assist children in meeting their developmental needs."[9] This means a higher order of teaching activities which harmonizes the subject-matter teaching with the perceptions of occupationally related learnings according to the maturity and interests of the learner. Goldhammer cautions us that "teachers in the career education mode must be prepared to use knowledge instrumentally to help children achieve *their* purposes."[10] This is an important point in preparing new teachers: it is the child who becomes the object of the curriculum, not the organized material. This is one of the key distinctions between career education and traditional subject-matter curricula.

Within the classroom, teachers will be expected to do more team teaching and work with other teachers and community personalities and resources. This organization might be adopted, in Goldhammer's view, with "some [teachers] prepared as educational diagnosticians, some as teachers of basic learning skills, some as specialists in child growth and development, some as specialists in guidance, some as specialists in areas of particular life roles, and some in a variety of other roles."[11]

The classroom setting will also change, with more emphasis on individual instruction, field trips, work study, programmed learning, and independent learning. The class will generally be more "open-ended," with a greater use of group and individual multimedia materials and performance-oriented instruction, both within the classroom and well beyond it.

While much of the change process in curriculum, teacher development, organizational structure, and goal-setting has been initiated locally in school districts and at state level, the movement has not been merely random. Without imposing standards, the U.S. Office of Education and the National Institute of Education have promoted by contracts and grants many curriculum-development activities to serve as models for adaptation nationally. As noted in an earlier chapter, the states have each designed one or more experimental systems of reform through career education, utilizing federal funds, comingled in many cases with state and local funds, but adhering to general federal guidelines.

The State Department of Education in Florida was among the leaders (along with Louisiana, Oregon, Arizona, Iowa, New Jersey, and others) in adopting statewide policies for career education, including the necessary in-service development of faculties. The following statement dated October 1973 is extracted from "Career Education in Florida: An Official Position Paper of the Department of Education":

> CAREER EDUCATION: TEACHER EDUCATION
> Challenges to teacher education inherent in the concept of career education are obvious.
>
> ALL teachers must be involved.
>
> No grade level, no subject area, and no service area can be left out. First attention for in-service and pre-service teacher education must be given to the development of awareness and understanding of career education. Teachers in traditional grade levels, subjects, and service areas may need to be regrouped into new and different patterns for exploration of career education. Regrouping may also be required for developing and learning to use the new materials and practices required for career education.
>
> • Teachers must have direct hands-on experiences in the non-school environment of the learners.
>
> Teachers must relate the content of academic subjects to career opportunities and also to the skills, knowledge and attitudes required in real life situations outside of school.

This presents a new challenge to both in-service and pre-service teacher education.

• Teachers must analyze their own fields of specialization.

Teachers must identify the nature and extent of career-relevant content and methodology in their fields of specialization. Teacher education must aid in this process. This exploration and analysis must be a continuing one. It must take into account technological and social changes and their implications.

Career oriented education for students is dependent upon proven performance of skills, knowledge and attitudes. Effective career education for teachers is dependent upon teacher education programs based upon demonstrated performance.

Developing a program of teacher education for implementing career education is both a challenge and an opportunity. It is an opportunity to make education more meaningful in the lives of teachers and students. It is an opportunity to reach more young people and adults with relevant educational experiences. It is an opportunity to inspire toward lifetime learning. These opportunities underlie a challenge which cannot be ignored by any teacher or teacher educator.

In Ohio, curriculum development in a specific occupational field, correlating the occupational teaching with academic teaching, has been performed under contract with the Office of Education. In this case the broad occupational field of Transportation has been the objective. (In other states similar large curricular objectives have been addressed and are now being field-tested.)

The Ohio design for the Transportation Curriculum, following the Office of Education's general format, addresses the middle school level with Exploration of Transportation Careers and the high school level with Preparation for Transportation Careers. The curriculum material, after field testing during 1973–1974, will be evaluated and, if found satisfactory, disseminated for nationwide adaptation and adoption. The following extract from the Ohio product gives some impressions of its scope:

> Transportation, the movement of people and goods from one place to another, employs over 13% of our nation's civilian working population. Almost 20% of our total expenditures for goods and services (GNP) is for transportation. Nearly 10% of our net civilian investment in privately owned tangible assets is for transportation facilities and transportation sources pay over 17% of our federal taxes.
>
> The Transportation Occupations Curriculum Project is producing four major publications: a teacher's guide and a student manual for the exploration of transportation careers, and a teacher's guide and a student manual for transportation career preparation. In the planning stage is a counselor's guide to careers in transportation.

The span of career themes on the transportation industry embraced by the Ohio curriculum development is displayed in the charts on pages 200 to 203.

The concept of career education, particularly at the middle school and high school level is quite lucidly expressed in Ohio's diagram showing the flow of learning experiences applicable to any occupational field:

To select specific states as providing good examples of developmental activities for the teacher and counselor is risky business. Much good work is going on in nearly all the states, but space allows only one or two more illustrations.

Governor William T. Cahill in New Jersey addressed the subject in his annual message of January 9, 1973:

> During the past year, the three pilot districts in the Governor's Career Education Project have expanded their efforts in the development of a K–12 Career Education system, and new pilot districts are being added to the project. The Department of Education has developed a new task force to coordinate career education efforts among the Divisions of Curriculum and Instruction, Vocational Education, and Research, Planning and Evaluation.

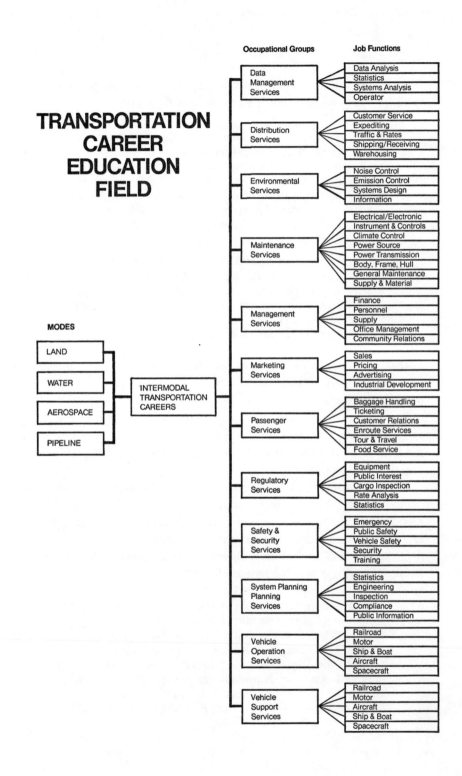

TRANSPORTATION CAREER EDUCATION FIELD

MODES

- LAND
- WATER
- AEROSPACE
- PIPELINE

INTERMODAL TRANSPORTATION CAREERS

Occupational Groups | **Job Functions**

Data Management Services
- Data Analysis
- Statistics
- Systems Analysis
- Operator

Distribution Services
- Customer Service
- Expediting
- Traffic & Rates
- Shipping/Receiving
- Warehousing

Environmental Services
- Noise Control
- Emission Control
- Systems Design
- Information

Maintenance Services
- Electrical/Electronic
- Instrument & Controls
- Climate Control
- Power Source
- Power Transmission
- Body, Frame, Hull
- General Maintenance
- Supply & Material

Management Services
- Finance
- Personnel
- Supply
- Office Management
- Community Relations

Marketing Services
- Sales
- Pricing
- Advertising
- Industrial Development

Passenger Services
- Baggage Handling
- Ticketing
- Customer Relations
- Enroute Services
- Tour & Travel
- Food Service

Regulatory Services
- Equipment
- Public Interest
- Cargo Inspection
- Rate Analysis
- Statistics

Safety & Security Services
- Emergency
- Public Safety
- Vehicle Safety
- Security
- Training

System Planning Planning Services
- Statistics
- Engineering
- Inspection
- Compliance
- Public Information

Vehicle Operation Services
- Railroad
- Motor
- Ship & Boat
- Aircraft
- Spacecraft

Vehicle Support Services
- Railroad
- Motor
- Aircraft
- Ship & Boat
- Spacecraft

STATE DEPARTMENT OF EDUCATION— OHIO (Middle School)

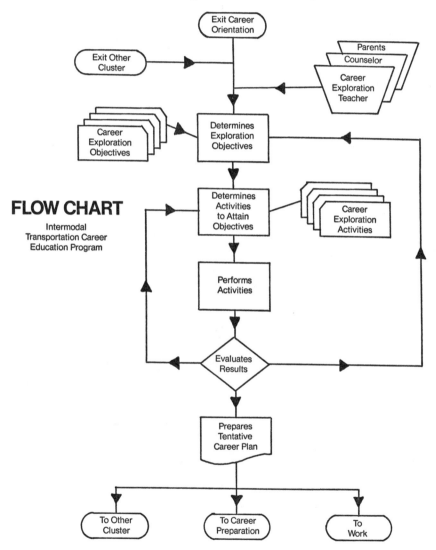

Exit Career Orientation

Exit Other Cluster

Parents
Counselor
Career Exploration Teacher

Career Exploration Objectives

Determines Exploration Objectives

FLOW CHART

Intermodal Transportation Career Education Program

Determines Activities to Attain Objectives

Career Exploration Activities

Performs Activities

Evaluates Results

Prepares Tentative Career Plan

To Other Cluster

To Career Preparation

To Work

STATE DEPARTMENT OF EDUCATION – OHIO (High School)

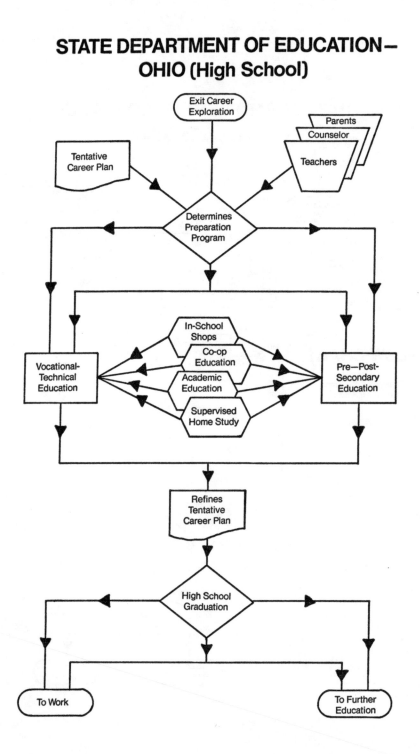

CAREER EDUCATION CONCEPT:
A LIFETIME OF LEARNING

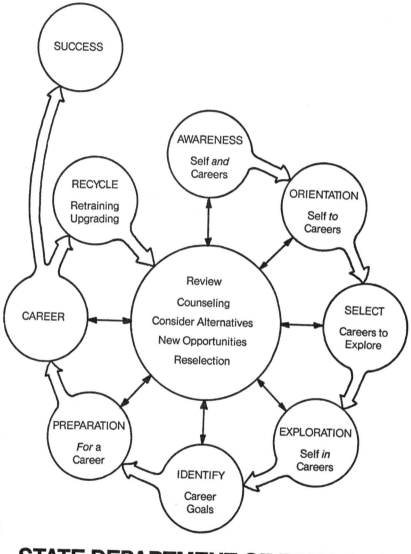

STATE DEPARTMENT OF EDUCATION
—OHIO

In addition, 18 county offices now have career education coordinators to assist in the establishment of K–12 programs in their respective areas.

More than 37,000 elementary school children have participated in the project since its inception. Approximately 600 teachers have been trained [in career education] and during the current school year, the program will be implemented in 76 new school districts involving an additional 500 teachers.

While the Office of Education has assisted in funding such curriculum-development and teacher-training programs as cited above, many school systems are proceeding under their own initiative, without federal support. Sheboygan, Wisconsin, for example, has established the Career Education Center, giving systemwide direction to the installation of career education. A guide to teachers lists six central components of the process, ranging from kindergarten to postsecondary education:

Self-concept
Career planning and preparation
World of work
Community
Postsecondary alternatives
Placement

The Sheboygan manual for teachers carries the following introduction:

> The Career Education Model is presented as a graphic description of Career Education. For effective implementation, the component parts of the model require input by parents, teachers, counselors, administrators, school boards, business, industry, government and the church.
>
> This Career Education Model identifies six major components that can be used to plan and organize for the implementing of Career Education. Most concepts and activities crucial to establishing Career Education are not only developmental, pre-school through adult, but are infused through all six of these components.
>
> These six components are presented to show the vast

scope and sequence of some of the activities necessary to implement Career Education. The project activities identified are usually very important to all six components, but we have listed them with only the most important component.

Implementation of any Career Education Model will require district-wide commitment to the Career development philosophy. Full-time leadership and responsibility must be provided by dedicated professionals in order to implement Career Education components.

While the Office of Education, consistent with its legal responsibilities, is encouraging the pragmatic development of materials and procedures, the National Institute of Education is, pursuant to its legal mandate, advancing more fundamental research toward refining the theory and testing the validity of the career education concept. The NIE work has important long-term implications for teachers and counselors. NIE has declared its present function in the career education field to include the following:[12]

- Provide national leadership in defining and describing career education.
- Serve as a clearing house for information on career education.
- Report overall development of career education programs and the findings from studies related to career education.
- Develop and test a limited number of curriculum materials and approaches as options for local and state educational authorities.
- Initiate research studies directed at the most basic and controversial issues in career education.
- Analyze policy implications of basic career education issues.
- Identify second generation research questions.
- Support research emerging from existing program development.
- Expand current models by helping initiate new program development activities and by supplementing the evaluation and documentation components of field-initiated projects.

- Maintain a bank of ideas from small-scale, exploratory-level studies.

- Stimulate career-related research in human learning, needs, educational goals and objectives, "life skills" and related concerns.

- Assess the capacity of career education to support educational reform.

More will be written about the current efforts of both the Office of Education and the National Institute of Education in a later chapter. The foregoing notes may be particularly useful to those concerned with the resources for teacher education.

While the message of this chapter has been focused largely on the development of elementary and secondary school *teachers*, all professional staff members of the school structure are inescapably engaged in the proposed reform. Obviously, school administrators, subject matter supervisors, and particularly guidance counselors are essential parties to the adoption of career education.

The counselor, especially in the secondary schools and colleges, becomes a very strategic resource to the change process. Historically, counseling found its headwaters in *occupational* counseling over fifty years ago. But, as noted in an earlier chapter, the evolution of the profession brought changing expectations, driving us almost exclusively toward *college* counseling. The reward system was clearly evident in this evolution. And now, it seems we are coming full circle, and asking that counselors rise above the implications of exclusive occupational counseling, or college counseling, and serve as the key people in orchestrating the two themes into one. It is quite likely that the ablest counselors have, consciously or subconsciously, regardless of how they were perceived, been doing this all along. But they have been doing it with *ad hoc* and intuitive resources, rather than in a system of education designed to serve the occupational aspirations as well as the immediate academic aspirations of the learner.

While it is noted that classroom teachers must now have larger appreciation for work outside the school, this expectation is even larger for the counselor. E. L. Tolbert, of the University of Florida, addresses the enlarged role of the counselor in his *Counseling for Career Development*:

> One of the counselor's most important responsibilities is to assist pupils with career planning. This responsibility, however, has been neglected by counselors and by the other members of the school staff. Considerable reorientation is needed, for humanitarian reasons and for practical ones—the public demands it. Alternative methods of guidance and counseling will be developed by others if career guidance services are not provided, and funds for current programs may be cut back. One way the public demand is articulated is through emphasis on accountability. This concept will have far-reaching effects on guidance, as well as on the whole educational establishment.
>
> Career education is another response to public demands. Current social and economic conditions underline the critical need for improvement in both the quantity and quality of guidance. Trends in the availability of jobs, the increasing complexity of the world of work, the large number of school dropouts, the high rate of youth unemployment, and job discrimination exacerbate the problem. Late changers and second-career persons also need assistance. Career planning skills are needed by individuals at all ages; school guidance could at least begin developing these competencies.
>
> The conditions that make career guidance and counseling necessary are not new. They existed at the turn of the century and gave rise to guidance as one aspect of a social reform movement.
>
> Career education based on vocational development theory provides a framework for identifying the major emphases of vocational exploration, planning, and decision making at the high school level and helps in specifying the career guidance services needed. Individual and group counseling are the central services. Others, such as group guidance and the information system, support counseling and also provide specific types of assistance to pupils.[13]

Soon after the concept of career education began to take the form of a national priority, the College Entrance Examination Board undertook a detailed analysis of the implications of career education for the role of the counselor. Warren Willingham, Richard Ferrin, and Elsie Begle took on the task in the winter of 1972, producing a worthy publication entitled *Career Guidance in Secondary Education*. One chart from this study is reproduced (pp. 210–211) with these comments by the authors:

> . . . The new models include a variety of emphases that will characterize new guidance programs over the next several years. Especially in demand will be curriculum materials and programs that involve students in real-life situations. Favored methods include simulation, self-directed activities, group guidance, use of new media, interdisciplinary cooperation, and multimethod integrated programs. The high priority processes are student-centered: planning, decision-making, and coping. It will be especially required that these student-centered services be directed to all students, individualized to their level of aspiration and vocational maturity, and designed to serve educational and career functions that students recognize as actually useful and realistic. With respect to content, special emphasis is now being placed on understanding the meaning of education and work—not just their outward characteristics. At this writing there are relatively few guidance materials that reflect these values. That will not be true a year from now.[14]

Drawing further upon the College Board study, the changing role of the counselor is analyzed developmentally by Willingham *et al.* under the rubric of "dominant ideas" in counseling:

> There are perhaps an indefinite number of ways to describe the dominant ideas that shape guidance in the secondary school. Of the eight listed in the College Board's Chart, the first two represent the traditional and somewhat antagonistic orientations—the so-called trait-factor approach and the more non-directive method of personal counseling. The two approaches represent different values (scientific versus humanistic), different emphasis in training, and different practices. Many coun-

selors have administered tests and openly preferred personal counseling, but the two certainly are not mutually exclusive. Both are criticized for different reasons. The trait-factor approach works much better in theory than in practice because it appears that multiaptitude tests have limited value in predicting career choice or success. Personal counseling has important status associations with psychology and psychiatry, but one-to-one counseling is now widely regarded as impractical for educational and economic reasons.

The next four ideas in Chart 1 represent substantive emphases that have gained much momentum in the past five years. It is now commonly felt to be essential that students learn more about the world of work—that the serious imbalance between guidance for college and vocational orientation be redressed. Closely related to this is the recognition that students develop career awareness over a long period of time and require different types of career guidance at different age levels.

Another important idea is the notion that young people must learn how to make decisions and how to recognize situations that demand decisions. Students require help in this process because it has become far more difficult to deal with career planning than it used to be, and such decisions involve more serious questions concerning values and life styles than students generally realize.

As a consequence of these ideas, there are new movements to alter the basic orientation of guidance in the schools. Since the mid 1960s, there have been concerted efforts by some professional leaders to move guidance into the school curriculum and to develop comprehensive systems approaches that would integrate services and objectives (last two items in the chart). As these movements develop they seem certain to alter basically the role of the counselor in the school and the way guidance services are coordinated.

Most of the observations and examples of this chapter have dealt with the needs of educators now engaged in elementary and secondary schools. This is a necessary and immediate response to the proposal for reform, because only those engaged explicitly in the affairs of the schools are capable of bringing it off.

DOMINANT IDEAS

IDEA	DESCRIPTION	HISTORY AND STATUS	IMPLICATIONS
Trait-factor approach is the scientific basis of guidance.	The essential task of career guidance is to match individual traits (abilities, interests, etc.) with important job factors (work requirements, necessary skills, etc.). Done effectively, this maximizes social benefit and likelihood of individual satisfaction and success.	The "matching men and jobs" concept of vocational guidance was originated by Frank Parsons in 1908 and dominated the field until 1950. It was advanced by psychometric development and job analysis of industrial engineers in the '20s and '30s. Greatly encouraged by multiaptitude movement (Louis L. Thurstone and Clark L. Hull), differential prediction of career success in military (Paul Horst, John C. Flanagan, et al.). Humanistic and developmental counterreaction was fanned by empirical evidence of poor results (Thorndike and Hagen, 1959). Still a fundamental basis for much career guidance—particularly out of school—but regarded as insufficient by most experts and dismissed by some.	• In broad outline the approach seems inescapable in any general model of career guidance, but traditional applications seem certain to meet resistance. • Psychometric methods must be integrated into developmental models of self/career awareness rather than choosing a job on the basis of an aptitude profile.
Guidance is primarily personal counseling.	Emphasizes view of guidance as concern for total development of individual, not just educational/vocational assistance. Goal of counseling is self-realization. Counselor must create climate in which client can solve his own problems.	Developed as a reaction against "actuarial" counseling (mechanized approach) and "saturation testing." Influence of nondirective psychotherapists (Carl Rogers, et al.) very strong. Krumboltz (1966) emphasizes behavioral change aspect of personal counseling. This is the prestige component of guidance profession still stressed in many training centers though strongly criticized by some observers.	• Continued conflict between social and professional interests—also between personal and career counseling.
Career awareness is an integral part of school guidance.	Complexity of socioeconomic environments walls off student. The job structure changes rapidly. Contrary to earlier times when career role models were readily observable, it is now necessary to teach students what the world of work is like.	Occupational information courses have a long and deadly history. Schools have come to neglect vocational preparation in favor of more glamorous college guidance, but recent emphasis by U.S. Office of Education promises to stimulate much new activity.	• Important component of career development; career-guidance services will have to be compatible with major career-information models.
Career choice and adjustment is a lifelong process involving developmental stages.	Career choice is not a one-shot decision. Individual moves through stages; important choice points occur at 9th and 12th grade. Vocational maturity at different stages is characterized by different values, different concerns, and different guidance needs.	Ginzberg (1951) was a catalyst for the developmental approach and theories of occupational choice. Super (1963, 1968) was an important contributor to ideas of self-concept in vocational decisions, vocational maturity, and the delineation of life styles. Crites (1971) and Gribbons and Lohnes (1968) have done extensive work in measuring vocational development. This general idea is currently quite important. Has the weight of the profession and the U.S. Office of Education behind it.	• Guidance services must be better integrated across grade levels. • Materials must be appropriate to the level of vocational maturity of individual students. • Periodic evaluation of vocational maturity itself may become an especially important objective in career guidance. • The largely untapped market of adult career guidance will likely receive much more attention. (Federal initiative may be the key.)

DOMINANT IDEAS

IDEA	DESCRIPTION	HISTORY AND STATUS	IMPLICATIONS
Career patterns reflect life styles	Occupational choices and career patterns are basic to the life style of the individual and reflect personality hopes, social background, etc. Career choice thus involves far more than matching abilities and job requirements. It is, in Super's terms, an expression of the individual's self-concept (and vice versa).	Influenced by sociological and developmental psychology. Charlotte Buehler's sequential development concept and Robert Havighurst's framework of life stages supplied groundwork for Super's (1969) work in career patterns. Important today to research sociologists and psychologists and to students, especially those who question work ethic and traditional values. Doesn't always filter down (Wilensky, 1964)	• Important consideration in materials and program design. Especially needed to add realism to career guidance.
A primary goal is to develop the student's decision-making skills	Career choice is a rational process—not determined by chance or social position but subject to scientific investigation, amenable to intervention, and responsive to training. The counselor's job is to make the student aware of alternatives and to develop his ability to make rational decisions	Outgrowth of vocational theory developed after World War II. David Tiedeman most important theoretical contributor—sees decision-making as a continuous process in which computers can be "mediators" (O'Hara and Tiedeman, 1971). Martin Katz developed an early practical model (1970). Gelatt (1962) created first school program based on this idea	• Very promising organizing theme for career guidance.
Career development must be incorporated in the curriculum	For educational and practical reasons career guidance must be an integral part of the student's formal education. This is necessary to obtain the time, the diverse teaching skills, and the continuity that are required to cope with this developmental learning problem	In 1917 George E. Myers was one of the first to argue that vocational guidance should be part of the curriculum. In recent years realization of the complexity of career development and disappointment with the limited success of present guidance practices has led to widespread agreement that career development principles must be moved into the curriculum (National Vocational Guidance Association, 1966). Present federal programs are heavily committed to this principle for all age levels	• Increasingly career-guidance components will be adopted by curriculum specialists to fill slots in designated curriculums
Guidance requires a systems approach	Multiple goals of guidance require complementary skills of different disciplines, coordination of large amounts of information, integrated program packages, and focused effort on specific objectives—that is, a systems approach that integrates resources.	Systematic analysis and coordination of complex activities had its birth in World War II and has been used in education only in the past 10 years (see Campbell et al., 1968). This approach now assumes a prominent role in the federal initiatives and most applications of computer technology	• Counselor will be increasingly required to serve as the administrator of a program that involves other members of the school staff and a variety of media. • Services not compatible with "the system" will become more difficult to adopt.

However, the eventual design for the reform of teacher education will rest with colleges and universities in their departments or schools of teacher education. There is little to be gained by a transformation of existing teachers and counselors, if young, newly employed teachers will enter the system with the traditional practices, beliefs, and philosophies now undergoing change.

This does not suggest a universal and singular "curriculum" for all teacher-education institutions. Rather it calls for a general learning environment for aspirant teachers which will equip them for ready adaptability to the concept of career education upon entering a system which has undertaken the career education design. Depending upon the level of grade and subject matter which the student-teacher is planning to enter, the college-level instruction will provide the developing teacher with a full grasp of the underlying meaning of career education, and will afford literal exposure to a variety of work situations which articulate with academic and occupational instruction. Student-teaching or internship experiences should be designed by the training institution to expose the candidate to successful ongoing career education classrooms as well as out-of-school, hands-on experience in other forms of work than teaching. Indeed, the development of the young teacher, perhaps when he or she, at whatever age, begins to formulate occupational goals, is in itself a first-rate example of career education, leading often through advanced professional degrees.

Apart from the specific teacher-education function of higher education, there is the added responsibility of research and development in career education. This opportunity is not limited to the school of education, but should properly cut across many parts of the college or university. Certainly the scholars of the social sciences have their place in this spectrum, as do those concerned with management, business, politics, and engineering. Their research will have a potential sponsor, among others, in the National Institute of Education, whose annual appropriations over time for this topic could run to tens of millions of dollars for allocation to promising scholarly inquiry.

Change does not come easily to any institution, whether in the business world, in government, in the applied sciences, or certainly in education. But change is inescapable in any enterprise. Teachers and counselors know this, and are ready and willing to change. Change in education has been slow, uncoordinated, frequently lacking the benefit of research and validation, and often counterproductive in the eyes of teachers whose hearts were not in it. It is possible, as some dependable observers now declare, that the unifying theme of career education and the systematic (though not directive) support for change through funding and research will for the first time in a long while give American teachers and counselors a central column of consistent pedagogical theory and philosophy around which to construct their own creative changes leading to general reform. Two million and more American teachers and counselors will not see career education through the same eyes, as they might be expected to do in some other countries where educational conformity is the rule. But if they see it clearly and adapt their beliefs and behavior to its message, they may well find a deeper satisfaction and professional fulfillment as the lives of the learners are brightened, made more meaningful, and enlivened by the implicit motivation to learn that resides in the learner's enlarged command of his own destiny.

Career Education
at the
College Level

Parents of high school- and college-age students are facing a swiftly rising tuition rate in all postsecondary institutions. Students, many of whom are partly self-supporting in college, are seeking a more immediate and material return on the investment of time and money devoted to the postsecondary years. Historically, the typical American parent, following the tradition of unquestioning support of the education ethos, has sacrificed readily and substantially to insure a college education for our young. While federal and state grants and loans have encouraged lower-income students to enter college, the members of the large middle- and upper-income sector of our society do not qualify for grants and face high interest rates on loans. There appears to be a quiet but persistent rejection of the "unquestioning support of the education ethos" that now calls for a more economically measurable outcome from the investments in college and university education. Heretofore, such an outcome was taken for granted. The level of cost and the evidence of dubious economic outcomes are combining to push institutions toward career education.

"Fashioners of career curricula must catch the spirit of liberal education and meld it inextricably with vocational and professional training at all levels," according to Stephen K. Bailey.[1] While Dr. Bailey's statement was aimed at the institutions of postsecondary education, he spoke the "all levels" message of a new harmony between academic learning and occupational development. Widely respected as a scholar in his own field, political science, he now serves as Vice President and Director of Research of the American Council on Education. Bailey's message in this esteemed higher education body will inevitably influence policy development in postsecondary education.

A number of colleges and universities, not without some uneasiness, are probing the new dimensions of career education as the concept affects higher education. This chapter will offer examples of developmental work now going on, to include four-year and two-year institutions.

As I address the topic of career education at the postsecondary level, I am mindful of a wider difference in mood from the spirit of consensus than appears to be emerging at the elementary and secondary levels. And certainly there is no unanimity in the lower schools! But in the colleges and universities career education *as a term* can be frequently cast in a pejorative context, especially by faculty members who perceive it as a threat rather than as a reinforcement to their field of teaching. As noted in an earlier chapter, the quick reader sometimes mistranslates career education into vocational education, and the scholar-professor understandably rejects it.

Accordingly, in this chapter I would suggest that the term *career education* be used as a generic reference to what I feel is a perceivable trend in higher education, rather than the more focused and specific programmatic reform being advanced in elementary and secondary schools. The institutions of higher education are, quite rightly, more diverse, more individualistic, more sensitive to the political and scholarly prerogatives of faculties, and accordingly far less organized for responsiveness to a singular theme of curricular reform than the public schools. It will be recalled, however, that even though more systematically organized for responsiveness, the elementary and secondary schools will not accept the reforms of career education effectively unless their implementation is a product of faculty determination. Suffice it to say that I will be dealing with a less discrete and more generic application of career education in this chapter than in most of the others.

Columbia University last year launched a major reform in its general education program so that undergraduates would receive more technical, career-oriented offerings, while graduate students in the professions would receive more attention in the humanities. Under this plan at Columbia—titled University Directions II—medical students, for example, following as they do a highly specific occupational or professional education program, would continue their general education past the undergraduate level and study the historical, legal, and ethical aspects of such questions as the right to health care, mental retardation, drug addiction, and abortion, in conjunction with the technical and clinical aspects of their field. Undergraduates would be able to start taking courses in the occupational and professional disciplines as early as their sophomore year, combining these courses with ongoing studies in general education that would extend into their graduate training.

> If there are any educational constants to be observed [says deBary], they are found in the need for both specialized (occupational) training in certain disciplines and liberal education in the humanities to start from the first years of college and continue through university education.[2]

This statement reaches to the heart of the present issue as career education reform makes its impact on colleges and universities.

One may question, quite rightly, whether the restlessness of parents and students vis-à-vis college investments is a good reason for changing the scope and purpose of higher education. The answer resides in sustaining the historic substance and values of the institution, and blending them harmoniously with the utilitarian expectations of the client.

Dr. de Bary, in his leadership of curricular reform at Columbia, has written powerfully and extensively on higher education's commitment to the liberal arts. Under the title *General Education and the Humanities*, he declares:

> General education, though a vital part of liberal educa-
> tion, is not the whole of it. Liberal education, most people
> would agree, aims to liberate the powers of the individual
> by disciplining them; and that discipline in turn im-
> mediately relates him to the values of his culture and
> certain social necessities. I do not, then, have any dif-
> ficulty in accepting even professional training or voca-
> tional education as contributing to those aims. The edu-
> cated man, the member of society, even the purported
> citizen of the world, needs this everyday discipline if he is
> to be liberated from a sense of total dependence on
> others. He must have something that he can contribute of
> his own to the work of the world, and if he learns to do it
> well, that will be part of his liberal education. It is not to be
> scorned as "mere vocationalism." For this reason I can
> appreciate the concerns which have given rise to the
> current drive for "career education." . . . [3]

DeBary notes the correspondence between Columbia's monu-
mental and trail-blazing curricular reforms of 1919 and the present major reform now in process. "The two events were not
unrelated: both were attempts to remotivate dissatisfied students
and dropouts." A weekly seminar, reports *The Chronicle*, conducted by Richard F. Kuhns, professor of philosophy, is devoted
to the examination of "common goals and values" within the
university.[4] Nearly half of the "students" are faculty members,
learning from their colleagues. According to Mr. Kuhns, "Faculty
interest is a legacy of the 1960s. . . . During the disruptions of the
university," he says, "students criticized professionalism, the
need to follow time-bound rules. . . . While the violence has
cooled, some professors are now facing up to the charges of
academic narrowness, and see Mr. de Bary's proposals as a way to
confront the issues."

In announcing the University Directions II (February 23, 1973),
Columbia University spelled out what it perceived were the
changes in their situation over the last several decades that
required the new program. Several of the points listed are

extracted from the Columbia statement, with the belief they have meaning for higher education at large:

> The trend toward specialization and vocationalism reflects not only social changes but the vast expansion of knowledge and the individual's difficulty in coping with it. There seems to be no way of achieving a sense of mastery or individual competence except by cutting out for one's self some manageable segment of the whole.

> There is less and less plausibility to the idea that one can define a liberal education by circumscribing a body of knowledge in such terms as "what every educated man ought to know."

> Survey courses, to the degree that they imply extensive coverage and generality rather than selectivity in regard to values and priorities, do not serve the purposes of general education.

> It is not practicable or desirable to think of general education or education in the humanities (broadly conceived) as something done in the first years of college and then gradually yielding to specialization. The needs of different programs vary and uniformity cannot be enforced; if there are any educational constants to be observed, they are found in the need for both specialized training in certain [occupational] disciplines and liberal education in the humanities to start from the first years of college and continue throughout university education.

> Because of the increasingly technological character of our society and the rapidity of social change, with a consequent bewildering flux in shared values, it is vital that undergraduates have some common experience of the humanities as a basis for their continuing education. There should, however, be a recognition that this process spreads outward from a human center and the humane scholar continues to be concerned with questions of value in the midst of increasingly specialized studies on the frontiers of advancing knowledge.

> For many students the relevance of the "humanities" may be best appreciated in relation to the study of contemporary social, scientific or technological problems in concrete form. An effective program in the humanities will seek to involve scholars and scientists capable of bridging

the gap between shared human concerns and new discoveries in the forefront of scholarship.

This reform calling for the harmonizing of occupational or "specialization" curricula with the liberal arts is the first major reform in universitywide curriculum since Columbia pioneered the concept of "general education" after World War I. That curriculum, which had wide influence on the policies of higher education in America, was called "Contemporary Civilization" and was initiated then to give students a broader grounding in the arts, natural sciences, and social history than did the unstructured system of electives offered at the time. It represented the beginning of today's familiar "required courses" that other institutions borrowed from Columbia's early reforms.

Columbia University is not alone in its new efforts toward reform. Claremont College in Claremont, California, has drawn up plans to combine undergraduate and graduate training in law and business administration. Many of the major colleges and universities in America have begun to take an interdisciplinary approach to a broad range of subjects, giving meaning to the philosophy of career education, whether employing the term or not. (See Clark Kerr, et al., *Less Time, More Options.*)

Professor Nathan Glazer of Harvard takes note of the continuing ambivalence between occupational development and the scholarly disciplines in what he calls the "minor professions."

> It has long been clear that schools that train for such professions as education, social work, city planning, and divinity, have a great deal in common. . . . [They possess] . . . certain characteristic conflicts that arise in remarkably similar form in the professional schools that train for each of these minor professions. . . . We characteristically have a situation in which a faculty drawn from scholars and researchers, with a base in one of the academic disciplines, teaches students who will become practitioners. . . . The major professional role for which students are being taught and trained is itself of inferior status. . . .

Glazer continues with an example:

The young man headed for a pulpit is taught by biblical scholars, theologians, and archaeologists. He knows that the main answers to his problems in dealing with a living congregation will not be found there. Yet it is in those fields that the school will look for a new faculty. Increasingly, it will daringly select men who have some competence in some area in which the clergyman will have practical problems, such as personal counseling, or congregational organizational management, but the heart of the faculty is still in Bible and theology.[5]

Patricia Cross has developed a forward-thinking conceptualization under the term "the learning society." She probes the emergence of a new design in higher education.

The learning society is likely to accelerate the education-competitive phase, at least in the beginning. In this transitional period we are in a buyer's market. Supply has caught up with demand, and students are in a position to get what they want. There will be a certain amount of threat to established institutions as well as a certain amount of stimulus for reform . . .

Higher education has, in the past, operated within fairly well-defined boundaries and limitations. The learning society breaks loose from those boundaries and learning pervades the entire community. There are some important distinctions between the pre-learning society and the mature learning society.

First, the pre-learning society devotes considerable attention to determining who is eligible for admission to college. The learning society places no limitations on who may enter college; all people are eligible for learning at the level that seems useful for them.

Second, the pre-learning society has clearly specified requirements for teachers. The mature learning society welcomes as teachers all who have knowledge or skills to share with others. A bank executive may teach banking; an auto mechanic may teach auto repair; a business-woman may counsel women seeking re-entry to professional education. In principle, the openness toward teacher qualifications already has been accepted by the establishment in the form of adjunct professors, paraprofessionals and peer tutors.

Third, the pre-learning society emphasizes accreditation for the official houses of learning. The learning society emphasizes the use of learning resources wherever they are found—in the home, on the job, in proprietary institutions, in museums, in a foreign country. In short, the pre-learning society is concerned with procedures, structures, qualifications and standards. The mature learning society is more concerned with learning itself.[6]

Prestigious Chatham College in Pittsburgh, perhaps a classic example among women's colleges with a progressive liberal arts philosophy, describes itself to prospective students.

You've heard the clichés about women liberal arts majors. They boil down to one sentence: "Major in the liberal arts and you can always get a job—as a typist." Once that might have been true. But no more. Certainly not for Chatham's liberal arts majors.

The fact is that the business world, for example, wants the leadership skills of Chatham women—skills developed through rigorous training in the liberal arts. Examples? The ability to think critically and analyze assumptions. To communicate precisely and effectively. To bring a sense of cultural and historical perspective to problem solving.

The statement continues:

. . . when it comes to setting the world on fire, you'll never find a better book of matches than the liberal arts. The only trick is in striking a balance between academic learning and actual work experience. . . . Our students can take career internships in business and nonprofit organizations all over Pittsburgh . . . Internships help to give our students the "real-world" experience needed to make intelligent, confident career decisions. . . . Each program covers a broad range of possible careers.[7]

Colleges and universities have begun to see, as de Bary states, that "general education and disciplinary training must be thought of as complementary and parallel pursuits, not competing or divergent ones. The former view of general education as a broadening experience in the early years of college, followed by intensive specialization, must give way to a conception of general education as continuing in later years, and of specialized [occupational] training as starting earlier, alongside of general education for those ready to make that commitment." The blending of the two threads into one fabric, is, in my opinion, the essential message of career education at the postsecondary level.

The shift of curriculum at Columbia and at other prominent institutions is to a great degree influenced by the realization that their clientele—the students—have changed dramatically in recent years. These "new" young people want to become usefully employed and financially independent early in life, and they are seeking to accomplish their goals in a time when society wants technically competent employees, and is increasingly selective in employment policies. They are the customers in Patricia Cross's "buyer's market." This condition, as noted earlier, is reinforced by the cost of "an education" at most four-year colleges, which is becoming a serious problem for most young people and their families, and pushes us all to make the investment more pragmatically attractive.

A recent study conducted by the College Scholarship Service of the College Entrance Examination Board, reveals that student costs, including tuition and all other expenses, have increased over the past five years as follows:[8]

Type of Institution	Increases over 5 years (1970-1971 to 1974-1975)			
	Resident		Commuter	
Public 2-year	N/A		$ 492	(34.4%)
Private 2-year	$1,237	(52.0%)	$1,453	(79.2%)
Public 4-year	$ 617	(34.6%)	$ 554	(36.2%)
Private 4-year	$1,065	(35.8%)	$1,301	(54.6%)

A university administrator declared in a meeting in the spring of 1974, "When people ask me whether I have children in college, I no longer say 'Yes, two.' I now say, 'Yes, $9000-worth a year.'"

According to Bailey, "as four-year college experiences become more and more costly to taxpayers and to direct users, and as the disjuncture between entering job requirements and baccalaureate status becomes clear, hostility to the traditional four-year college will increase as threatened pocketbooks induce a psychic compulsion among parents and students to denigrate those instruments of social status that have 'opportunity-costed' themselves out of the market of the many."[9]

Now, at the postsecondary level the community colleges are, to a degree, filling the gap and preparing students, through a wide range of occupational offerings combined with academic studies, for the world of work. They have responded quickly to the needs of the students, adjusting their programs to prepare students for what *they* want out of school. Less constrained by tradition and protocol, the community colleges are able to move more fluidly and flexibly to meet students' needs. Students who once scorned the community college as a lower order of the education establishment are finding pragmatic satisfaction in its classrooms and laboratories. Marvin Feldman, president of The Fashion Institute of Technology, a well-respected community college in New York City, reports that his two-year institution has been obliged to impose a quota on the percentage of bachelor-degree holders it will accept in its occupational offerings. This is a strange and interesting twist of the term "graduate studies."

Dr. Marie Y. Martin, the director of community college education in the U.S. Office of Education, recently wrote: "The common goal of community colleges is to respond to the student's specific, immediate educational needs in a manner that serves his long-term aspirations for a satisfying and meaningful life after his schooling is ended." (I would have preferred that she use a verb other than *ended*; *suspended* or *interrupted* would have been closer to the career education idea of "lifelong educational opportunities.")

Dr. Martin examined in detail what was happening at the community-college level in reflecting the career education theme. She focused on six colleges in various parts of the country. The summaries that follow are based on her personal observation; extensive interviews with administrators, faculty, and students; and materials supplied by the individual institutions.

Pasadena City College, in Pasadena, California, offers sixty-four career-oriented courses—from commercial airline pilot training to metal processes technology. Such courses engage about half of its 14,000 students, with the other half taking transfer courses in preparation for entering four-year colleges.

Typifying the stress placed on interdisciplinary cooperation between the academic and occupational skills, each year at Pasadena the students build and sell a model home to the highest bidder—enlisting as they do so the interest and cooperation of representatives of the professions, labor, and business.

Students studying architecture or architectural drafting develop a range of designs, with the best being chosen on a competitive basis. Students in structural specifications then take over, drawing up the formal specifications and making sure they are followed by the students in construction classes. Students of interior design select the color schemes to be used and decide upon the colors, drapes, and furnishings. The printing and lithography students prepare advertisements and brochures. Business classes participate in preparing bid specifications and managing the affairs of the accounting and sale of the structure.

There is also an advisory committee composed of practicing architects and experts from the construction unions, trade associations, utility companies, and furniture stores who assist the project.

Pasadena has seventy-one off-campus educational sites in churches, schools, parks, and vacated factories, where classes are offered in courses ranging from the sawing of lumber to grocery store operations. A key component of this Pasadena community-education program is a mobile career guidance unit. Moved from place to place in low-income neighborhoods, it serves as a center for job aptitudes testing, counseling, and information about subjects available at Pasadena City College main campus and the satellite campuses.

New York City Community College of the City University of New York, located in Brooklyn, serves a student body of 15,000 in thirty-four different career-education and college-transfer courses. About 80 percent of the students have chosen one or more of the occupational offerings, which are offered both day and evening.

The overall career program at Brooklyn Community College has three components—general education, orientation, and training in specific skills, with the curriculum for the latter being determined largely by the entry-level requirements of industry or by the state's licensing boards.

Student needs and industry demands have an important impact on NYCCC's offerings. Located as it is near the center of the advertising industry, for example, the college has developed programs responding to the continuing demand for people trained in commercial art, graphic arts, and advertising technology.

Of the students participating in cooperative education programs in engineering technologies, data processing, and accounting, better than 80 percent were offered permanent jobs in 1973 (a difficult placement year, generally) by the companies with whom they had been gaining experience.

Central Piedmont Community College, in Charlotte, North Carolina, never closes its doors on its 8000 students. Its instructional program runs around the clock, partly to make full use of expensive facilities and handle heavy class loads, partly to accommodate students who have jobs during the day. Thus, an automobile mechanics course, for example, gets under way at midnight and runs until 7:00 A.M.

For these same reasons, Central Piedmont is a year-round institution, and about 70 percent of the students who attend during the regular academic year enroll in summer classes to complete trade and vocational courses.

In all, Central Piedmont offers thirty-four occupational programs. One of the most recent to be added to the curriculum is a Human Services Associate degree program geared to employment in day care centers, nursing homes, orphanages, and other welfare-related service agencies.

Moraine Valley Community College, in the southwest suburb of Cook County, Illinois, has an enrollment of 3800 with 42 percent enrolled in the career-education curriculum, blending occupations with general education. The college offers twenty-seven programs leading to an associate degree in applied science or to a one-year certificate in a given field.

In an exemplary program in Industrial Engineering Technology devised by the MVCC faculty and one of its community-consultant committees, each student individually pursues speci-fied, measurable objectives organized according to particular job factors.

This means that, if a student completes only part of the program, he will still be qualified for a job in one of the industrial-technology fields—though at a lower level—because he has mastered at least an established portion of the required skills. The program is organized in such a way as to make it possible for all students to be working on different tasks at the same time and to select their own individual modes of learning and time allocations for the accomplishment of the prescribed task.

Community College of Denver has 7200 students enrolled on its three campuses, and of them 64 percent are participating in career programs. The average age of CCD's students is twenty-seven, and 75 percent hold full- or part-time jobs. As a response to this unusual student body, the college has defined career education as education which meets the needs of the individual as determined by the individual himself.

Particular help in making that determination is provided by a *career center* which operates on the theory that the individual's chance of choosing a satisfying career is directly proportional to the number of occupations he knows about and understands. In developing the informational material necessary to serve that purpose, the center has become a major learning resource not only for the students and faculty but also for high school and junior high school counselors and for the community at large.

Recognizing that many students need experiences in a variety of career fields before they can settle intelligently on one, the college allows students to develop schedules that permit them to try out introductory courses in a number of different occupations, moving at any time from one program to another if they find that their initial choice has proved unsuitable. This exposure is not unlike the elementary and secondary system, which emphasizes career surveys and exposures at the middle school level. But it is unlikely that young adults in college today had this opportunity in the middle schools and high schools of a few years ago. The future, if career education becomes a general reality, will not need to provide introductory explanatory offerings beyond high school.

One of the basic elements in Denver's effort to assist individuals with career choices is a group of instructional laboratories covering basic academic skills. Most instruction is either individualized or carried out with very small groups. Some students enroll in the academic laboratory and at the same time pursue their career program, while others concentrate on acquiring basic skills before they enter the program.

Lane Community College, in Eugene, Oregon, was established as the career education center for the state's southern Willamette Valley. The college serves nearly 20,000 full- or part-time students each year. Lane offers some forty-two separate career-oriented fields, each designed to lead directly to employment at the end of a one- or two-year period of preparation.

Courses are added or deleted at Lane to reflect shifts in the job market, and the emphasis of instruction has moved to a concentration on the personal needs of the individual. A key step in achieving that goal has been the development of more than 850 "V.I.P.s"—Vocational Instructional Packages designed by the faculty with the assistance of experts from business, labor, industry, and the professions.

An open-entry/open-exit instructional strategy allows the student to enter a program at any time, accomplish his objectives at his own rate, and exit the program no sooner and no later than the time he meets the requirements of the job he is pursuing. Placement services are provided, and the college maintains constant liaison with the business community and with the Oregon State Employment Office, enabling students to receive up-to-the-minute information about job opportunities and current wage levels. All students receive on-the-job experience before completing their program.

One could go on citing many other two-year institutions

engaged in the career education design. The community college is, at this point, perhaps the most apt example of the effective harmonizing of occupational and academic learning, paced according to the needs and interests of the learner.

Nominally, consistent with the Education Amendments of 1972, proprietary schools are a recognized component of the postsecondary education system. They will be treated only in passing here, since they do not address the theme of career education, confining their purposes to the occupational component. Yet, they are a force to be reckoned with, and indeed respected, as institutions offering very pragmatic and sometimes huckstered attractions to young people.

Indeed, the proprietary schools are only one element of the large system of education, especially for mature learners, that lies beyond the conventional institutions. And the "peripheral" system is growing, devoting itself primarily to the occupational development of the learners. Moses reported from his studies of 1970 that enrollment in conventional institutions in 1940 for the full span of kindergarten through graduate school was about 30 million, compared with about 17 million, or roughly one-half, enrolled in the *educational periphery institutions* such as business, churches, proprietary schools, television offerings, and unions. He predicted that by 1975 the number *in* the conventional system will be about 67 million learners with 82 million in the programs offered *outside* of schools and colleges.[10]

A wide range of skill training is offered at proprietary schools for people seeking skills to gain employment. They are perhaps the most likely competitors among the peripheral institutions for the time *and money* of the young person seeking solely utilitarian skill development. The official number of such institutions formally accredited is about 1300, enrolling about one million students. But unofficial numbers, including nonaccredited proprietary schools, reach to the 8000–9000 range, and in the educational system of the United States they are an increasingly significant component.

Another component of the skills-development system is the very significant *area vocational-technical school,* a quasi-postsecondary public institution. These schools, heavily supported by federal funds and operated by state and local public school authorities, do not, strictly speaking, conform with the career education theme, since they do not pretend to equate formal general education with occupational education. Yet these trade and technical schools are beginning to be "accepted" by the education establishment for the valuable skill training they provide. As Ewald B. Nyquist, Commissioner of Education for New York, said at the Eighth Annual Conference of the National Association of Trade and Technical Schools, "Education sure is learning how to live a life—a sensitive, creative, compassionate, human life, but it is also learning how to make a living." The proprietary schools and the public postsecondary vocational-technical schools, geared as they are toward industry, are places students can learn to make a living. The line between the public vocational-technical schools and the community colleges is dime-thin in terms of purpose and governance. It would seem to me that all such schools would profit by adapting to a community-college mode and definition, reflecting the academic as well as the occupational substance of learning.

The major concern of this chapter is the four-year institutions—the colleges and universities where most of the students are, and where expectations for reform are most keenly felt. I remind the reader that the term *career education* is used generically in the higher-education setting, describing a process of change that may be discernable, but not necessarily under such a specific name or rubric as "career education."

Alvin Toffler, addressing the Association for Supervision and Curriculum Development in 1973, decried the "teachers and professors who . . . wrongly believe that the future [of education] is going to be pretty much like the present." He declared of teachers and professors that the "trend of the majority is to organize to protect their jobs."[11] Toffler may be correct in his tough line. I share his view that education at all levels will change, but I believe that faculties by the very nature of their profession want to increase the effectiveness of the learning going on under their tutelage. Career education is a *process,* not a different curriculum. It enhances the learner's purposefulness in learning and, accordingly, the instructor's effectiveness and personal satisfaction.

The support of occupational objectives within the curriculum of colleges and universities is not new. As Bailey notes in an essay celebrating our bicentennial year:

> . . . higher education purposes have not remained steady over time. The original functions and curriculum of Harvard were a far cry from later definitions of collegiate purpose there and elsewhere. Harvard's first commencement program stressed the founders' longing ". . . to advance learning and perpetuate it to Posterity; dreading to leave an illiterate Ministry to the Churches, when our present Ministers shall lie in the Dust." This did not mean, as Professor Samuel Eliot Morison has pointed out, that Harvard was only a theological school. The founders provided for the teaching of the arts, sciences and good literature as well as theology. Presumably others besides clergymen could profit from the higher learning. But educating clergy was surely the essential purpose of the early Harvard for ". . . the advancement and perpetuation of learning was one and the same with a succession of literate ministers in the churches." Seventy percent of Harvard's graduates in its first century went into the ministry.[12]

But the years since Harvard's career-oriented founding in 1636 have produced a separation of academic learning from occupational development in many institutions. While any generalization about professional behavior is risky, it may be fair to say that professors have tended over the years to teach their subject content *qua* subject content because that was what they knew well, and as far as a career was concerned it was *their* career.

For students not planning to become college professors, the relationship of the subject to other useful purposes was left to chance or the creativity of the students. This is not meant to be harsh or negative toward teachers, but rather to contemplate a condition that I believe has evolved in higher education, especially in the schools of liberal arts.

Students' attitudes and actions offer the most visible testimony that points us toward this conclusion. John Carusone, student body president at Brown University, said in response to curricula reforms, "I represent the mainstream of student sentiment in seeking career goals and moving away from intellectual finger painting. People realize that the world is a competitive place in which perseverance is more a virtue than cardboard piety."[13] This does not, and I believe must not ever, suggest that Brown or any other college or university should be concerned solely with occupational objectives. Nor should the humanities or the liberalizing arts and sciences, which are the heart of higher education's contribution to our society, be debased or diluted of their scholarship. But the need is for history or art or philosophy or poetry or science that fortifies our students in what they find to be meaningful relationships for their ultimate effectiveness and wholeness as businessmen, attorneys, and workers of all kinds, and well-developed, responsible human beings with instincts for self-fulfillment.

Faculties across the land, whether enthusiastic or not about the fact, are acknowledging that students are asking for practical outcomes as a product of their university years. In a critical and eloquent review of Sidney Hook's book *Education and the Training of Power,* Paul Lauter, professor of American studies at the State University of New York, Westbury, observes:

> In an era in which the struggle for universal access will continue and broaden, many students will be job-minded, since they believe educational credentials to be passports to upward mobility. But if they are not to be trapped into dead-end jobs, at the mercy of shifting currents of technology and management, if they are to be able to win control over their workplaces and their lives more generally, if they are to combat the forces that have kept many blacks, women, and working people as second-class citizens, then they and we must work for a curriculum that combines genuinely relevant general education with vocational preparation. To do that we must understand the historical failure of what has come before.[14]

There is always the possibility that the "search for relevance" (and "relevance" *is* a dependent word, as Kingman Brewster notes) will pass. There is the danger that overreaction by institutions can weaken the foundations of scholarship in all fields, especially those that *appear* on the surface not to offer relevance to life situations and work. Richard Lyman, President of Stanford University, observes, "A few years ago we seemed greatly supplied with amateur rhetoricians and street corner moralists. Now there seems to be a danger of our becoming once again oversupplied with careerists and technocrats of one kind or another."[15] Harvard's undergraduate assistant dean Robert T. Keily notes that students are "moving from purely academic programs to those that lead to professional training." He reports "tremendous increases in bio-chemistry and biology." "The liberal arts universities," adds Keily, "are becoming pre-professional and pre-technical schools. People are very worried about jobs." Dean Keily does not say which people are worried about jobs— students or faculty; I suspect both. At the risk of seeming repetitious, this need not be, and indeed must not be, an either-or issue. The professor who may be worried about his job is a product of the pendulum that may be saying *or* instead of *both*. The student, voting with his feet, *perceives* some subjects at this point as not meaningful to his occupational goals. The nexus of career education in the college or university lies squarely on this issue. The institution must not let itself forswear its foundations in the humanities and the liberal arts and sciences for the passing and still-unmatured perceptions of students. The marketing preoccupations of colleges and universities in a time of financial duress can overshadow the ultimate and immutable values upon which our institutions were founded. Rather the course offerings should be so clearly and intrinsically responsive to students' appetites for meaning that both worlds will be served, and the student will perceive the whole.

Erwin Steinberg, professor of English at Carnegie-Mellon in Pittsburgh, calls on his humanist colleagues to "apply their skills to interdisciplinary problems as a way of breaking out of the specialization that seems to alienate students who do not wish to pursue . . . the humanities."[16] He urges them to become "colleagues of the social scientists and engineers." Pointing to the needs of urban centers for well-developed practitioners of the humanist's craft, Steinberg says, "They could become chroniclers and analysts of urban problems; collector-analysts of ethnic literatures, urban popular literature . . . popular music, folklore, customs and value systems; collectors and analysts of urban speech patterns, consultants to urban school systems and cultural centers." With lively relationships to real issues, Steinberg notes, "the humanities may well be revitalized and certainly will be less susceptible to charges of elitism and irrelevance."

This is not a "how-to" book, and certainly I possess no credentials for counseling professors of the humanities in survival techniques. But as a general educator and respectful observer of the historic eminence of general education and its faculties in our colleges and universities, I plead for them to hear the call and meet the students and society on their own ground, with their own transcending knowledge of their discipline and *communicate* it, proudly. There is nothing demeaning or materialistic in a professor's enthusiastic concern for insuring that his particular discipline be perceived by students as important and *useful*. But to wait for the student to discover this virtue, in the pragmatic mood of the seventies, appears to be hazardous.

Peter Drucker may have some useful clues:

> . . . what is taught in classes today is, at best, information. In most cases, it is raw, undigested data. Information becomes knowledge only when you can do something with it—either in the sense of having an effect on the outside world or having an effect on yourself inside. . . .
>
> I hope we will recruit people from the outside who have made their mark and want to teach. . . . They don't have to argue relevance. They are living it.[17]

Drucker was expressing for professors the theme of career education that draws upon the "community," as does the elementary school teacher, to make learning meaningful. He continues, "Faculties are both the pride and despair of learning and teaching. They are understandably dedicated to their discipline and, therefore, heavily oriented toward things which are of little value to their students, either [academically] or vocationally . . . most of the existing disciplines, which were invented in the late nineteenth century, are by now obsolete . . . departmentalization and narrow specialization have not worked out."

Dr. Joseph Cosand, a leader of the community-college movement and a respected champion of higher education at the University of Michigan, has said:

> Career education must be an integral part of most collegiate programs and ideally would be combined with a broad general education which would prepare for both employment and cultural appreciation, combined with a sense of responsibility to society as well as to self. Career education may end with the completion of high school, or with any semester or nine years of college. The career may be built upon a narrow skill such as an auto body repairman or be the difficult sophisticated profession of a psychiatrist. In any case there is no cause to look down upon the word career or occupation or vocation. All of us who are employed have an occupation or a career and those students who desire to prepare themselves for employment should have the opportunity to enroll in that institution which can best do the job—be it public, private or proprietary.

As we look to the future of the colleges and universities, reform is now visible and its shape is the shape of career education. One of the most pervasive trends is the open or nontraditional university, by whatever name it goes. Here the learner can be accommodated on his terms, probably while engaged in full-time employment, and still progress through the institution's offerings. This is literally career-related learning.

New criteria for *access,* including the facilitation of entry, exit, and reentry are likely to transform institutions. I believe that the folklore, heretofore governing both the lower schools and the universities, which declares all learning to come in yearly multiples of four will be set aside. The young person should be free to exit purposefully, without being classified as a dropout, and with equal ease reenter after a time of work or travel. Increasingly the institutions will recognize academic or occupational competence, as measured by "credit by examination."

The College Board's CLEP program (College Level Examination Program), which started only five years ago, now reaches over 1500 colleges and universities. In 1971–1972 CLEP examinations for college credit were administered to about 20,000 learners. In

1974 probably 90,000 tests will be administered. This again is compatible with the spirit of entry-reentry that implements career education's lifelong learning philosophy. It may well be that the immediate future will find as many mature part-time adult learners in the classrooms as conventional students. This may be a major solution to some of higher education's economic problems.

Ernest L. Boyer, Chancellor of the State University of New York, writes:

> . . . colleges have focused almost exclusively on one age group, students who have come in just four sizes: 18, 19, 20 and 21. We have scheduled classes Monday through Friday from ten to four, colliding with the world of work. . . . Clearly, the rigid life cycle is breaking up, and the implications for colleges and universities are enormous. Higher education must be viewed not as a pre-work ritual, but as a resource for everyone from 18 to 85 and beyond.[18]

One final illustration of a career education theme which may emerge in the near future is the "G.I. Bill in Community Service." A product of the Newman Task Force, this idea capitalizes on the good experiences of the post–World War II period when mature veterans returned to higher education. The Task Force report offers the following challenge to Congress and to the leaders of higher education:

> . . . Despite the G.I. Bill's success, no attempt has been made to expand the concept to anything beyond military service. We believe that the changes that have taken place in higher education and in society as a whole make the idea of extending the concept of the G.I. Bill more urgent than ever before.
>
> We, therefore, propose a legislative initiative for providing limited education benefits to those people who voluntarily choose to step out of formal education in order to participate in selected national, regional, and local programs of community services. The benefits, modeled after those of the G.I. Bill, would accrue during the period of service and would be used later whenever the volunteer chose to enroll at a post-secondary education institution.

The Fellowship would recognize and reward community service. At the same time, it would communicate to students, parents, and faculty that youths engaged in such activities were planning their educational careers rather than drifting into them; that as volunteers they were building a stock of experience with which to make a more personal and more intense commitment to formal education at a later time. It would help begin the reversal of the negative stereotype of the "drop-out." It would take a step toward making college opportunities more valued and better used.[19]

Here indeed would be a clear expression of legitimate work experience leading to purposeful and calculated academic and professional objectives in colleges and universities.

Whether we call it career education or some other name, or no name at all, the reform of our postsecondary systems is taking place. It is happening in part because wise and responsible leaders are shaping the future of our institutions, as Columbia did in 1919 and is doing again. It is happening in part by default, as students opt for a different drumbeat. It is happening more swiftly and with increasing numbers of students in the community colleges. It is happening because parents are finding the costs of higher education so demanding as to call for better evidence of economic outcomes.

But the theme that seems to permeate all higher education is one of a new inclusiveness, as distinct from historic exclusiveness. This not only means the inclusion of people of all ages and aptitudes, but also the inclusion of valid occupational objectives as distinct from prescription of what was once *the* required curriculum. The question is whether the great centers of intellect and scholarship, which our institutions are, will have the adaptability and creativity to meet the new expectations for human fulfillment with respect to work, leisure, and purposeful learning, without giving an inch of ground in their dedication to academic excellence.

Linking School and the Work Place

From the beginning of my own commitment to career education, I have found a ready and supportive spirit from the business and labor community. During my period of service as superintendent of schools in Pittsburgh in the mid-1960s and before the term career education had come into general usage, we had upwards of seventy advisory councils serving our vocational education programs. These councils were made up of prominent and not-so-prominent citizens representing the great variety of occupations to be found in any large city. They gave unremittingly of their time and wisdom to assisting teachers in the construction of curricula and to the overview of teaching, equipment and job-placement.

This condition is not uncommon across America. Illustrations in earlier chapters cite similar cooperation in New Jersey, Los Angeles, Oregon, and Dallas which are quite exemplary.

However, serving on advisory committees or accepting a limited number of students in cooperative work-study programs is one thing. The scale of engagement by business, industry and labor in the full implementation of career education theory is quite another. Much more will be expected of the work place. I have good reason to believe that the work place will respond.

Today, there are at least four factors favorably influencing the increased commitment of the business sector (for brevity I will use the term *business* in this chapter as embracing all parts of the work site, including industry, labor, government, nonprofit institutions, and community agencies—any enterprise where work is performed):

1. Most business enterprises carry a vested and appropriately self-serving interest in sustaining a good economic environment in the community in which they are located. They have capital investments, not easily relocated, which they wish to sustain, and which call for a healthy community of employed people for direct or indirect environmental stability. Banks, department stores, public utilities, transportation systems, hospitals, manufacturing plants, small businesses are typical of the enterprises necessarily dependent upon a citizenry of well-developed people. This is especially true in large cities where decay has set in. Reversal of this trend is seen by progressive business and labor leaders as largely dependent upon good schools, related consciously to the economic and manpower futures of the enterprise.

2. Business looks to its future for its market potential. It needs to produce goods or services to stay in business, and it must have a market for those goods and services. Locally based enterprises such as banks, libraries, utilities, stores, and service agencies need customers, clients, and consumers. The business will prosper or not, depending upon the nature and prosperity of the people being served. Bluntly, the schools are regarded, quite rationally, as the source of developing increased consumer capacities in the generations that follow. The better the schools do their job, the better will be the market area for the local business enterprise.

Large businesses with nationwide sites such as the steel industry, garment industry, airlines, computer manufacturers, insurance companies, and food chains are equally or perhaps even more conscious of the upcoming population, not only in the immediate communities where they are located, but also in the larger nationwide scope of their marketing interests. They have everything to gain by the increased purchasing power and sophistication implicit in generations passing through the schools and colleges.

3. Perhaps the most obvious and immediate relationship between business and education derives from the manpower needs of the enterprise. Whether in a bank, a factory, a building contractor, a telephone company, a hospital, or an insurance company, the personnel office looks to the schools and colleges for its staffing needs. Recent years have revealed an earnest demand from the business sector for better-educated young people, especially those leaving high school directly for the work site. Not only does business find some applicants weak in basic skills, but in attitudes toward work, in self-discipline on the job, and in work habits such as grooming and promptness as well. In responding to this charge the schools must point out that the business sector, in evaluating the immediate post-high school applicant, is evaluating a quite different person from the graduate of five or ten years ago. Many of the type of young people who entered the work force directly from high school are now entering college, as the percentages of college entrants have doubled in the past decade. Thus, the remaining students naturally tend to be less strong academically.

But that is not a sufficient answer to the real needs of the work place. High school graduates should have a good command of the basic skills of reading, writing, and arithmetic, as well as a ready attitude toward work. Career education is seen as a response to both weaknesses. It is a hypothesis, yet to be proven, that the implicit *motivation* in career education will greatly improve the command of basic skills on the part of all learners, starting in the elementary schools. Evidence from the Oregon demonstration (Chapter 10) gives substance to this proposition. As for work habits and attitudes, these are clearly and specifically a part of the career education design. Employers are becoming aware of this, and accordingly are contributing their efforts to the advancement of the concept.

4. All of the foregoing "factors" giving reasonableness and purpose to the business community's support for career education may be viewed as at least partly self-serving (better environment, better market, better employees). But I believe there is another, possibly larger motivation now being demonstrated by business, industry, and labor. This factor, in my judgment, can be broadly described as "social responsibility." Quite apart from enlightened self-interest, corporations are increasingly taking on risky and selfless responsibilities that are not necessarily "good business" but are desirable and important to the social good. The Bell System has been especially prominent in this new dimension of social responsibility. The voluntary engagement of many industries in the regional renaissance enterprises of Baltimore, Pittsburgh, and St. Louis are expressions of this higher order of commitment, as is the Economic Development Council of New York City and the National Alliance of Businessmen.

Chrysler Corporation in the Detroit high schools, Chase Bank in the Bronx and Manhattan high schools, the Bell System and Olin in the New Haven schools are examples of large investments of corporate resources in man-years and experience as well as money. These are engagements of a much larger scale than service on an advisory committee. No immediate, short-term profit or self-serving advantage can be detected in these commitments by industry to help meet a social need.

This degree of corporate concern for education entails a possible public relations risk to the business, and probably entails a short-term fiscal "loss" in the bottom line. But it is a new and visible force that is clearly marked "altruism," and it is a force that educators must welcome and embrace more warmly than they have.

It is clear that career education will not become a working philosophy in the classrooms of our schools and colleges without the active support of the business, industrial, and labor communities. These indispensable forces are needed to provide work experience and work/study opportunities for students and teachers. *Neither students nor their teachers can learn what they need to know about the world of work only through a textbook.*

Additionally, any direct involvement with the business-industry-labor community helps students make an easier transition from school to work. It is necessary that a higher level of cooperative arrangement be established beyond the present spotty and incidental arrangements, notwithstanding the several good examples to be found here and there across the land.

In spite of a willingness on the part of the business community, educators have been slow to exercise initiative in forging more elaborate and sophisticated linkages with the work place. David Rogers notes in his very searching appraisal of vocational and career education:

> Various cooperative education and work-study programs are at least preliminary examples of some of these concepts. . . . There is widespread agreement that employers are at best only passively involved. . . . Nobody has yet developed explicit norms as to what the nature and extent of [business's] participation might be. And educators are often very wary of having employers come in, lest they be unreasonably critical of existing programs and management and attempt to take over. . . . Some employers on their side, have tended to be insensitive and tactless in the past as they freely voiced their criticism [of the schools].[1]

Returning to Rogers: "The issue, then, is not whether schools can interest employers in education, but rather how educators can be induced to respond to the interest already there, to harness the resources business has to offer."

I would be less harsh on the educators than Rogers, but these views serve to sharpen our awareness of how educators may be perceived. While recent years have brought an increased spirit of partnership between the business sector and the schools and colleges, there remains a very large gap, even in the most progressive schools, between what is and what might be.

The Los Angeles Unified School District, in developing its comprehensive career education model, realized its limitations and formed a relationship with the business, industrial, and labor sectors. This program involves a consortium of approximately a hundred corporations, companies, and government agencies and is identified as "Project 70's, Community Alliance for Career Education." Project 70's has set up task forces to coordinate five types of industry help:

- Career information, under which industry representatives provide students in grades six through twelve information on the kinds of jobs that are apt to be available upon graduating and to point out what courses to take in preparation. This career information program includes brochures, speakers, and company-conducted tours.

- Tutoring in basic subjects, with volunteers supplied by participating companies and instruction given at schools, homes, tutorial centers, and company offices.

- Work experience, to provide part-time jobs at participating companies for the eleventh and twelfth graders and exposure to jobs an hour or two a day for class credit in the ninth and tenth grades.

- Teacher and counselor training, in which company people bring school employees up to date about industry needs through summer jobs related to teaching specialties and summer workshops for firsthand observation of business operations.

- Aid to school administrators, using internships, training programs, and consultation, to give school officials a better understanding of business-world techniques in budgets, purchasing, personnel, wages, and insurance.[2]

The aim of Project 70's is to reach 175,000 junior and senior high school students—one-quarter of those attending schools in the City and County of Los Angeles by 1975.

The effectiveness of Project 70's in California is an example of what cooperative efforts can bring to the process of educational reform. Education cannot be accomplished within the walls of the established schools or solely in a work place. Even the Los Angeles model is considerably short of what might be the total scope of the business sector in career education. The real world of work outside the formal educational system must become part of the total educational design. Career education recognizes that, in our post-industrial occupational society, education and work must function together. Kenneth Hoyt counsels us: "More is required than simple cooperation with the formal educational structure, leaving it the primary responsibility. Rather, business and labor must become an integral part of the program."[3]

One major step toward the objective of a much closer association occurred in late February and early March 1973, when 240 leading businessmen, educators, and labor leaders met in Washington to participate in the First National Conference on Career Education, sponsored by the Chamber of Commerce of the United States. The following pages will draw heavily upon the report of that conference, since the report has not likely been available to many readers of this book.[4]

As part of this Conference, which was directed by Dr. Hoyt, participants were placed in small discussion groups to resolve a set of ten basic questions centered on the role of the business-education-labor community in career education. Each small group was asked to consider the desirability, practical probability, and practical limitations of one concept. Each group was also asked to develop suggestions for converting the concept into an action program. The results of these meetings, as published in Hoyt's report, "A Handbook of Action Suggestions," are an accounting of the discourse around ten concepts that represent a concrete proposal for involvement of the business-labor-industry community in a comprehensive career education effort.

According to Thomas P. Walsh of the Education and Manpower Development Committee of the U.S. Chamber of Commerce, "The Handbook is intended only as a beginning, and the action suggestions found in the handbook are only illustrations. We have been primarily concerned about specifying concepts to be considered and with providing broad, beginning suggestions for action. Specific program planning and implementation must be done in each locality. We need to begin now."

The ten concepts discussed by the Chamber of Commerce Conference are truly a good beginning for any local community developing a career education program. It will be seen that they reach beyond the present order of magnitude in any business-education linkage. We quote them here in full:

1. THE CONCEPT OF EXCHANGE PROGRAMS BETWEEN BUSINESS-LABOR-INDUSTRY PERSONNEL AND SCHOOL PERSONNEL

Basic Idea

It has been proposed that exchange programs be initiated whereby schoolteachers, counselors, and administrators would spend anywhere from a few days to a few months working for pay outside of education and that business-labor-industry personnel be invited to spend some time teaching their occupational skills to high school students and adult education students.

Assumptions

1. School personnel often lack an understanding or appreciation of the world of work outside of education. Many have never worked outside the school. If educators are able to teach students about the broader occupational society, it is essential that they actually experience what it is like to work in the free enterprise system.

2. Business-labor-industrial personnel have many things to teach students about work that today's teachers are not equipped to teach. In addition, some occupational skills needed by today's students aren't taught in public schools, but could be taught by workers possessing such skills.

Problems

1. Could industry afford to pay educators for the work they do in the business-labor-industry setting? If not, who should?

2. Do jobs exist that would provide educators the kinds of experience they need and still require a short enough training period so that educators could be productive on such jobs?

3. Could industry afford to release some skilled personnel to work in schools part of the year? Could equipment required for teaching also be made available? Should the training be done in school buildings or at the actual work site?

4. Should teacher certification requirements be changed so that business-labor-industrial representatives could be employed part-time as teachers?

Action Suggestions

1. Make two inventories: (a) an inventory of persons with occupational skills who are willing and can be released for a time to teach in the schools; and (b) an inventory of occupational skills (such as math, typing, etc.) possessed by school personnel that industry might need. Given both inventories, it should be possible to set up exchange programs where neither the school nor the industry suffers.

2. Get school personnel involved in working with industry on such things as BIE days or Junior Achievement programs. School and industry people need to know each other better before we try to set up any ambitious exchange program of school with industry personnel.

3. Exchange programs will work best when a specific need exists on the part of either the schools *or* industry for skills the other might possess. It is unrealistic to expect that each will need the other at the same time. However, both should and could be flexible enough to respond to needs of the other for personnel. Don't expect exchange programs to work when *neither* schools nor industry feel they need personnel from the other. One or the other should know what they need, why they need them, and what they want them to do.

4. Exchange programs will work better if both schools and industries set up internal teams to work with persons who come to them on an exchange basis. The "exchanged" person is certain to have many questions and needs a quick, easily identifiable resource to turn to when such questions arise.

5. Consider initiating an exchange program by assigning one personnel specialist from industry to work, say, with one elementary school. He could help all teachers in that school incorporate career implications into their teaching. Teachers could

then be assigned, on a rotating basis (a few weeks at a time for each) to the personnel department from which the industry man came. Teachers should have enough skills to partially fill the gap left by the personnel man.

2. THE CONCEPT OF FIELD TRIPS FOR STUDENTS

Basic Idea

Career Education advocates have proposed that extensive field-trip programs be developed so that students (and their teachers) from K–12 have a wide variety of opportunities to observe workers actually performing in various kinds of occupations and work settings. In the elementary school, pupils could learn to appreciate work and the necessity for work. In the junior high school, pupils could see occupations in each of the fifteen USOE occupational clusters. In the senior high years, students would observe workers in their tentative areas of occupational choice.

Assumptions

1. Most students will be more likely to enter jobs in the geographic area where they are growing up. Thus, it is important that they learn about work in that area.

2. Pupils can't learn about the world of work only in textbooks. They need to see work being done at the worksite.

3. Teachers would acquire some much-needed information about occupations and implications of their subject matter for those occupations if they take students on field trips.

Problems

1. How could industry handle constant calls for field trips so that some work settings are not so bothered as to hamper productivity while others never have visitors?

2. How could industry and school personnel work together so as to ensure that new learnings result from such field trips and duplications of students' experiences are avoided?

3. Who would or could answer student questions raised during field trips? Follow-up questions are sure to come after the field trip is over.

4. What kinds of practical plant safety requirements argue against the desirability of field trips?

5. Would it be better to have small student committees, rather than entire classes, make field trips?

6. Do field trips for students affect industry insurance rates?

Action Suggestions

1. Before field trips are taken, the school and the business or industry to be visited should *jointly* agree on *objectives* to be sought by the field trip. Too many field trips take place where school officials don't know what they are looking for and industry doesn't know what to show them.

2. Encourage industries to set up community resource workshops for teachers. In such workshops, teachers could be made aware of what the industry has to offer during a field trip, who the contact person is, and special provisions that need to be made before bringing students in for a field trip.

3. Establish a community-resource occupational bank listing occupations and industries willing to be involved in field trips for youth. The local chamber of commerce could establish such a bank. It should contain a description of the experiences possible on a field trip and the name of a specific industry person to contact for making field-trip arrangements. Such a data bank could be shared with out-of-school youth groups such as Boy Scouts or youth church groups as well as with schools in the area.

4. It is too expensive for industry to service all students through field trips. Videotapes could be made showing some students on field trips. These could then be played for other students in lieu of their actual visiting industry. If industry representatives could be present in the school to "rap" with students who have watched the videotapes, they might be just as effective as field trips.

5. Feedback after field trips is essential in which industry repre-sentatives are present in the school to respond to questions students raise regarding what they saw on the field trip.

3. THE CONCEPT OF WORK EXPERI-ENCE FOR ALL HIGH SCHOOL STUDENTS

Basic Idea
It has been proposed that some systematic means be provided to ensure that no student leave high school without some actual work experience, paid or unpaid in nature, that would let him or her actually know the rewards and satisfactions that can come from work. Too many students are now passing through our schools who have never worked. They find themselves forced to make occupational choices before they even have experienced what it is like to work.

Assumptions
1. High school students have typically made some tentative occupational choices. By having a chance to work in a setting where that occupation exists, they will acquire a more realistic basis for the choices they have made.

2. If prospective college students acquire some work experi-ence while in high school, they will be more motivated to think about college as preparation for work. In addition, they will gain more respect and appreciation for persons whose work does not require college attendance. Finally, they may be more motivated to work while going to college.

3. Students in the general curriculum need work experience even though they are not acquiring specific job skills in vocational education. Vocational education students need work experience even if it is not in the field for which they are being trained.

Problems
1. Can enough jobs, paid or unpaid, be created so that *all* high school students can get some work experience? How much should they have? Should they have some each year?

2. When would high school students work? Must we think of an extended school day? Should we think only of a summer program?

3. Should work experience be *required* of all students or should it be offered as an elective? If it is required, what do we do with the student who doesn't want to work?

4. Should work-experience programs establish a goal that every student is paid for the work he or she does? Many aren't capable of producing enough to really earn today's required minimum wage. Can reduced wages be paid?

5. Would massive high school work-experience programs result in firing of some currently employed person? If so, what is to be done about this?

Action Suggestions

1. Some type of reward system must be established for students participating in a work experience program. The reward could be in the form of money, or students could be paid in academic credit. If only observation of others at work is involved, perhaps no pay of any kind is necessary but, if students really work, some reward system will be essential.

2. If our goal is work experience for *all* high school students, then work will have to be made available in the public as well as in the private sector. The private sector alone cannot be expected to provide enough work stations for *all* high school students.

3. It would be unwise to *require* work experience for all high school students. It will be difficult enough for industry to provide meaningful work experience for students who want to learn what it is like to work. It would not be feasible for industry to take, in addition, responsibility for motivating the student who does not want to work.

4. One work station could serve several students on a rotating basis with each student working, say, only two hours per day. If each, in addition, was expected to undergo the work experience

for only part of the school year, it might be possible that one work station might effectively serve up to twenty students.

5.   Some provision should be made for rotating work stations to which students are assigned so that they gain different kinds of work experiences. If these are adequately described to students, students could elect different kinds just as they now elect different subjects in school.

6.   Careful study should be given to ways through which work experience could be provided students beginning at age fourteen. To wait until age sixteen will be too late for many.

4.   THE CONCEPT OF SCHOOL-INDUSTRY JOB PLACEMENT PROGRAMS

Basic Idea

It has been proposed that every high school and post-high school educational institution build, in cooperation with the business-labor-industry community, an aggressive job development and job placement program. Career education advocates are fond of saying that, whenever a student leaves a school, he should either be ready for a job or for further education. The ratio of youth to adult unemployment, having risen for the last several years, is now over 5:1. Career education will be a farce if it succeeds in helping youth want to work, gives them the skills required to work, but fails to help them find work when they leave school.

Assumptions

1.   The United States Employment Service (Department of Labor) system of youth job placement services is not now and shows no signs of becoming adequate to meet the needs of youth for work and the needs of employers for qualified applicants.

2.   Both employers and school systems would have much to gain from cooperative efforts to establish an aggressive and effective job placement program. Motivation should be present.

3.   If really effective job placement programs existed, youth

unemployment statistics would decline sharply from their current levels. It is *not* assumed that youth unemployment can drop as low as adult unemployment.

Problems

1.   How could a placement data bank, containing current, valid data regarding both job-seekers and job vacancies, be established and maintained?

2.   Should USES be asked to participate in the program? To coordinate the program? To pay for it?

3.   Should schools and the business-labor-industry community share the costs of the job placement program?

4.   What system could guarantee job placement services for the former student who wishes to work in another part of the country?

5.   Should we be thinking of a program that concerns itself with the total problem of transition from school to work—including follow-up of new workers—or is a job placement program as much as we can handle?

6.   Who is responsible for the student who, after leaving school, can't find a job?

7.   Should all students be required to register at the placement office, or only those who will shortly be seeking work?

Action Suggestions

1.   Don't try to operate a placement program without seeking to involve the local public employment office. There is nothing to gain by trying to set up a placement service in competition with USES. Because USES efforts have, by themselves, not always been fully effective is no reason to ignore them in this effort.

2.   Problems of youth unemployment are great and grow in severity each year. The ratio of youth to adult unemployment continues to rise. The only direct solution we see is for both the public and private sector to allocate a certain number of job slots for youth. Youth cannot be expected to compete effectively with adults for jobs in a tight labor market.

3. Each school system should have a central placement office with satellite centers in each school within that school system. Data concerning job applicants should be fed from the satellite centers to the central placement office and, from that office, be made available to industry. Similarly, job vacancies from industry should be fed through the central placement office to each satellite center.

4. The local chamber of commerce could, in cooperation with the school system, act as a record center from which information from job applicants could be made available to employers. Such records should indicate the abilities, goals, and aspirations of each student seeking full- or part-time employment. School counselors could collect such information from students who seek employment and transmit it in accurate form to a placement office at the local chamber of commerce.

5. THE CONCEPT OF ESTABLISHING OCCUPATIONAL RESOURCE PERSONS FROM THE BUSINESS-INDUSTRY-LABOR COMMUNITY

Basic Idea

Many career education programs, through both parental and local civic associations, have established large lists of workers from a very wide variety of occupations. Each worker has volunteered to respond, through either phone calls or personal contacts, to requests for information about his or her occupation that come from students, teachers, or counselors. In addition, some volunteer to present information and answer questions before groups of students in the classroom.

Assumptions

1. Workers are the most valid source of information about life styles involved in occupations. It is better to find out what an occupation is really like from one who is in it than from an article describing it. Employed workers who are successful in their jobs can serve as effective models for youth.

2.   Many employed workers will be willing to volunteer their efforts to help youth have more intelligent vocational choices.

Problems

1.   To what extent do workers need special training in order to perform this service? Who will provide it?

2.   How can we be sure that persons volunteering to participate are the kinds of individuals we need?

3.   Should both workers who are happy and those unhappy in their occupations be on the list? If only fully satisfied persons are selected, are we unduly biasing youth?

4.   Should more than one worker from each occupation be chosen? Since each is in a different *job,* do we need more than one so that an *occupation,* rather than a *job,* can be discussed?

5.   Will industry let people off to speak to students in schools?

6.   Many of these contacts will result in students asking to see the worker at the job site. Is this something that can be done effectively or should it be discouraged?

Action Suggestions

1.   Study Portland, Oregon's, program. They collected names of specific workers from 176 different occupations representing 95 percent of all Oregon occupations. Schools were given this list and can call on any one of these people.

2.   Occupational-resource persons from industry need to be trained to perform this function. Their training must enable them to discuss life styles associated with their occupations as well as the ability to describe the work they do and the preparation required for it.

3.   The climate for this program must be established in the business-industry-labor setting. If chief executive officers from a number of industries form an executive committee (as in Los Angeles' Project 70s), they can establish a climate that will encourage volunteers for the occupational resource program. Workers volunteering must feel that their company supports them and will provide them time to participate.

4. A program calling for occupational-resource persons from industry to visit in schools requires a central organizational structure. The local chamber of commerce might provide this central organization or it could come from a consortium of employers. The school system, too, needs a central organizing agency for this program to work. Both schools and industries need to have contact persons who can be called quickly when problems or questions arise.

5. A number of occupational-resource persons from each occupation needs to be recruited for this kind of program to work. You can't keep calling on the same person time after time. Some feedback system is essential so that occupational-resource persons can learn how to function more effectively. Such a system will also provide for replacing ineffective occupational-resource persons. You can't expect all of your volunteers to be successful when they try to relate with students and teachers in the school setting.

6. THE CONCEPT OF THE YEAR-ROUND SCHOOL RUNNING 16 HOURS A DAY SIX DAYS A WEEK AND STAFFED PARTLY BY BUSINESS-LABOR-INDUSTRIAL PERSONNEL

Basic Idea

The year-round high school seems essential to many advocates of career education. Under this concept, school facilities would be open sixteen hours a day six days a week, twelve months each year, and would enroll both youth and adults. Advantages inherent in this concept include: (a) Students could choose their school hours based, in part, on when they could get work experience or work-study arrangements in the business-labor-industry community; (b) Business-labor-industry personnel could teach in the school program without losing time from their regular jobs; (c) Academic teachers could get work experience in industry on a staggered basis since they would be employed on a twelve-month basis; and (d) Students would be graduating each month during the year (rather than only in June), which should make the job-placement problem easier.

Assumptions

1.   School buildings are too expensive to be utilized only part of the day or part of the year.

2.   Putting teachers on twelve-month rather than nine-month contracts would be more efficient and, in the long run, save taxpayers money.

3.   Public schools must take much more responsibility for adult education and education of current out-of-school youth than is currently being done. This would save money over the cost of running remedial manpower programs.

4.   Personnel from business-labor-industry are capable of teaching their vocational skills to others.

Problems

1.   Is industry ready to support the concept of the year-round school? Initially, it might mean higher taxes. It certainly would demand full cooperation of the business-labor-industry personnel in making available both equipment and personnel.

2.   Is there a place for industry's effort to upgrade and retrain workers in the concept of the year-round school?

3.   What would be the public's reactions to find (a) students on vacation at various times during the year; (b) some students going to school at night rather than during the day; and (c) some classes that contained a mixture of high school students and adults?

Action Suggestions

1.   This will require a major public relations campaign before it can be sold to many communities. Examples of pilot-school systems where the year-round school is now working are badly needed.

2.   To sell the concept of the year-round school, cooperation of a wide variety of groups, including the local chamber of com-

merce, service clubs, PTA, and industry advisory councils will be required. These are the kinds of groups that should spearhead such an effort. If the push for the year-round school comes from such a coalition, school boards will be forced to listen.

3.   The year-round school concept involves many headaches and tough administrative problems. Different children from the same family will require similar schedules so that their vacation periods coincide with those of the parents. Many schools will have to be air-conditioned. Higher education would have to alter its patterns of admission and graduation to coincide with those of the high schools—and that isn't practical unless most high schools were operating on a year-round basis. Great flexibility would have to be built into student schedules so that the constant coming and going of students will not interfere with the development of any particular student. These are but a few of the practical problems to be faced.

4.   The year-round school will be essential if work-experience programs for all high school students are to become a reality. It will be equally essential to the success of a youth job-placement program.

7.   THE CONCEPT OF USING RETIRED WORKERS AS RESOURCE PERSONS IN SCHOOLS TO ACQUAINT STUDENTS WITH THE WORLD OF WORK

Basic Idea

Several career education programs have placed great emphasis on using retired workers as resource persons for career education. They have identified such persons from a wide variety of occupational fields. Once identified and solicited, such persons meet with students, teachers, and counselors to discuss their former occupation as it might apply to today's students. They talk about the work values that are meaningful to them, demonstrate the specific vocational skills they used on their jobs, and express their personal opinions regarding their former occupation and the life style it led to.

Assumptions

1.   Retired workers have a strong need to continue feeling useful and valuable. To ask them to participate in career education offers them a way to enhance their own personal feelings of self-worth and provides students with valuable insights regarding life styles associated with various kinds of careers.

2.   Even if the skills of the retired worker are no longer in demand, students can learn much from such workers regarding the values of a work-oriented society. Additionally, students can receive graphic illustrations regarding ways in which technology speeds occupational change.

Problems

1.   To what extent can retired workers give high school students a realistic view of work and occupations in our current society?

2.   How valuable is it to have a retired worker talk about his former occupation without being able to show students the actual work place itself?

3.   How valid a view of today's occupational society can be expected to be presented by retired workers? Is change occurring so fast as to make their memories irrelevant to the informational needs of today's youth?

4.   Can and should the business-labor-industry community work with schools in recruiting retired persons for career education?

Action Suggestions

1.   Multiple ways exist to identify retired workers for this program. These include seeking names from Golden Age Clubs, civic organizations (who usually list retired persons separately in their directories), from company directories that list retired former workers, and from labor unions.

2.   Employers will be happy to supply lists of persons about to retire. Such persons can provide a ready tie-back to their former

employer that will help schools in many ways. It may also ease the shock of retirement for some persons who are looking for something to keep them busy.

3.   A referral file of retired persons will be essential for use by school personnel. Such a file can be maintained by a retired person's association or by the local chamber of commerce. If a person's name is on the list, it is essential that someone see that he or she is called upon to serve.

4.   Retired executives may be especially interested in working with gifted and talented students who are thinking about entering the business world.

5.   Use a person *just* retired from a company and one who left several years ago from a similar position to show high school students how rapidly jobs and occupations change.

6.   Conduct a career day using retired people as resource persons. Ask them to discuss their entire *career* (not just their last job) so that students will better understand the concept of "career" as a succession of choices made through life.

7.   Use retired former workers as classroom aides who will help teachers discover ways to emphasize the career implications of their subject matter. Retired workers can teach teachers a great deal about the world outside of education.

8.   Establish training programs to train retired persons with respect to how to work with teachers and with students from the elementary school through the high school.

8.   THE CONCEPT THAT WORK SHOULD BECOME MORE PERSONALLY SATISFYING TO THE INDIVIDUAL WORKER

Basic Idea

The goals of career education are to make work *possible,* *meaningful,* and *satisfying* to each individual. We know we can make the concept of work *meaningful* and, for most persons, we can make work *possible*. However, the extent to which work can be *satisfying* is a function of the work place itself. Studies of worker alienation and causes of worker dissatisfaction are currently very popular. People seem to delight in talking about the inhuman treatment given workers. They speak about the need to give workers more autonomy, more variety in their work tasks, and a clearer picture of the importance of each man's work to the "big picture." Many educators are currently resisting career education's emphasis on *work* because they feel that to ready youth for today's work place would be to condition them to expect inhumane treatment. Others question whether the situation in the work place is as bad as it has been pictured.

Assumptions

1.   Worker satisfaction should lead to greater productivity and so should be a goal of employers as well as educators.

2.   The goal of making work more satisfying to the worker is a valid and viable one for career education to embrace.

Problems

1.   If work is made more possible and meaningful to individuals, is it likely that it will automatically also become more satisfying? If additional tasks are involved, what are they?

2.   How can one give workers more freedom to make their own work decisions while still maintaining the essential concept of the discipline of the work place? How far can you go in letting workers "do their own thing" and still make it clear that everyone has a "boss"?

3.   Can and should school systems be involved in the task of making work more satisfying—or is this strictly up to the business-labor-industry community? If school systems have a role to play here, what is that role?

4.   Is the problem of current worker dissatisfaction really a major one? Or is this something that has been overemphasized?

Action Suggestions

1.   Students in schools should learn that hardly anyone is always satisfied with his job. Most people have some days when they like

their job and other days when they do not. This is a valuable lesson for youth to learn and think about.

2.   Youth should understand the difference between satisfaction with a *career* and satisfaction with a particular *job*. There are some distasteful things about some job tasks involved in particular careers, but the career itself may be very satisfying nevertheless.

3.   Youth should be taught that job satisfaction is intimately related to satisfaction with one's total life style. If a person doesn't like his job, it may mean he doesn't like the life style he finds himself involved in. Changing jobs may allow one to develop a different life style. The question of job satisfaction or dissatisfaction is part of a much larger question for most people.

4.   Job satisfaction of employees can be increased if employers will communicate to each worker the importance of his job as part of a total team effort. All employers should do this.

5.   Young workers need to understand that, at times, their job dissatisfaction will exist because of demands placed on management that are unavoidable. Schools can help if they teach students concepts of responsibility faced by management and concepts of responsibility faced by workers. This isn't done often enough.

9.   THE CONCEPT THAT EVERY STUDENT LEAVING SCHOOL SHOULD BE EQUIPPED WITH A MARKETABLE JOB SKILL

Basic Idea
One of the most pervasive ideas of the U.S. Office of Education's career education emphasis has been that the student should not leave the educational system without a marketable job skill. Some will, of course, go right from high school to college, but, even when *they* leave college, they should have a marketable job skill. This emphasis has grown out of a realization that, at both

the secondary-school and collegiate levels, many students are currently being graduated who have no specific job skills. With less than 25 percent of today's high school graduates becoming eventual college graduates, this idea can become a reality only if vocational education programs are greatly expanded at both the secondary and at the postsecondary school levels.

Assumptions

1. It is possible to provide school-leavers with marketable job skills even though they may not be sufficient for a very long period of time.

2. This *is* a worthy goal for American education.

3. The general public will support the vast increases in vocational education called for to convert this goal into a reality.

Problems

1. Does this goal ignore the potential of OJT (on-the-job training) and apprenticeship training in the business-industry-labor community? If so, what is industry's answer to this goal?

2. Is it realistic to suppose that we know enough about the changing nature of the occupational society so that we could, given sufficient resources, *really* give every school-leaver an immediately marketable job skill?

3. Should not some students feel free to enjoy a purely liberal arts education without feeling guilty that, by doing so, they are acquiring no specific marketable job skills?

4. Does industry really want entry workers with specific job skills, or would they prefer to develop such skills after the man or woman is employed?

Action Suggestions

1. If this concept is to become a reality, some form of OJT will be needed. Some vocational education students are now enrolled in work-study programs where they spend part time studying job skills in schools and part time learning more about them as they try to apply job skills in a real work setting. To apply that concept

to all students will require that "work-study" become a method of instruction for all students, not a special kind of program for only some students. This means that the method will have to be used with college students as well as high school students. Most students cannot acquire a marketable job skill operating only within the walls of the school.

2.　This concept could become a reality if the business-labor-industry community worked with the schools in establishing simulated job training in the school itself. These simulated jobs would be supervised cooperatively by school and industry personnel. It would require additional facilities and equipment over and beyond what is now available in most schools. Industry could work with schools in making such equipment available.

3.　The term *marketable job skills* should not be considered independent of "employability skills." Youth need to know more than how to do a job. In addition, they need to know good work habits and have a basic understanding of how work can give them a more satisfying and rewarding total life style. Career education should not focus on just marketable job skills. This is too narrow an emphasis.

4.　Schools cannot provide youth with marketable job skills by themselves. To attain this goal will demand total community involvement—parents as well as the business-labor-industry community. It is too big for schools to try alone.

5.　Begin defining "marketable job skills" in terms of performance evaluation. Paper-and-pencil tests coupled with grades in school are not enough. Industry should work with school personnel in developing performance evaluation measures.

10.　THE CONCEPT THAT EVERY STUDENT LEAVING SCHOOL SHOULD, IF HE DESIRES, BE ABLE TO FIND WORK

Basic Idea

Career education seeks to help all students acquire a *desire* to work. An essential ingredient here is a promise, either explicit or implicit, that those who want to work *can* find work to do. With the ratio of youth to adult unemployment having risen each year since 1960 (from 2.2:1 to 5.5:1), it is obvious that it will be difficult to guarantee work, in the form of paid employment, to each youth who may desire to work. At the same time, it is obvious that it is a farce to instill in students a desire to work and provide them with job skills, but ignore the actual availability of paid employment. To try to solve this problem by convincing youth that volunteer, unpaid workers are always in demand will not "wash well" with today's youth culture.

Assumptions

1. The current rate of unemployment, for both youth and adults, is capable of being reduced.

2. The trend of the last thirteen years toward a higher and higher ratio of youth-to-adult unemployment can be reversed.

Problems

1. Is it realistic to promise availability of work to youth in view of the current labor market conditions?

2. Can career education appeal to youth if we fail to promise that work is available to the adequately prepared?

3. If we promote a concept of work that includes volunteers as well as paid employment, do we run the risk of giving youth an unrealistic view of work?

4. Should the government initiate youth work programs for those unable to find paid employment in the free-enterprise system?

5. Is the creation of an all-volunteer armed forces a necessary ingredient for giving viability to this concept?

Action Suggestions

1. This concept can become a reality only when we have the year-round school. Work should be made available to youth in the private sector through the Chamber of Commerce and, in the public sector, through government.

2. Consider revision of the educational system so that high

school students could elect a three-month school experience followed by three months' work experience, then back to school for three more months, etc. This would make the *concept* of work meaningful to students before they leave school. That concept will be helpful to such students whether they seek paid employment or volunteer work after leaving high school.

3. Career education programs must begin in the elementary school if this concept is to become a reality. If we continue to wait until the senior year, many students will not only fail to find work but, in addition, will not even be properly motivated to work.

4. No one should tell students that all who desire work upon leaving school will be able to find it. We cannot, and should not, pretend to guarantee work to all youth who may seek it. Public service jobs for youth will be essential in large numbers if we are to come close to converting this concept into a reality.

5. Attention must be given to revising compulsory school attendance laws and child labor laws. As both are now written, this concept cannot become a reality.

6. Consider establishing a kind of "apprenticeship" for all kinds of work. It is time we ceased restricting apprenticeship to just the trade and technical fields.

The foregoing listing of "issues and answers" is especially useful to the creative educator as he sets about the very crucial process of designing a systematic linkage with the worksite. He should proceed on the assumption that the business, industry, and labor leaders are ready and waiting for his initiative.

Business, industry, and labor are ready and willing to take a much larger role in the implementation of career education. The U.S. Chamber of Commerce has given consistent and powerful support to the career education concept from the time of its first expression as a priority of the U.S. Office of Education. The then president of the Chamber, in September 1971, wrote to President Nixon as follows (in part):

"Mr. President, we are pleased by what seems to be a new thrust by the U.S. Office of Education to make career education a high priority. . . . The basic principles advanced by [the office] to reform career education in America's schools are to be encouraged and applauded."

When all is said and done, the career education theory declares that education should include knowledge and experience literally related to work. Growing up to work is an economic and psychological necessity for virtually all people. Accordingly, we ask for a *much* larger and more operational relationship between schools and colleges and the work place.

The reason is very simple. Work in its comprehensive and economic context takes place outside the classroom. If it is to be a part of the education of all people, including an increased command of its specifics by teachers, and a hands-on, literal experience by students, there must be forged a new relationship that actually makes the work place a component of the education system. This will call for radical change in the perceptions of educators, substantial enlargement of the business community's present level of commitment, and a system for reallocation of public funds to meet the out-of-pocket costs incurred by business in meeting this new obligation.

Most important, there must be models invented and put in place at the community level. While the National Institute of Education in its employer-based model has opened the door on this subject, the NIE model is necessarily and correctly viewed as an *alternative* system. It does engage the business sector to provide the learning site for students choosing this alternative. But the mainstream of school and college education will, for the foreseeable future, remain in the existing institutions for the great majority of school and college-age learners, as distinct from *total* alternative institutions.

It is to this large segment of as many as three to five million young people a year, from grades ten through the baccalaureate degree, that the new dimensions of business and education linkage must be addressed. The field is open, there is readiness on the part of the business sector, there is need on the part of the educational structure. There remains the creative task of putting the pieces together in the construction of a totally new social form.

Form, Function, Feds, and Funds:

THE NATIONAL INSTITUTE OF EDUCATION

When in the fall of 1973 I left the federal government to join the College Entrance Examination Board, there were many letters and innumerable queries—"What will happen to career education?" Throughout my service as Commissioner, and later as Assistant Secretary, I had shunned vigorously the personalization of career education around my own name, stating repeatedly that the concept had been hovering around education long before my time. I cared too much about the success of the enterprise to risk its derogation as a passing fad attributed to a transitory government official. I nevertheless readily acknowledge that my years in Washington were dominated by my concern for advancing and facilitating the career education philosophy.

But I saw no threat to career education's forward movement in my separation. Nor do I today, several months later. If anything, the conviction in HEW is stronger, the human and fiscal resources are more firm, and the likelihood of continuity as a federal priority more evident than when I left. This sense of assurance derives from the demonstrated philosophies and values held by the key individuals in the Office of Education and the National

Institute of Education, and by the clear evidence in the ongoing performance of the agencies in their support of career education. Indeed, the theme is sufficiently established in state and local performance to be beyond damage by a federal withdrawal. But withdrawal is unlikely.

For those who enjoy tracing the genealogy of events, there follows an extract of the document that put the career education notion into place as the first step in federal support, shared with the states. Since this chapter will come primarily to a treatment of the National Institute of Education as the principal *research and development* force for career education, the early research and development antecedents to NIE are given attention at the start.

Dr. Robert W. Worthington, serving ably as Associate Commissioner of Education for Adult Vocational and Technical Education, followed up the "history-making" agreement with the chief state school officers in June 1971 with a proper official instrument, setting forth conditions and guidelines which gave substance to our bargain. Dated September 9, 1971, Worthington's memorandum was addressed to State Directors of Vocational Education and Executive Officers of State Boards for Vocational Education:

> In his letter to the Chief State School Officers dated September 7, 1971, the U.S. Commissioner of Education announced his decision to turn over to the States a supplemental allocation of $9 million from his discretionary funds, for use in vocational research and development projects focused on the establishment of comprehensive career education model programs. The Commissioner also mentioned in his letter that the Bureau of Adult, Vocational, and Technical Education would provide the States with guidelines for the utilization of this supplemental $9 million allocation. The purpose of this Policy Paper is to set forth the guidelines to which the Commissioner referred.
>
> These research and development projects are to be designed to enable each State to establish its own demonstration, testing, and development site for a career education program.
>
> Each of these research and development projects will focus on establishing a meaningful, comprehensive,

well-developed career education program, with a strong
guidance and counseling component. It is expected that
each project will involve, in addition to the guidance and
counseling component, the development, testing, and
demonstration of one or more of the following:

1.   Programs designed to increase the self-awareness
of each student and to develop in each student favorable
attitudes about the personal, social, and economic significance of work.

2.   Programs at the elementary school level designed to
increase the career awareness of students in terms of the
broad range of options open to them in the world of work.

3.   Programs at the junior high or middle school level
designed to provide career orientation and meaningful
exploratory experiences for students.

4.   Programs at grade levels 10 through 14 designed to
provide job preparation in a wide variety of occupational
areas, with special emphasis on the utilization of work
experience and cooperative education opportunities for
all students.

5.   Programs designed to insure the placement of all
exiting students in either (a) a job, (b) a post-secondary
occupational program, or (c) a baccalaureate program
. . . ."

Worthington's memorandum contained the stipulation that a
number of general criteria, consistent with the then-emerging
federal design for career education, had to be met in a state's
plan. The guidelines were consciously nonprescriptive, giving the
states considerable latitude for their own inventiveness for reform under the authority of statutes supporting research and
development in occupational education. The memo continues:

States wishing to utilize their portion of the supplemental
$9 million allocation, as itemized on the attached table,
should submit a letter of assurance to the U.S. Commissioner of Education on or before November 1, 1971. . . .

Every state and territory responded with the prescribed plan
and assurance. Accordingly, the first federal funds allocated to
the advancement of career education as a state initiative resulted

in the following distribution. Modest though the sums were, as deployed according to enrollment numbers, they were a start. Most states overmatched the federal investment very substantially.

SUPPORT FOR RESEARCH AND DEVELOPMENT PROJECTS IN VOCATIONAL EDUCATION FOR FY 1972 UNDER THE SUPPLEMENTAL $9 MILLION ALLOCATION FROM THE U.S. COMMISSIONER'S DISCRETIONARY FUNDS FOR CAREER EDUCATION

(Allocation by states)

State	Amount	State	Amount
Alabama	$197,115	Nevada	$ 15,850
Alaska	12,039	New Hampshire	31,243
Arizona	85,421	New Jersey	254,114
Arkansas	106,580	New Mexico	57,852
California	705,568	New York	591,380
Colorado	98,979	North Carolina	294,703
Connecticut	99,227	North Dakota	35,229
Delaware	20,143	Ohio	459,697
District of Columbia	23,700	Oklahoma	132,525
Florida	280,556	Oregon	94,491
Georgia	255,831	Pennsylvania	498,124
Hawaii	37,058	Rhode Island	36,583
Idaho	40,804	South Carolina	161,613
Illinois	382,790	South Dakota	35,594
Indiana	223,021	Tennessee	213,211
Iowa	128,938	Texas	578,266
Kansas	109,014	Utah	57,627
Kentucky	178,740	Vermont	20,781
Louisiana	208,042	Virginia	241,777
Maine	49,626	Washington	145,680
Maryland	151,322	West Virginia	100,304
Massachusetts	194,120	Wisconsin	186,774
Michigan	359,043	Wyoming	16,440
Minnesota	167,391	American Samoa	1,940
Mississippi	136,091	Guam	7,245
Missouri	207,297	Puerto Rico	162,778
Montana	36,439	Trust Territory	4,930
Nebraska	65,299	Virgin Islands	3,055

TOTAL $9,000,000

The National Institute of Education had not yet been established at this time, in the summer and fall of 1971. Its research and development authority were not to emerge in law for another year. Hence, the Office of Education, still carrying the research and development authority, was anticipating the role that NIE would assume in investing risk money in pursuit of national goals.

A similar and possibly more fundamental event occurred in Pinehurst, North Carolina, in early March 1974, with most of the same players present. There, all the chief state school officers who could schedule the event, amounting to over two-thirds, gathered to review the issues and to point to the future of career education. Benefiting by this date from research and development work launched by the National Institute of Education, along with the developmental investments allocated by the Office of Education directly to the states, every state by this time had in one degree or another undertaken its own research and development of career education.

Sponsored by North Carolina State University's Center for Occupational and Vocational Education and by Craig Phillips, North Carolina's talented Superintendent of Public Instruction, the conference devoted three days solely to the career education concept. This conference itself is a good example of the general support afforded by the National Institute of Education for establishing centers of intellectual and experimental strength throughout the country.

The chemistry of that meeting is noteworthy. Clearly, the chief state school officers were the principal parties. They correctly view themselves as the ultimate responsible agents of education in the United States. Yet, there are fifty states, all different, and fifty equally different and consciously independent state leaders. The concept of career education had been, in varying degrees, under development and limited implementation in all states for at least the period since the consensus of June 1971 and the subsequent allocation of federal funds.

In a few states the concept without the title had been under development longer. Consensus on any social theme is difficult enough even between two intelligent and concerned professional companions, not to mention fifty. On such a complex and loosely defined theme as career education, consensus is more than one should expect. Yet, for all their different styles and political environments, variant depths of comprehension of the concept, and disparities in resources, experience, and tenure in their posts, the chiefs present came to closure. They went home more earnestly mindful of the educational reform now in motion, and more deeply convinced of the essential leadership implicit in their fifty offices, than when they had left home for Pinehurst.

The clear message of the meeting was the reaffirmation that career education is a reality, that its advancement is a state responsibility, notwithstanding the diversity of our system, that some states had traveled much farther than others, and that there was no turning back.

Among those from outside the circle of state leaders upon whose wisdom we drew were John Ottina, U.S. Commissioner of Education and my successor; Eugene Sydnor, Vice President and Education Chairman of the U.S. Chamber of Commerce; Willard Wirtz, former Secretary of Labor and now President of the Manpower Institute; Albert Quie, Congressman from Minnesota and minority leader of the House Subcommittee on Education; Tom Glennan, Director of the National Institute of Education; Nelson Jack Edwards, Vice President, United Auto Workers, representing labor's viewpoint; William Pierce, Deputy U.S. Commissioner of Education for Occupational and Adult Education; and others whose prominence and experience formed a fabric for deliberation not equaled in my memory for contemplating the educational and occupational needs of the country, when blended with the power of the chief state school officers.

The voices of esteemed scholars and practitioners in vocational education, such as Rupert Evans and Lowell Burkett, were blended with those of higher education such as Aaron Warner, Dean of the College of General Studies at Columbia, where reform is already in motion. To leave out the names of any of the lively and wise contributors to this conference is offensive, yet this is not the place for a personnel directory. The illustrations are meant to illuminate the many ingredients of the discourse that dramatized another benchmark in career education's evolution.

John Ottina and Tom Glennan made it clear that, concerning the

federal role in career education, the National Institute of Education as well as the Office of Education was deeply committed to
the theme and would continue its support with funds, technical
assistance, research, dissemination, and leadership.

Eugene Sydnor, bringing a business leader's perceptions to the
sessions, reaffirmed the readiness of the business world to enter
a larger and more meaningful partnership with education. He
accepted the reality of career education's dependence upon a
higher order of magnitude in the businessman's partnership with
the schools and colleges. He pleaded for more aggressive action
by educators to exploit the business world's willingness.

Jack Edwards, speaking not only as a voice from the labor
movement but as a concerned Black citizen of Detroit, declared
that labor, for all its uncertainties about the implications of career
education, must rise above its traditional posture and join hands
with the schools. He put down as irrelevant the concerns that
have been expressed by some of his fellows in labor that we
should guard the anachronistic and outmoded child labor laws
and prohibit unpaid work experience by young people in school.
He urged that Blacks seize career education as one of their most
promising opportunities.

Congressman Quie, who probably knows more about and has
done more for occupational education than any other recent
member of Congress, urged that we rise above our narrow
differences, imbedded in such terms as *vocational* education,
industrial education, *occupational* education. Half in jest, but
half-serious, he declared, "Let us abandon those terms, and deal
solely with the larger term, career education." He insisted that
more funds should be appropriated for research in career education, and restated his commitment to a federal governance
system that would combine appropriate agencies into a Cabinet-
level Department of Education and Manpower. He pledged
continued legislative support to the chief state school officers,
observing that they were becoming a force to be reckoned with
on any issue in which they should combine their strength.

Willard Wirtz brought a spirit of destiny to the meeting that few
others in America have the credentials to do. He reinforced the
proposition that change in education was desperately needed,
but that the sprawling federal government, for all its good

intentions, was an inhibitor of change. He placed the burden for change squarely upon the states, and in turn upon localities. He said that the reforms implicit in career education would not come easily, drawing upon his political and managerial experience: "There are no fast bucks to be made in career education; no relief from taxes; no vocal constituency; no singular leadership that is clear; no national crisis forging a national response." He urged that we get over petty differences about definitions, develop good demonstrations of career education, evaluate them with thoroughness, and capitalize on successes through national dissemination.

As in the beginning, the states are the responsible parties to educational reform. Their function is generally focused toward elementary and secondary education, but their influence on postsecondary education is increasing. This is particularly true in the case of community colleges where career education is of paramount importance, linked through curriculum and philosophy with the secondary schools.

But, notwithstanding the preeminence of the states in the governance of education, the federal area is a very crucial component of any reform. Therefore, the weight of this chapter will deal with what is, and what should be in the future, the federal engagement in career education—with particular emphasis on the research and development function as now firmly established in the National Institute of Education. The Office of Education will receive equal treatment in the following chapter.

While the federal government contains several agencies which are identifiable with education, the primary agency is the Education Division of the Department of Health, Education, and Welfare. The two major components of this division are the Office of Education and the National Institute of Education. Both have a clear and dynamic role in career education. But their roles, as established by law, are different and they behave in different ways. Congress intended that they be different, as declared in the Education Amendments of 1972, which removed the research function in education from the Office of Education and gave research an equal status in HEW with the Office of Education through the creation of the National Institute of Education.

The Director of NIE has rank and authority comparable to that of the Commissioner of Education. While the agencies are dissimilar in size and appropriations they have, and in my judgment should have, equal authority and responsibility. Oversimplified, the differences are those of a funding agency (OE) with comprehensive and explicit authority to carry out many statutory programs of an *operational support* nature (disadvantaged, handicapped, student loans, bilingual education, etc.) as distinguished from a research agency with broad, discretionary authority to perform or support research in education. NIE has few, if any, of the categorical mandates that govern the Office of Education. But one salient feature of NIE's statute is the expectation by Congress that the agency will perform research and development functions on career education and disseminate the results of such research and development.

While the Office of Education had been committed to the career education concept for well over a year before NIE was born, the logical treatment of these two agencies would suggest that NIE be viewed first in the chronology of these concluding chapters. The architects have an axiom that says *form follows function.* Therefore, under ideal conditions, the concept of career education should have been developed by NIE through research, experimentation, validation, evaluation, field testing, and dissemination *before* the operational phase, as suited to the statutory authorities of the Office of Education, should be undertaken.

Educational reform, as a *national* enterprise, however, is a very untidy system. The federal government as an educational policy-making instrument is a very untidy system. The bureaucracy, however, within governments, including state and local as well as federal, is a reasonably tidy system. It is quite self-contained; it lives and works by rules and regulations; its tidiness is threatened only by change or reform. Like elephant seals from the Antarctic on their breeding beaches, the members of internal government structures rise in self-righteousness and anger to challenge any intruder on the beach. They understandably want to keep the system tidy. And as long as tidy systems are kept tidy at federal, state, and local bureaus of America's educational structure, there will be little change. Untidiness is a necessary and, to some, painful and even impossible accommodation to make, even for the alleged promises of career education.

Soon after I joined the Office of Education in late 1970, I asked Dr. Harry Silberman, newly appointed Associate Commissioner for Research and Development, to undertake a major research effort to analyze, describe, test, and validate the feasibility of the career education theory then emerging. Ideally, form would follow function. He put staff to work on this topic, and good beginnings were discernable. But, in keeping with the untidiness of government, Congress, with my earnest supporting testimony, was engaged at the same time in passing legislation to create NIE and accordingly to separate the research and development function from the Office of Education, over which I presided at the time. I was more anxious to see education research elevated to a place of its own in the government hierarchy than to keep it contained as a subsystem of the Office of Education. The untidiness is evident in the fact that Dr. Silberman and others were engaged in a research task (career education along with other topics) of considerable importance, knowing that in the months ahead their bureau would be dissolved and a new agency, NIE, would take over. They also knew that congressional colloquy was clearly saying that "different" people would be expected to occupy and run the new institution.

To compound the problem, I put upon Dr. Silberman the added task of planning the implementation of the expected legislation to put the National Institute of Education into place. His credentials as a first-rate researcher and psychologist compelled me to place these tasks (start the research on career education, and plan the establishment of NIE) on him. He did them well, and upon their conclusion he turned over to the newborn NIE a set of options for putting its organization together and a well-started structure of commissioned research in career education. All of this happened in the winter of 1971–1972 and on into the spring. In June 1972, with the passage of the Education Amendments, NIE came into being, and Dr. Silberman, having served his country well, returned to private scholarly pursuits.

It would have been fine management theory and practice to have let career education remain a research topic in the still-emerging NIE for two or three or four years until its validity had been tested, its assumptions formulated, its effectiveness demonstrated and evaluated, and its dissemination systematically performed. But there was not much time. There still is not enough time to meet the needs of the young people who are in our schools and colleges right now, and who are not being well served. We could not wait for the tidy arrangements to catch up. Career education, by whatever rubrics of behavior, was happening—without the benefits of a formal conceptual framework and validated models.

Theoreticians tell us that reform follows a sequential process of (1) conceptualization, (2) creation of a delivery system, and (3) installation of a new process. The reform of education does not fit neatly into these protocols as might apply in medical or engineering research. They may be useful in reforming, say, people's shampooing habits with a reformed soap; but the structure of education resists someone else's "conceptualization," an intervening "delivery system," and an "installation" of a process in which the practitioner has no voice.

Thus, while the research was going forward we started a parallel, or tandem, system in each state. The differences between the Office of Education and NIE were manifest. The federal research initiatives as vested finally in NIE quite explicity contracted for the design and creation of conceptualization, experimental models, curriculum research, and validation measures, including evaluation. At the same time, the Office of Education, by persuasion as distinct from authority, provided funds for each state to undertake its own developmental and experimental efforts. Thus, two systems were in place at the same time, doing roughly the same things, albeit the NIE system was probably more sophisticated, scientific, and controlled. To add to the complexity, by the fall of 1972 many school districts, quite independently of state or federal funding or even open encouragement, had begun to develop experimental models and curricular designs, consistent with the career education message. There was, and remains, a spirit of experimental chaos. And it is not at all bad.

The National Institute of Education, headed by Dr. Thomas Glennan, a brilliant and seasoned research administrator, has had a stuttering start as a new government agency. The infant Institute has suffered delays and reverses in staffing, governance, and funding that it does not deserve. Yet, in spite of organizational and fiscal adversity, NIE has gathered a staff of competent and dedicated scholars and practitioners around the career education mandate. Dr. Corrinne Reider, Assistant Director for Career Education under Glennan's direct leadership, is a scholarly, dedicated, and skillful researcher and manager. Dr. Reider is not a conventional educator either from the lower schools or from higher education, though she is at home in both. By the nature of NIE's conscious *difference* from what had been educational research at the federal level, she has determinedly and successfully sought to address career education as researcher as distinct from practitioner. In doing so, she initially set some nerves on edge in the conventional educational community. But her dedication to the philosophy of career education and her wit and intellect have earned the respect of traditionalists and she will, I believe, make her mark as a major contributor to educational reform.

As an example of Dr. Reider's initiative, requests for proposals (RFPs) were published in the spring of 1974 calling for a national competition among scholars and researchers to produce four basic publications for wide dissemination to schools and colleges as resources for unifying and systematizing the burgeoning information on the subject of career education:

> 1) *Instructional Materials*—a compendium of information about printed materials, audio and/or visual products and other diverse instructional materials which relate academic and career learning for children and youth.
>
> 2) *Facilities*—a handbook for the locating and/or planning the use of space and equipment for operational programs that relate the world of education and the world of work.
>
> 3) *Learning Resource Activities*—a teacher's guide to field trips, community resources, speakers and other less formal learning resources which increase the learner's career information base level of career awareness and opportunities for career exploration.

4) *Case Studies*—case studies and an annotated listing of a diversified. cross-section of ongoing educational programs that address the future career needs of children and youth.

The purpose of this Request for Proposals is to elicit proposals from interested parties for the issuance of a contract or contracts to develop, produce and prepare for dissemination four resource publications in the areas described above. Together, these publications will serve educators and learners who have need for topical and current information about career-related instructional materials, facilities, learning activities and ongoing programs.

Although the definitions of the concept of career education are innumerable and vary widely, the NIE's Career Education Program has advanced the following as its present perception of the basic parameters of the effort:

> Career Education is the development of knowledge and of special and general abilities to help individuals interact with the economic sector. Learning in this context would occur in both formal and informal situations which motivate the learners by causing them to experience work directly and/or relate in-school learning activities to their career implications for the student.

A common element in most definitions of career education is that all individuals, during and after their formal schooling, should be exposed to materials and experiences that:
- lead to a better understanding of the world of work
- assist them in discovering their own competencies
- assist them in acquiring the basic skills necessary to enter and progress in the world of work
- train or retrain them in specific job skills when necessary

Activities sponsored for youth thus far by the National Institute of Education include the development of curriculum and guidance units, training materials for teachers, community involvement techniques, administrative guidelines, academic credit work experiences with high school students outside the traditional school setting and increased emphasis on reading, mathematics, career guidance and community organization development in a large urban, minority, low-income area of Washington, D.C. These products and processes are evolving and some of them are expected to be ready for dissemination in 1974–75, following thorough field testing and revision.

While program development and testing efforts are underway to provide long term outcomes, a great area of immediate concern is the present need for resources which provide information about available resources which might be utilized by program developers and participants in efforts to better relate educational processes to their application in a career setting. The National Institute of Education is primarily interested in publications that will be used in schools or by personnel outside the schools who are interested in career education efforts. Yet, the publications may be of interest and use to a larger audience also and should be considered a significant addition to the knowledge base for career-related education at all levels.

Necessarily, NIE approached the vast territory of career education by de-limiting its terms to segments that were realistically manageable for research. The substance of this de-limitation took initial form in a report developed under Dr. Reider by NIE's Career Education Development Task Force, published as a discussion draft in April 1973. The report,[1] reproduced in part here, is intended to display the focus and "researchable themes" to which NIE has declared itself:

FOCUS AND DEFINITION

(Discussion Draft)

NOTE: The several pages following are extracted selectively from the document.

A fundamental premise for the career education program has been that programmatic research and development must be undertaken within the framework of a definite problem focus. *The initial emphasis for the NIE career education R&D program*

*will be the responsiveness of career education to the problems
people experience in finding the right jobs and advancing within
them.* As more is understood about this fundamental element
and its impact on other aspects of life development, additional
factors can receive R&D attention.

More specifically, career education is defined as the development of knowledge and of special and general abilities to help
individuals and groups interact with the economic sector. Economic and psychological incomes from employment comprise
the long term outcomes which are proper questions for research
and development. In other words, NIE will begin its career
education efforts by concentrating on how people earn their
living: do they earn enough to maintain a decent standard of
living, and do they like what they are doing? This focus has been
chosen because:

- Resources are limited and must be concentrated on priority issues. A world without work *may* be imminent and
  persons *may* seek career education that will address their
  "nonwork life." Yet, there is also sizeable evidence that
  persons expect educational systems to prepare them and
  others for gainful employment.

- How people earn a living (Do they earn enough? Do they
  like what they are doing?) is of primary concern with
  reference to the well-being of individuals and Nation as a
  whole.

- Data about the economic sector of society, and the
  development of individual careers within that context, are
  more accessible than the knowledge base for other aspects of societal or individual activity—e.g., use of leisure
  time, citizenship responsibility, homemaking, aesthetic
  development, spiritual growth. While these aspects of life
  are important, the research and development community
  is faced with a considerably smaller and less accessible
  bank of information.

A Conceptual Framework

The first step in developing a program plan is to analyze the
problem and its history. With these data planners are better able
to trace connections between perceived problems and possible
research and demonstration activities.

The NIE–CEDTF intends to examine the assumptions that people often are educationally and vocationally unsuited to enter and successfully navigate a technologically oriented labor market. Many are concerned about maintaining their ability to earn a living. Others are concerned with finding and holding a satisfactory job. Education in this context is viewed as a comprehensive delivery system composed of both formal and informal resources (schools, colleges, broadcast media, business-industry-commerce, labor, youth organizations and the like).

Our conceptual model for career education explores how educational and other processes affect the labor market and, eventually, the financial and psychological rewards of employment. There are at least two elements affecting this latter aspect of one's life work: career entry and career progression.

When examining the problem of career entry there appear to be at least two impinging forces that must be dealt with: (1) aggregate employment factors—that is, situations in the economic life of society over which individuals have little control (e.g., federal monetary and fiscal policies that affect inflation, minimum wages, supply and demand) and (2) structural problems—e.g., no workers with skills to fill available jobs, unrealistic job requirements, discrimination, the extent to which people know about jobs.

In choosing structural problems for analysis, there are probably several tacks that could be taken. One approach would be to alter policies and adjust existing practice in the private sector. A reasonable course for education in ameliorating the structural problems associated with career entry and progression is the provision of the following, among others:

1. *Information*, primarily guidance and counseling about careers and the job market.

2. *Specific and General Skills*, which are either minimal requirements or influences on job entry and advancement.

3. *Rewards* for career development and recurrent education, including financial support (e.g., entitlements, scholarships, continuing free public education, worker sabbaticals) and social/psychological support (e.g., acceptability and rewards for career

exploration, occupational and educational discontinuities and midcareer change).

4. *Matching and Placement Systems* which relate individuals and local or regional employment resources and opportunities.

However, to address these kinds of problems for *all* persons would be unrealistic. Limited R&D resources will be directed at two target groups most affected by problems of career entry and progression: youth and midcareer adults, particularly women. For youth, emphasis will be on employment access and entry; for adults, emphasis will be on distribution of employment and career progression.

The Career Education Models

The present career education models are examined:

- To suggest how these projects might be integrated coherently into the overall program and
- To match the current projects with the conceptual analysis to facilitate additional high priority research and development initiatives.

During the period since mid-1971, four career education "models"—actually a series of projects based on common themes and assumptions—have attracted considerable attention and resources:

Model I: School-Based Comprehensive Career Education Model (CCEM)

The Center for Vocational and Technical Education at the Ohio State University is the prime Model I contractor. Associated with the Center are six local school district sites that serve as focal points for the development and field testing of career education materials—curriculum units, guidance units, teacher training manuals, public information and administrative guidelines. The major problem focus of the project is youth's alleged lack of preparedness for employment, further study and adult life. The project attempts to reform the curriculum of the established public school system by infusing career development concepts into the entire K–12 curriculum. In grades K through six career awareness is emphasized; in grades seven through nine, career exploration and in grades 10 through 13, career preparation. By the end of 1973, 98 curriculum units are to be completed; all will have been tried out in the various cooperating school systems. They will be ready for dissemination in FY 75, following more rigorous field testing. A staff development package to accompany the completed units, a guidance and counseling package and a placement component also will be ready for dissemination.

Model II: Employer-Based Career Education

There are four Model II contractors: Appalachia Educational Laboratory, Far West Laboratory for Research and Development, Northwest Regional Educational Laboratory and Research for Better Schools, Inc. As with Model I, the major problem focus is the unpreparedness of youth for employment, further study and adult life.

Model II projects are designing a comprehensive alternative to the public secondary school. The education setting is shifted from the existing school system to an adult, employer-based and action learning environment. Special emphasis is placed on the development of career planning, guidance and learning resources outside the school and close to employers.

When fully developed, this model will provide comprehensive data on the benefits and limitations of utilizing educational opportunities within economic institutions. Analyses will be given of the readiness of employers to involve themselves in comprehensive education programs, the necessity and/or potential of various incentives to employers, the learning potential of specific economic institutions, and jobs and methods of high school equivalency certification.

Model III: Home-Based Career Education

The Education Development Center, Inc. (EDC), conducts the only Model III project. EDC is working in Providence, Rhode Island, with the problems of adults and adolescents who are neither employed nor in school. Unlike the other models, this Model III project is not attempting to teach skills and attitudes directly. Rather, the project is designed to inform individuals about existing work and training opportunities in the community and to apply mass communication media to the outreach and assessment of the career interests of selected home-bound populations.

Model IV: Rural-Residential Career Education

Model IV is being developed by the Mountain-Plains Education and Economic Development Program, Inc. The project focuses on chronically underemployed multi-problem rural families. It represents a "total" intervention in that it attempts to influence all significant activities of the family, not only education-related activities. The major goal is to make the family unit economically viable through career counseling, training, remedial education and guidance for the children; homemaking and family development skills for the parents and job placement.

During these early months of operation most projects have successfully created a variety of program activities which give promise of reaching each model's objectives. The programs also have developed effective strategies for solving the many problems of implementation. Reviews of the models reveal some major difficulties, however. Foremost of these is an imbalance toward development, particularly day-by-day operations. The portfolio is typified by little emphasis on documentation, research and analysis, absence of common variables and planned variations, insufficient concern with implementation strategies, a narrow range of contractor types and lack of a systematic plan for summative as well as formative evaluation. Also, assessed against the conceptual framework, current contracts appear to address systematically only a few of the career entry and advancement problems outlined in the conceptual framework.

The FY 73 and FY 74 Program Plan

The NIE career education program will test the conceptual framework and develop knowledge, techniques and delivery systems consistent with its aims. A program plan including research and development activities derived from the conceptual analysis and suggestions for improving the models programs is proposed. During FY 74, the Task Force will follow that conceptual framework in managing existing programs. It also will test the validity of the framework by spearheading a variety of new activities.

A. **Management of Current Models**

The current models will continue to be a central element of program development activities.

According to earlier workplans, initial products from Models I, II, III, and IV will be available by the end of FY 73. In FY 74, NIE proposes to support program revision and a second round of development, during which the Career Education Development Task Force will test the effectiveness of materials developed in FY 73. The second round of program development and testing will be conducted primarily through internal evaluations.

Planning to test whether the program is transportable and cost effective will begin in FY 74. In FY 75, implementation of tests to determine if programs can be reproduced and if they are cost effective will be conducted via external evaluations and experiments. Results from these studies will be available by the end of FY 75 and mid-FY 76.

Having declared the general scope and constraints affecting the NIE role, the Plan continues with more explicit research and development objectives: only the topical themes are listed here, revealing the scope of research invited by NIE in 1974 under *field initiated studies* and *directed contracts*:

.... B. **New Activities**

1. *Research : Activities undertaken to gain understanding of cause/effect relationships and to increase basic knowledge in career education*

YOUTH
ADULT   a. Field-initiated studies

YOUTH
ADULT   b. Studies developed from current projects

ADULT   c. Studies relating to job satisfaction

ADULT   d. Implications for career education of differing adult learning patterns and styles

2. *Policy analyses: Research to generate and compare ways of making program decisions*

YOUTH a. Studies relating to legislative and other barriers to career education

YOUTH
ADULT b. Studies of alternative financing and governance patterns for career education

YOUTH
ADULT c. Studies directed at the development and refinement of the conceptual framework as it affects target groups

ADULT d. Studies of the nature and effect of job redistribution as a worthwhile mechanism for improving employment opportunities and work satisfaction

3. *Planning and Program Development: Invention of educational products that can be used by practitioners or as a component of a large-scale experiment*

YOUTH a. Development of programs related to the roles and functions of postsecondary institutions in extending educational and career opportunities

YOUTH b. Studies focused on the unique problem of hard-to-reach youth whom the schools may have failed to serve adequately

YOUTH c. Planning studies leading to program development in the area of counseling, guidance and placement

YOUTH
ADULT d. Development of new and/or synthesized career education models based on research findings and policy analyses

ADULT e. Studies centered on the development of the potential of cable TV and other media for the delivery of career education into the home and other settings

4. *Experimentation: Large-scale intercession into a real-world setting to answer with considerable certainty a question of major policy significance*

YOUTH a. Studies relating to the transportability of remedial basic skills programs available in the non-school domain for delivery of entry level foundation education

YOUTH b. Studies focused on the strategy of "infusing" career education into ongoing school curricula

5. *Dissemination: Provision of information and guidelines for career education planning and research utilization*

YOUTH a. Development of a "whole earth catalog" on career education, containing material, activities and resources for teachers, counselors and administrators is suggested

YOUTH b. Studies resulting in suggestions for media developers to guide their presentation of careers in the world of work, with particular references to sex and ethnic stereotypes, are proposed

ADULT c. To draw on existing resources of other governmental subdivisions, an interagency group on adult learning is proposed, similar to present interagency activities on early childhood and adolescents

By the terms of its enabling statute, NIE is obliged to evaluate the products of research and development. While the art of educational evaluation is still quite primitive, the following elements of the Plan address this objective:

. . . C. Evaluation

1. High priority is given to strengthening project evaluation. Consultants are reviewing currently funded formative and summative evaluation efforts. Initial recommendations for strengthening the overall evaluation component were adopted in 1973, and are increasingly operational for all career education research.

2. Methodological studies of procedures for program development and product testing are needed. (Standards appear extremely variable and the term "fully field tested" often reflects little more than the first round of developmental activity.)

3. Development of intermediate and long term criteria for career education is underway. Measurement problems have been reported in almost all areas including job preparedness, ability to plan and make career decisions and career information.

4. Funds are requested for support of high opportunity situations such as evaluations of career education programs not supported by NIE (e.g., Cleveland placement service, California alternatives to the 12th grade).

5. Development of a National, State and regional reporting system for career education indicators, using existing data systems and possibly additional surveys.

. . . D. **Other Projects**

A variety of educational projects which lend themselves to educational research and development are currently being monitored by the NIE Task Force on Career Education. These include:

1. Career education-related programs at regional laboratories and research and development centers

2. Use of community aides and development of specially targeted curriculum in Washington, D.C.

3. Operation of a Child Study Center providing intramural research opportunities for general child development in terms of the overall NIE mission

4. Special workshops and activities deemed necessary to support and advance the field of career education.

Implementing the Program Plan

The career education program's success depends on the policies that guide its organization and management.

- The program will strive to support balanced activities involving a variety of disciplines and institutions.

- The program will provide limited and carefully controlled institutional support but also will strive for continuity in project support, given adequate performance.

- The program will provide some support to short term projects with a high probability of success.

- The program will fund projects directed by skilled program developers who can achieve success in career education and let invention lead research by investigating the determinants of such success.

- The project will not assume responsibility for widespread implementation of career education discoveries but will work with Federal, State and local agencies to plan ahead for product utilization. . . .

(Here, again the Office of Education will take the lead for *installation*, as form follows function.)

Dr. Reider's comprehensive and ambitious plan for the initiation of research and development in career education was circulated widely in draft during 1973. Responses led to refinements and modifications which the Task Force incorporated in their subsequent planning. This first plan, I felt, was very ambitious, in spite of Reider's conscientious measures for delimiting the scope of the research effort. But the Plan served and continues to serve, with variations, as the conceptual base for NIE's approach to career education.

About a year later, in February 1974, with the fiscal year half gone, NIE published an accounting of how it had begun to address its new tasks, including a progress report following its 1973 Forward Plan for Career Education.[2] Funds expended by NIE for all forms of research and development support under career education totaled $14.8 million in fiscal 1974, by far the largest single line of the NIE $75 million budget. For fiscal 1975, the sum of $21.3 million is requested for career education research and development, again the highest line item, at 18 percent of the NIE budget. Highlights of the 1974 publication concerning career education follow (These passages, are, again, drawn selectively from the NIE report):

The belief of the American people that education and economic opportunity are related is reflected in national polls, statistical surveys, and research documents. When those interviewed in the 1972 Gallup Poll of Public Attitudes Toward Education were asked why they wanted their children to get an education, 44 percent replied, "to get better jobs," and 38 percent said, "to make more money, achieve financial success." An NIE-sponsored survey of public views on the objectives of secondary education found job skills rated more important than four other choices, including academic skills, by at least a two to one margin.

And, while there are repeated calls to improve the ability of schools to help children meet career objectives and to develop new approaches to relate learning and work, there are also persistent questions about the capacity of education to influence an individual's economic future.

NIE's strategy, therefore, calls for activities to:

- Improve our understanding of the relationship between education and work.

- Improve access to careers by improving the contribution of education to career awareness and exploration among children and helping young people to make a wise career choice, prepare for a job, and then obtain one.

- Improve progression in careers by improving career choices among adults starting second careers or preparing for advanced positions and helping them gain access to education by examining its responsiveness to the career-related needs of adults.

In Fiscal 1975, NIE will try to attain these objectives in three ways. First, research will be conducted to close gaps in our understanding of the relationship between education and work. Second, the development, testing, and dissemination of career education programs transferred from the Office of Education will be continued and, in most cases, nearly completed. Third, in areas where the present knowledge base is relatively firm, new programs will be initiated.

Improve our understanding of the relationship between education and work

One of the more controversial issues in education is the influence of schooling on children's future occupational success. Many factors—not the least of which is common sense—suggest that education contributes to the career choices available to adults and their ability to earn more money in more desirable jobs. On the other hand, some research suggests that a parent's education, occupation, and income have the greatest influence over how much education a young person completes and his or her ease in finding employment and later success. Still other studies suggest that neither family background or schooling explain many individual differences in occupational attainment.

Therefore, NIE will continue to support field-initiated research to increase our understanding of education and work, as well as directed studies to:

- Improve definitions and measures of such concepts as "careers," "job satisfaction," and "economic returns."

- Assess the ability of educational institutions to adjust to changes in labor market demands for specialized manpowers.

- Understand the relative merits of providing young people with a general "ability to learn," as compared to job-specific skills.

- Evaluate the timing and sequence of education. Should the compulsory period during which children are required to attend school be lengthened or shortened? What would happen if more young people were released from school or encouraged to work and go to school?

To improve access to careers

Continuing programs already have contributed greatly to our understanding of how to improve curriculum materials that increase children's career awareness and how to provide young people with work experience that offers both specific skills and an understanding of career options.

For example, the school-based career education model has offered thousands of elementary and secondary school children an opportunity to learn about careers as an integral part of their arithmetic, history, science, and physical education studies. From the children and their teachers, NIE has learned how to improve these K–12 materials, which will be disseminated nationwide in Fiscal 1975. In another project, researchers, high school students, employers, and workers in four states created an innovative experience-based career education program. This project varies from most work/study programs, in that students are provided individualized schooling tailored to their work experience. Participating young people received academic credit for their work experience, which was above the entry level usually available to youth. Employers and workers also learned more about the contributions young people can make to society. It also was learned how to assess the learning potential of the work site, how to match the student and the job, and requirements for participation incentives and costs.

Several recent reports, including the Panel on Youth of the President's Science Advisory Committee (*Youth: Transition to Adulthood*) and the National Commission on the Reform of Secondary Education (*The Reform of Secondary Education*), have suggested that young people are not prepared to make a smooth transition from school to work because their schooling unduly segregates them from adults and is not conducive to their full development. One new initiative to address this issue will be a grants program to design experiments on promising innovations by local education agencies to improve general and specific skill instruction, break down barriers to age integration, foster specialized schools, and encourage out-of-school programs that provide opportunities for occupational exploration and preparation.

Other major demonstration projects, which will closely involve schools in the design and implementation processes, will be planned to address these issues with funds from the Fiscal 1974 appropriation. The experiment would become operational in Fiscal 1976.

Improve career progression

Ongoing and new programs are intended to provide adults with improved information about career opportunities and educational requirements and resources; financial support for living expenses as well as education-related costs; and education services more responsive to their needs.

For example, in Providence, Rhode Island, in one year 1900 adults who wanted to re-enter the labor market or a new career focus received career counseling by phone. Many were worried about the obsolescence of their skills; others didn't know what help they needed until they received assistance. From this project, information was provided about the stages in career choices for adults and the ways in which guidance and counseling approaches designed for young people are—and are not—adaptable for adults. The project is also providing information as to whether existing job and educational opportunities are adequate for adults and as to whether counseling to provide access to those opportunities is sufficient to meet adults' needs.

Another program, the Mountain Plains rural residential model in Glasgow, Montana, has served 1440 individuals in 380 families since operation began in 1972. Heads of households are provided specific skills needed in the six-state region served by the center, such as ski-lift repair and food handling. Counseling and guidance are provided to their families. Ancillary services, such as dental and medical care and alcoholic and financial counseling, also are offered. Costs of the program are high—about $16,000 per family—but if the project is successful in putting families back on their feet it may be a cost/effective alternative to welfare and other forms of public dependency caused by severe employment problems. An evaluation of the program is providing evidence about the sorts of problems it can deal with effectively as well as suggesting improvements in such residential-based programs.

New initiatives in Fiscal 1975 will include:

> A study center for adult career counseling, which would survey programs of continuing career education, guid-

ance, and counseling services for adults outside educational institutions, and produce handbooks and other
informational material.

Evaluation of alternative ways to finance recurrent education for workers, such as guaranteed loan funds, tax
incentives, insurance programs, entitlements, or changes
that would make work hours more adaptable to study
programs. . . .

NIE shows strong promise of making major contributions to our
knowledge about work, occupations, job-satisfaction, and the
relationships between education and work. But research is a slow
and labored process. We should not expect significant findings
on the deep and plaguing problems being addressed for some
years. In the meantime, less sophisticated but equally earnest
work goes forward in state and local school systems and in
colleges and universities, with the encouragement and support of
the Office of Education.

The tandem advancement of the research and development
phase of career education, untidy though it may be, with NIE
moving deliberately, necessarily slowly, and scientifically on the
one hand, and OE, working with states and school systems to
push ahead more pragmatically than scientifically on the other,
has an analogy. If the grain farmers of the Midwest had stopped
growing corn years ago in anticipation of the labored, scientific
research that finally produced hybrid seed, the grain farmers
would have gone out of business. Ingenious farmers kept trying, I
am sure, to grow a better and more efficient crop with what they
had. When the hybrid seed finally was produced, even then with
some skepticism they tried it, sparingly at first. So it will be, I
believe, with research for career education.

Form, Function, Feds, and Funds:

THE OFFICE OF EDUCATION

This closing chapter shows how the power of the Office of Education can be assembled around a central idea to give national leadership to problem-solving. The central idea, of course, in this case is career education.

When all is said and done, the Office of Education is a place where money is distributed to serve educational needs as established by Congress. The Office does not operate schools; only very tangentially does it teach classes (as in workshops for educators); it makes no rules about teaching and learning; and it is forbidden by law from intruding into the establishment of curriculum. While it is governed by and in turn governs the administration and execution of over a hundred different federal laws and programs, its leadership, influence, and discretionary authority are considerably circumscribed by the closely guarded state powers. I support this arrangement.

Thus, as noted earlier, nearly all federal influence for reform resides primarily in *persuasion*, fortified by relatively minuscule sums of money which can be targeted toward national goals. "Minuscule" in this analysis means, in 1974 terms, a total of $6 billion in the $90-billion education enterprise. When the sums, as constrained under law, allocated to the encouragement of career education are counted, they are very small indeed, as will be demonstrated in the pages that follow. Yet these small sums, actually well below $100 million a year for the past three years, or less than one-tenth of 1 percent of the annual costs of education, have served as the germ of the career education movement. The Office of Education provided the small capsule of yeast that is now beginning to influence all learners and their institutions, business and industry, labor, families and social institutions in this country, and to a slight degree a number of countries abroad.

The time is now at hand for the Office of Education to set about the task of refining the present generalizations and announcing more specific, definitive terms for the clarification of career education. The concept is widely recognized, much individuality and local creativity have been released for diverse yet compatible interpretations, and the movement is sufficiently advanced to have its own momentum, not likely to be dampened or inhibited by a perceived federal "control." The generalizations have resulted in Rorschach interpretations of the concept, not only in state and local school systems and colleges, but in the Office of Education as well. People saw what they wanted to see in adapting career education to their own values. This is not all bad, if it does not go on too long without some central consensus of meaning.

When it became clear in the spring of 1971 that indeed the Administration (especially the White House reinforced by Secretary Richardson) was taking our priority statement of career education seriously, we requested all components of the Office of Education to target all possible funds, within the limits of the statutes, on programs that could support career education.

With a considerable spirit of unanimity, all parts of the Office searched for applicable discretionary or categorical programs that could lend their weight to career education's still broad and loosely defined criteria. The result, by June 1972, was the following tabulation[1]:

FUNDS IDENTIFIED IN SUPPORT OF
CAREER EDUCATION, FY 1972
(adapted from Office of Education report)

Appropriation & statutory authority	Funds identified by program staff as advancing career education
Vocational & Adult Education	
Grants to states	$ 62,500,000
Vocational Education	
Discretionary programs	21,000,000*
Higher Education	
Cooperative Education	1,700,000
Other	
Dropout Prevention	2,000,000
Education Personnel Development	6,900,000
Research & Development (scheduled for transfer to NIE at end of FY 1972)	19,900,000
	$114,000,000

*These were the funds first identified at the meeting of Chief State School Officers in June 1971 as the bargaining sums which I agreed to assign to states provided they agreed to match "the Commissioner's" discretionary funds with their own and to undertake the construction of career education models in their states during fiscal 1972.

The $114-million figure was more of a bookkeeping exercise than a true allocation of resources. It was more shadow than substance, for relabeling is a custom familiar to government staffers who dutifully try to follow administration policy. Actually, apart from the discretionary programs at $21 million, little real federal money went specifically to career education from the Office of Education that first year. But it was a start, and the staffers in the Office knew we were serious.

By fiscal 1973 a much more searching analysis was made of the funding support for career education, and a wholly accountable sum of $43,200,000 was expended from various program components of the Office of Education. In November of that year the post of Assistant Secretary for Education was established, and I was moved to it from the Commissioner's post, where John Ottina succeeded me. The National Institute for Education also came into being at the same time, with the appointment of Thomas K. Glennan as Director. The Assistant Secretary is charged by law with "general supervision and direction" over both the Office of Education and the National Institute for Education, but does not have direct authority over these agencies operating programs. Yet, there was no doubt of the deep commitments held by Ottina and Glennan toward career education.

The preceding chapter noted that during fiscal 1973 NIE invested about $18 million in career education, thus bringing the combined federal effort in that year to over $61 million. In passing the 1975 budget, Congress appropriated, for the first time, the sum of $10 million (specifically for career education). Up to fiscal 1975 the administration has not pressed with vigor and documentation for large funding for career education as a line item—but I believe it soon will, and that Congress will be cordial. The fact remains that from 1971 through fiscal 1974 all career education support from federal resources has been through the concentration of the very limited discretionary funds, both for research and for operations.

In July 1973, a statement was hammered out by the principal planners and managers in OE in cooperation with the Assistant Secretary's office, giving substance and design to the federal role in support of career education. The following extract from the statement cites the distilled terms used for the internal management-by-objectives system in force throughout HEW:

> The career education objective of the Office of Education will be developed over a four-year period beginning in July 1973 (the beginning of fiscal 1974):
>
> • 1974: a diagnostic and developmental assistance focus designed to advance the state of the art, along with involvement in the support of two National Institute of Education models (school-based and employer-based) for demonstration purposes.

- 1975: first-phase installation efforts, emphasizing (1) planned variations in a variety of settings, (2) staff development and improved preservice and in-service teacher training models for career education, and (3) getting improved products and processes ready for the field. These ongoing programs will center on elementary and secondary education but will include the beginning of a major effort directed at institutions of higher education. These programs will yield lessons which will be applied to:

- 1976–77: major installation demonstrations combining public and higher education systems and trying for systemic change within target areas.

The document developed under the leadership of Dr. William Pierce, Deputy Commissioner for Occupational and Adult Education, who joined the Office in January 1973, and Dr. William Smith of his staff elaborated upon the immediate objectives of the Office for fiscal 1974:

> *First*, OE will conceptualize and further define the career education movement at the same time that it identifies problems, assumptions, and processes that underlie career education. There is a need to define the concept more carefully before designing a federal role for it, and this must be done so that career education does not come to have so exclusive a meaning as to stifle creativity, which is so important a part of educational reform. Thus, while a consensus position on career education is not necessary, career education concepts are badly in need of further refinement and clarification if intelligent planning, technical assistance, and expenditures are to take place.

> *Second*, with the conceptual effort will be diagnostic and analytical studies to describe the status of career education programs throughout the country, to see what lessons are being learned. The results of these studies on what schools and colleges and other agencies are doing in career education will be made available throughout the education community. Case studies of exemplary programs and projects will be conducted, and their findings will be shared at workshops and conferences, along with information on demonstration and installation activities.

Third, support will be given to pre-installation activities to bring about the orderly expansion of career education programs in state, local, and other educational agencies. These activities will include: (1) developing a design for a unified management control and information system, (2) providing support for state planning activities, (3) implementing pre- and in-service career education staff development programs, (4) developing a national network of institutions of postsecondary education to provide leadership, and (5) extending the second generation development and demonstration of the National Institute of Education school-based model sites.

The *fourth* major step is program evaluation. Since the career education program is a demonstration effort, designed to produce replicable products and processes which will be used by local and independent agencies and institutions without federal assistance, comprehensive evaluation is critical to the success of the program. These evaluations will have three purposes: (1) to track the process of installation; (2) to measure the impact of major demonstrations; and (3) to act as a monitor of quality control within each effort. Program plans for 1974 call for an emphasis on conceptual development, diagnosis, and developmental assistance—a decision which dictates that immediate 1974 evaluation efforts should focus on process evaluations. These will be planned and to a large extent conducted during 1974, concurrently with the developmental activities themselves. In addition, plans will be laid during 1974 for longer-term process and impact evaluation of the installation projects.

The career education installation program will represent a refocused effort in 1974. It will be the primary effort in the Office of Education directed specifically at advancing the career education concept and, as such, will have the primary responsibility for advancing the implementation of career education. However, there are a number of other programs under various legislative authorities which have supported career education efforts. Most of these career education-related programs have focused on two major needs: curriculum development and educational personnel development. These activities will continue in 1974, in cooperation with the career education program itself.

As the plans for fiscal 1974 were being formulated, standards were established for reviewing the extent of fund allocations made throughout the Office during fiscal 1973. As noted earlier, considerably more disciplined criteria were established to foreclose the "relabeling" technique. Quite appropriately this action not only insured an accurate accounting of expenditures during fiscal 1973, but pushed the staff further toward refinement and definition of the concept. The Education Amendments of 1972 had elevated the vocational education bureau to higher status in the Office of Education hierarchy and identified career education as one of its responsibilities. Deputy Commissioner William Pierce, heading the new Bureau of Occupational and Adult Education created the Center for Career Education in August 1973, as the first legally authorized organizational (though unfunded at the time) structure within OE to carry forward the responsibilities for career education. (This Center has subsequently, by OE reorganization of November 1973, become the Division of Career Education Programs, as a unit of the Office of Career Education.)

In an accounting of its work during 1973, the Office described the important steps taken to move toward a rationale for the federal role, and a conceptual base for analyzing fund allocations:

> Since the Office of Education publicly advanced the idea of career education in January, 1971, it has sought to avoid a prescriptive and premature definition which might stifle the creativity and diversity necessary for the development of this broad concept. Accordingly, OE units have neither been encouraged nor required to conform to a common plan or definition. The result has been a wide range of activities conducted under a variety of legislative authorities.
>
> While such diversity is a source of strength conceptually and programmatically, it makes analysis difficult. Estimates of the total OE effort in career education thus vary immensely, depending on how one answers the question: what do you mean by career education? Any attempt to realistically analyze career education activities thus requires at least some agreement on what is meant by the term. Consequently, the Center for Career Education developed a set of criteria which separated OE activities into two categories:

1. *Comprehensive Career Education Projects*—those activities which, for all students in the educational levels served, seek to: (1) develop and expand career awareness; (2) provide opportunities for exploration and/or skill attainment in careers of their choice; (3) provide career-oriented guidance and counseling; (4) provide career placement services; (5) improve cognitive and affective performance through restructuring the curriculum around a career development theme; and (6) provide training for educational personnel to enable them to meet the preceding objectives.

2. *Career Education Support System Projects*—those activities which contain one or more of the following as their *only* objective(s): to (1) provide training for educational personnel to improve their capability to design, operate and/or evaluate one or more aspects of a Comprehensive Career Education Project; (2) design, develop, test, demonstrate, or disseminate career education curriculum materials; or (3) design, develop, test, demonstrate, or disseminate career education management materials (e.g., case studies, evaluative designs, etc.).

Thus, Comprehensive Career Education Projects are operational models serving students in various grade levels while Career Education Support System Projects indirectly serve students through the development of materials and staff training.[2]

As a result of this more systematic process, a rigorous analysis of career education funding was conducted, starting in July 1973, immediately following the close of fiscal 1973. This analysis resulted in the following accounting for Office of Education investments in career education for the period July 1, 1972, to June 30, 1973[3]:

It is clear from the facing table and the criteria governing fund identification that in fiscal 1973 over $43 million was devoted either to the direct funding of state and local career education projects or to the development of supporting activities such as faculty development, curriculum materials, or related supporting activites. This sum is a significant order of magnitude for the introduction of change in education if carefully targeted, as this was. It should be noted that while the bulk of the moneys,

FUNDS IDENTIFIED IN SUPPORT OF CAREER EDUCATION, FISCAL 1974
(adapted)

| Appropriation and Statutory Authority | TYPE OF CAREER EDUCATION ACTIVITY | | | | Total funds | Total projects |
| | Comprehensive CE | | CE Support | | | |
	Funds	Number of identified projects nationally	Funds	Number of identified projects nationally		
Vocational & Adult Educ.	$16,296,818	126	$13,984,440	489	$30,280,258	615
Manpower Dev. & Training	399,439	1	—	—	399,439	1
Educ. Personnel Development, General	10,538	1	834,476	34	849,014	35
Higher Education (incl. Part E EPDA)	—	—	8,508,500	160	8,508,500	160
Elem., Secondary, & Handicapped Education	1,968,360	72	1,235,995	64	3,204,355	136
	$18,674,617	198	$24,567,411	747	$43,241,566	947

totaling about 70 percent, was drawn from Vocation Education Act resources, virtually all major components of the Office of Education were in realistic, budgetary terms, engaged in the career education priority. Even where authorizing legislation (such as in the education of the handicapped) gave no specific statutory authority for career education, the managers and planners were able to target funds in accordance with the agency-wide objective. A total of sixteen separate statutory authorities was assembled in the 1973 effort.

Of the 947 individual projects, the largest number were directed to comprehensive programs encompassing grades kindergarten through the community college in selected school districts. Also drawing heavily on the "comprehensive" resources were kindergarten–grade twelve projects, while the remaining were distributed over kindergarten–grade six, grades ten–twelve, and adult education. Substantial sums, especially under the "support" activities, went to colleges and universities engaged in developmental and service programs in career education, particularly in teacher education in-service and curriculum development.

While by far the largest sums were allocated to states for the development of working models, significant sums were obligated directly by the Office for curriculum construction. Dr. Elizabeth Simpson addressed the enormous task of formulating curriculum concepts and commissioning the actual construction of materials to scholars and practitioners throughout the country. In collaboration with Sidney High, Michael Russo, and under the leadership of Robert Worthington, Dr. Simpson developed in 1971 one of the early curricular conceptualizations that has served during the ensuing years to bring system and order to the vast array of occupations. The Department of Labor lists over 23,000 definable occupations in the United States. Dr. Simpson's curricular design has reduced these to fifteen job clusters for purposes of school and college offerings. These clusters embrace the majority of the 23,000 occupations in terms of knowledge and skills essential to job performance.[4] The following table arrays the fifteen clusters and their fiscal support along with general support allocations for career education's curricula over the first three years of the effort:

DISTRIBUTION OF PART I FUNDS BY OCCUPATIONAL CLUSTERS, 1971-1973			
CLUSTER	FY 1971	FY 1972	FY 1973
General Career Ed.	0	$1,137,661	$ 273,729
Agribusiness	$ 149,913	260,000	0
Business and Office	200,000	0	520,314
Communications & Media	570,000	0	241,830
Health	0	200,000	500,000
Hospitality, Tourism, and Recreation	103,012	0	0
Consumer & Homemaking	164,383	195,724	162,144
Fine Arts & Humanities	0	0	26,109
Construction Occupations	150,000	71,705	262,786
Environment	296,236	0	0
Marketing & Distribution	0	24,000	189,853
Manufacturing	150,000	0	250,000
Public Services	150,000	0	229,707
Personal Services	200,000	0	0
Transportation	150,000	49,396	250,000
Marine Sciences	0	0	0
Other	150,000	200,000	570,835
TOTALS	$2,443,544	$2,138,486	$3,477,307

Earlier chapters have identified transportation and construction occupations clusters in some detail as illustrations of state and local activities supported by this authority. At this time, six of the clusters have been completed, and are being field-tested and disseminated. By 1976, major curricular development will have been completed for all fifteen clusters. These curricula are designed, consistent with the career education theory, to interface with the corresponding academic programs. They will cover the span of related academic content from kindergarten through grade twelve. In addition, postsecondary curricula have been developed in several fields of expanding occupational opportunity including biomedical equipment technology, nuclear medical technology, electromechanical technology, and allied health services. These curricula are being widely used in community colleges, helping to carry forward the career education concept in the context of "supportive services" as defined earlier in this chapter.

Typically, two to four years are required for the development, testing, printing, and dissemination of a federally initiated curriculum. These complex instruments covering thirteen or more grade levels are excellent examples of how the power of the federal office can provide a critical mass of intellect, experience, and money for the confrontation of a national need. No single community, or even state, could muster the human or material resources in the cost-beneficial context described above. Yet, true to the rules of conduct in federal education enterprises, the curricula are not imposed. Their adoption by the universe of education will rest upon their quality and their usefulness as viewed by practicing scholars, teachers, and administrators. Having been created with the lively participation of scholars, teachers, and administrators, the likelihood of their wide adoption and adaptation to local conditions is high.

Throughout this book there have been numerous references calling attention to the work of Dr. Kenneth B. Hoyt as a protagonist of career education in his post as professor at the University of Maryland. Over the six or seven months that I have been a part-time author, a number of events have overtaken my writing. One of the most important of these was the appointment of Dr. Hoyt to the new post of U.S. Associate Commissioner of Education, Office of Career Education, by Commissioner John Ottina. Hoyt took on his new duties in the early spring of 1974, and I predict that education in America will prosper for reason of his presence in the center of the career education movement.

In a draft document, being circularized for review by associates in and out of government, Hoyt, very early in his tenure, stakes out a number of important hypotheses.[5] A few extracts follow, leaving the real heart of the document for more detailed scrutiny by those who wish to read it in whole—which it deserves:

Career education represents a response to a call for educational reform. This call has arisen from a variety of sources, each of which has voiced dissatisfaction with American education as it currently exists. Such sources include students, parents, the business-industry-labor community, out-of-school youth and adults, minorities, the disadvantaged, and the general public. While their specific concerns vary, all seem to agree that American education is in need of major reform at all levels. Career education is properly viewed as *one* of several possible responses that could be given to this call.

A Generic Definition of Career Education
As with any educational concept, "career education" has been operationally defined in a wide variety of ways. In a generic sense, its definition must obviously be derived from the ways in which the two words, "career" and "education," are defined. Here, "career" is defined as the totality of work one does in his or her lifetime. "Education" is defined as the totality of experiences through which one learns. Thus, "career education" can be defined generically as the totality of educational experiences through which one learns about work. "Work," with the definition cited above, obviously includes unpaid activities as well as paid employment. Education, as defined here, obviously includes far more than "schooling." Thus, this generic definition of career education is purposely intended to be of a very broad and a very encompassing nature. Career education emphasizes education as preparation for work as one of the basic goals of American education. In no way does career education try to say that this should be the only goal or even necessarily the most important goal for any student or for any educational system.

Basic Concept Assumptions of Career Education
Based on the generic definition of career education and its rationale as cited above, the career education movement has embraced a number of basic concept assumptions. These assumptions include:

1.   Since both one's career and one's education extend from the preschool through the retirement years, career education must also span almost the entire life cycle.

2.   The concept of productivity is central to the definition of work and so to the entire concept of career education.

3.   Since "work" includes unpaid activities as well as paid employment, career education's concerns, in addition to its prime emphasis on paid employment, extend to the work of the student as a learner, to the growing numbers of volunteer workers in our society, to the work of the full-time homemaker, and to work activities in which one engages as part of leisure and/or recreational time.

4.   The cosmopolitan nature of today's society demands that career education embrace a multiplicity of work values, rather than a single work ethic, as a means of helping each individual answer the question "Why should I work?"

5.   Both one's career and one's education are best viewed in a developmental, rather than in a fragmented, sense.

6.   Career education is for all persons—the young and the old; the mentally handicapped and the intellectually gifted; the poor and the wealthy; males and females; students in elementary schools and in the graduate colleges.

7.   The societal objectives of career education are to help all individuals: a) want to work; b) acquire the skills necessary for work in these times; and c) engage in work that is satisfying to the individual and beneficial to society.

8.   The individualistic goals of career education are to make work: a) possible, b) meaningful, and c) satisfying for each individual throughout his or her lifetime.

9.   Protection of the individual's freedom to choose and assistance in making and implementing career decisions are of central concern to career education.

10.   The expertise required for implementing career education is

to be found in many parts of society and is not limited to those employed in formal education.

Taken as a whole, these ten concept assumptions can be viewed as representing a philosophical base for current career education efforts. Career education makes no pretense of picturing these assumptions as anything more than the simple beliefs that they represent. Certainly, each is debatable and none is yet sufficiently accepted so as to be regarded as educational truisms.

> . . . in formulating action plans for career education, we are not, even at this point in time, forced to operate out of complete ignorance. While much more research is obviously needed, it seems safe to say that we know enough right now to justify the organization and implementation of comprehensive career education programs. The call for educational reform, to which career education seeks to respond, does not have to wait for further research before it can begin to be answered. Further research is badly needed, but we need not and should not wait until such research is completed before undertaking the installation of career education programs.

The actions of students, educational personnel, parents, and members of the business-industry-labor community, no matter how well-intentioned, cannot bring about educational reform so long as the basic policies of American education remain unchanged. None of the basic educational policy changes advocated by career education are either new or untested. Yet, none has as yet become common practice in a majority of educational systems. No one of these changes can or should come quickly. Each will require considerable study, debate, and public acceptance prior to its initiation. In spite of the obvious difficulties and dangers involved the following basic educational policy changes are each championed by the career education movement:

1. Substantial increases in the quantity, quality and variety of vocational education offerings at the secondary school level and

of occupational education offerings at the post-secondary school level.

2.   Increases in the number and variety of educational course options available to students with a de-emphasis on the presence of clearly differentiated college preparatory, general and vocational education curricula at the secondary school level.

3.   The installation of performance evaluation, as an alternative to the strict time requirements imposed by the traditional Carnegie unit, as a means of assessing and certifying educational accomplishment.

4.   The installation of systems for granting educational credit for learning that takes place outside the walls of the school.

5.   Increasing use of non-certificated personnel from the business-industry-labor community as educational resource persons in the educational system's total instructional program.

6.   The creation of an open entry-open exit educational system that allows students to combine schooling with work in ways that fit their needs and educational motivations.

7.   Substantial increases in programs of adult and recurrent education as a responsibility of the public school educational system.

8.   Creation of the year-round public school system that provides multiple points during any twelve-month period in which students will leave the educational system.

9.   Major overhaul of teacher education programs and graduate programs in education aimed at incorporating the career education concepts, skills and methodologies.

10.   Substantial increases in the career guidance, counseling, placement, and followup functions as parts of American education.

11.   Substantial increases in program and schedule flexibility that allow classroom teachers, at all levels, greater autonomy and freedom to choose educational strategies and devise methods

and materials they determine to be effective in increasing pupil achievement.

12. Increased utilization of educational technology for gathering, processing and disseminating knowledge required in the teaching-learning process.

13. Increases in participation in educational policy-making on the part of students, teachers, parents, and members of the business-industry-labor community.

14. Increases in participation, on the part of formal education, in comprehensive community educational and human services efforts.

Program objectives declared by the Office in the spring of 1974 to take effect with the beginning of fiscal 1975 (July 1974) are listed as follows (these objectives are tentative and subject to budget action):

1. To maintain and further encourage state and local efforts aimed at implementation of career education programs.

2. To strengthen career education leadership potential present in state educational agencies.

3. To advance the practice of career education in settings beyond the elementary school. To explore and demonstrate means of extending the career education concept in settings where implementation efforts have, to date, been largely lacking.

4. To further refine the conceptualization of career education and to seek consensus on results of conceptualization efforts.

5. To test the adequacy of a design for short-term evaluation of career education's effectiveness and to assemble evaluation data resulting from such testing.[6]

Such funds as may be appropriated by Congress will be heavily targeted toward the first objective: support of state and local initiatives. Calling at least for matching funds, the Office of

Career Education will encourage participating state and local systems to address the following activities:

1. In-service education of educational administrators employed at the K–12 level.

2. In-service education of instructional and guidance personnel employed at the K–12 level.

3. Career education program activities at the K–6, 7–9, and 10–12 levels in local educational agencies.

4. Modification of pre-service programs for preparation of educational personnel in ways reflecting a career education emphasis.

5. Involvement of the home and family structure in career education.

6. Involvement of the business-labor-industry community in career education.

7. Career education program activities at the post-high school level.

8. Efforts to reduce race and sex bias in career opportunities and choices.

As the Office of Career Education continues the refinement of definition and the extension of the concept, it declares among the objectives for 1975 the identification and illumination of exemplary programs in the fields listed below:

a. Career education for handicapped persons
b. Career education for gifted and talented persons
c. Career education for minority persons
d. Career education for females
e. Career education and parents
f. Career education and the business-labor-industry community
g. Career education for out-of-school youth and adults
h. Career education in teacher education

i. Career education in the community college
j. Career education in the four-year college or university setting
k. Career education's influence in teacher education programs
l. Career education in the elementary school
m. Career education in middle and junior high schools
n. Career education in senior high schools
o. Career education and career guidance
p. Career education's role in placement and followup
q. Career education and the all-volunteer armed forces
r. Career education and the Comprehensive Employment and Training Act

During fiscal 1975, according to the plans of the Office of Education, increased emphasis will be placed upon postsecondary education. Grants will be awarded to four to ten community colleges and four-year institutions for funding demonstration career education programs, including programs of teacher education. Further, the Office intends to award grants to two or more demonstration community career education resource centers for the development of model services to out-of-school learners.

Federal leaders, under the 1975 plans, will conduct a series of conferences addressing numerous facets or issues of career education such as *career education and the minorities; career education for the gifted and talented; career education and parents.*

While examining the short-term future of career education as an objective of the Office of Education, it is important to view the total effect of the combined energies and resources of the full Division of Education, including the National Institute of Education and the Fund for the Improvement of Post-Secondary Education, all under the general jurisdiction of the Assistant Secretary for Education. In the winter of 1973–1974, the essential collaboration between these quite different and complementary federal agencies was increased. (I had left the Assistant Secretary's post in November 1973.)

Dr. Constantine Menges, Deputy Assistant Secretary for Policy

Development, was charged during my tenure with the staff responsibilities for federal policy analysis in all education activities and with coordinating the cross-agency programs such as career education. A staff paper of November 28, 1973, by Dr. John Alden of his staff, gave an accounting of "the past and present directions of the career education effort within the Education Division." Extracts of this summary follow, giving expression to the continuity and forward movement implicit in the Division:

> The overwhelming response to the challenges of Career Education during the 1969–1972 period led to a reaffirmation of federal intentions for continuing and creative initiatives.
>
> In the summer of 1973 in order to move forward in positive directions and to synthesize the results of the first few years, the USOE, the NIE and the Office of the Assistant Secretary for Education (ASE) collaborated to formulate an operational definition of Career Education. Concurrent with this decision, the three units joined together to define a series of programmatic initiatives which might accomplish the major social purposes of Career Education. These suggested federal Career Education programs were fully conceptualized and designed to specify budgetary requirements, operational requirements, intended program beneficiaries and expected results. Careful attention was devoted to the explicit action steps required in 1974 and future years in order to arrive at recommendations for a focused federal Career Education program by the spring of 1974.
>
> The clear lessons of the last ten years of federal social policy efforts are convincing of the importance of intensive analysis and consideration of program implications in moving from diverse development activities into deliberate Career Education strategies. The complex nature of Career Education, encompassing intricate relationships between school and work, further underscores the need for thorough thinking about the impact of specific programs within all segments of the economic and educational systems. The Education Division, for that reason, has taken upon itself the difficult and absolutely essential task of objectively exploring the personal economic and insti-

tutional success probabilities of its suggested Career Education programmatic initiatives before taking the next step of recommending specific budgetary commitments in the spring of 1974 to the Secretary of HEW (for the FY '76 budget).

To accomplish this, the Education Division has moved to actively apply the results of the state and local career education activities of the last several years. The Center for Career Education is providing leadership for extracting the learnings of past Career Education experiences within the USOE. The Center (and USOE) are now assuming responsibility for systematically clarifying Career Education: (1) by engaging in further articulation and refinement of the concept; (2) by developing the conceptual framework for organizing priorities; (3) by encouraging support for program development; (4) and by designing evaluation studies of present USOE programs.

The NIE has likewise committed itself to the extraction of relevant major findings from its current research projects. At the same time that we are attempting to summarize and focus the lessons of past efforts, we have identified a series of major analytical issues deriving directly from the specific federal career education programs now under consideration. The collaborative efforts of NIE and OE, coordinated by the Assistant Secretary for Education, have been pledged to ensure that thorough and objective analysis is completed by mid-summer 1974, as a prelude to final recommendations on these suggested future programs.

The challenges posed by increased numbers of individuals moving through the educational system and the high aspirations of all individuals for meaningful work has touched educators at many levels who recognize the timeliness of the Career Education goals. The good efforts of the initial years merit the best and most careful analysis in order to build upon the strong beginning that has been achieved in Career Education. The coming months of intensive analytical effort will shape specific federal leadership. The large promise of Career Education challenges us all to apply our best and most creative skills to this endeavor.[7]

This book does not have a "conclusion." For, at this stage,

career education does not have a conclusion. It barely has a beginning.

Further, it does not have, in the manner of most books about education, a list of inspired "recommendations." The recommendations I would offer are either implicit in the text or premature.

But if I were to speculate about the short-term future of career education, I would offer a few final observations:

1. Our education system is crying out for change, renewal, reform—call it what we will. Our students, their parents, our own professional colleagues, our business and labor constituencies are calling for a better system of developing our people, young and old.

2. Career education, broadly and flexibly defined, yet sufficiently disciplined in conceptualization at all levels of instruction, can be the central rallying theme for reform. This has been the message of this book.

3. Given sufficient evidence of promise, as a major theme for reform, through tight evaluation of the models now in place and being put into place, the concept could become the next major national investment in domestic policy. In this context it would follow the pattern of educational legislation of the mid-sixties which aimed especially at the poor and the educationally disadvantaged. But to travel that road of federal money-throwing again without the discipline of validated program direction would be a mistake.

4. There is now on the books an adequate authority in federal law for very large-scale support of this reform. The Amendments of 1972 contain the Occupational and Adult Education title, viewed by its authors in Congress and by the managers and planners in the Education Division as wholly compatible with the goals, both implicit and explicit, of career education. The *authorizing* legislation now only awaits *appropriation* legislation. The scale of appropriation should be large, once the design for the federal system of support is clear; it should become clear over

the next two years, as experimental evidence and the results of evaluation flow in.

5. In addition to "education law," there is new authority in the Department of Labor which must have an implicit and explicit effect on career education. The Comprehensive Employment and Training Act of 1973 (CETA) is a potentially powerful companion to career education. Educators at high school and college level should capitalize upon this new resource. It affords the means and the system for bridging between education and employment—certainly a basic theme of career education.

6. The debate over the extent of federal revenue sharing with education governance at state and local level could be resolved through a major federal support system surrounding career education. The system would be broad enough and general enough, still within the career education rubric to avoid the stigma of "another categorial program." But it would be sufficiently specific to warrant the federal role as "a response to a national need"; i.e., the reform of education from the early years to adulthood.

7. It is premature to predict the scale of dollars that could be justified in the federal budget for the support of career education. This analysis must await further evidence from the trials. To give some impression of the order of magnitude which might be found valid, however, let us consider the sum of an add-on of 10 percent to the average cost-per-student at elementary and secondary level. Current average cost-per-student is about $1000. The $100 average add-on for new programs and services (counseling, teacher development, facilities, equipment, community out-reach, etc.) would apply to roughly 46 million students. (Costs would be lower in elementary schools and higher in secondary schools.) That comes to a federal budget total of $4.6 billion.

8. If the Administration, now or in the future, and Congress became truly interested in redressing the disparities of support between federal, state, and local funding for elementary and secondary education this would be a splendid and wholly rational

vehicle for increasing the federal share. That share, at roughly $3 billion, is now about 7 percent of the $43.5 billion costs of the operating expenses in our schools. If we were to follow the illustration of the $100 add-on, the $3 billion plus the $4.6 billion would produce perhaps 15 percent of the upgraded costs and quality. This would be a significant start toward the oft-stated goal of "30 percent federal support" for elementary and secondary education.

In attempting to give an accounting of the promise and progress of a reform of our schools and colleges through something called career education, I have been shooting at a moving target. Even as I have been putting thoughts on paper, many of these thoughts have been overtaken by events. There is now in motion in our land a very large and complex educational idea. It has its advocates and its adversaries, as every important idea should. It is possible—just possible—that this idea will be found sufficiently worthy after a year of two more of hard work to deserve the awesome implications of the word *reform*.

References

Chapter 1

1. Paul A. Mort, *Principles of School Administration* (New York: McGraw-Hill, 1946).
2. Ralph W. Tyler, *The Unfinished Journey* (New York: John Day, 1968), p. 181.

Chapter 2

1. *Kappan*, September 1973, p. 38, 42.
2. Stephen K. Bailey, unpublished paper for Washington Internships in Education, 1972.
3. D. J. Prediger, J. D. Roth, and R. J. Noeth, "Report #61: Study of Student Career Development" (Iowa City: American College Testing Program, November 1973), p. 9.
4. Gordon P. Miller, *College Board Review,* vol. 86 (Winter 1972–1973).
5. James S. Coleman *et al., Youth: Transition to Adulthood,* report of the Panel on Youth of the President's Science Advisory Committee (Washington, D.C.: Office of Science and Technology, June 1973), p. iv.

Chapter 3

1. Henry Borow, "Shifting Postures Toward Work: A Tracing," *American Vocational Journal* (January 1973), p. 28.
2. Hannah Arendt, *The Human Condition* (Garden City, N.Y.: Doubleday, Anchor Books, 1959), p. 74.

3. Kenneth B. Hoyt, "What the Future Holds for the Meaning of Work," *American Vocational Journal* (January 1973), p. 35.

4. Borow, *op. cit.,* p. 29.

5. *Ibid.*

6. *Ibid.*

7. James S. Coleman *et al., Youth: Transition to Adulthood,* report of the Panel on Youth of the President's Science Advisory Committee (Washington, D.C.: Office of Science and Technology, June 1973), pp. 2, 5, 6.

8. *Ibid.,* pp. 2, 5, 7.

9. Judson Gooding, *The Job Revolution* (New York: Walker, 1972), p. 12.

10. *Ibid.,* p. 2.

11. *Work in America,* report of a Special Task Force to the Secretary of Health, Education, and Welfare (Cambridge, Mass.: MIT Press, 1973), p. 3.

12. Hoyt, *op. cit.,* p. 35.

13. *Work in America,* p. 5.

14. Grant Venn, "Man, Education and Manpower," (Washington, D.C.: American Association of School Administrators, 1970), p. 76.

15. *Ibid.*

16. Charles Winick, "Atonie: The Psychology of the Unemployed and Marginal Worker," (Washington, D.C.: U.S. Department of Labor, 1964), p. 18.

17. *Work in America,* p. 13.

18. Abraham Maslow, *Motivation and Personality* (New York: Harper, 1954).

19. Robert L. Kahn, "The Meaning of Work: Interpretation and Proposals for Measurement," in A. A. Campbell and P. E. Converse (eds.), *The Human Meaning of Social Change* (New York: Basic Books, 1972).

20. *Work in America,* p. 17.

21. *Ibid.,* p. 18.

22. Gooding, *op. cit.,* p. 7.

23. *Ibid.,* p. 10.

24. *Work in America,* p. 20.

25. *Ibid.,* p. 21.

26. Hoyt, *op. cit.,* p. 36.

Chapter 4

1. George Kerschensteiner, "Three Lectures on Vocational Training" (Chicago: The Commercial Club of Chicago, 1911), pp. 2–3.

2. Daniel Yankelovich, *The Changing Values of Campus: Political and Personal Attitudes* (New York: Washington Square Press, 1972).

3. James S. Coleman *et al., Youth: Transition to Adulthood,* report of

the Panel on Youth of the President's Science Advisory Committee (Washington, D.C.: Office of Science and Technology, June 1973).

4. *Ibid.*

5. Kenneth Keniston, "Youth, A (New) Stage of Life, *American Scholar,* vol. 39, no. 4 (Autumn 1970), p. 631.

6. Ivar Berg, *Education and Jobs: The Great Training Robbery* (Boston: Beacon, 1971), pp. 68, 192.

7. Fred Wilhelms, "What Should the Schools Teach?," Phi Delta Kappa Educational Foundation pamphlet (Bloomington, Ind., 1972).

8. Quoted by W. Richard Stephens in "Social Reform and the Origins of Vocational Guidance" (Washington, D.C.: National Vocational Guidance Association, 1970).

9. Frank W. Parsons, *Choosing a Vocation* (New York: Agathon Press, 1909), p. 122.

10. Edwin L. Herr, "Review and Synthesis of Foundations for Career Education" (Columbus: ERIC Clearing House on Vocational Education, The Ohio State University, March 1972).

11. Stephen K. Bailey, "Higher Education, American Style," *American Education* (U.S. Office of Education, 1974).

12. W. Theodore deBary, *The New York Times,* January 16, 1974, p. 16.

13. Richard M. Millard, "Address before Northwest Association of Secondary and Higher Schools, December 3–6, 1972" (Iowa City: American College Testing Program).

14. Nell Eurich, "View from the Year 2001," *The Chronicle of Higher Education* (October 30, 1972).

15. Coleman *et al., op. cit.*

Chapter 5

1. Robert L. Darcy and Phillip E. Powell, *Manpower and Economic Education* (Denver: Love Publishing Co., 1973), p. 148.

2. *Ibid.,* p. 347.

3. *Ibid.,* p. 348.

4. *Ibid.,* pp. 231, 257.

5. *Ibid.,* p. 212.

6. K. Patricia Cross, "The Learning Society," *The College Board Review* (Spring 1974).

7. James S. Coleman *et al., op. cit.,* p. 73.

Chapter 6

1. David Rogers, "Vocational and Career Education: A Critique and Some New Directions," (New York: *Teachers College Record,* vol. 74, no. 4. May 1973).

2. Edwin L. Herr, "Review and Synthesis of Foundations for Career Education" (Columbus: ERIC Clearing House on Vocational Information, The Ohio State University, March 1972).

3. Kenneth B. Hoyt, "Selected Current Definitions of Career Education" in 1973 *Yearbook* of the American Vocational Association (Washington D.C.), p. 16.

4. *Ibid.*, p. 19.

Chapter 7

1. "What Is Career Education?," Occasional Paper No. 20 (Washington, D.C.: Council on Basic Education, 1972), p. 28.

2. James P. Spradley, "Career Education in Cultural Perspective," in *Essays on Career Education* (Northwest Regional Educational Laboratory in cooperation with U.S. Office of Education/National Institute of Education, April 1973), p. 10.

3. *The New York Times,* February 10, 1973, p. 50.

4. David Rogers, "Vocational and Career Education: A Critique and Some New Directions," *Teachers College Record*, vol. 74, no. 4 (May 1973).

5. Lowell Burkett in *Bulletin of the National Association of Secondary School Principals* (March 1973), p. 81.

6. Lawrence F. Davenport, "Career Education and the Black Student," in *Essays on Career Education*, p. 177.

7. Edmund W. Cordon, "Growing Up Aware" (Los Angeles Unified School District, June 1973).

8. George R. Quarles in the *Bulletin* of the Office of Career Education, New York City Board of Education (1973).

9. "Career Education, Implications for Minorities," Proceedings of a National Conference (Washington, D.C.: U.S. Office of Education, June 1973).

10. Robert C. Weaver, "The Urban University," address delivered at the opening of the Boston Campus, University of Massachusetts, April 27, 1974.

11. Shirley Chisholm, address before the Office of Education's National Conference on Career Education for Minorities, June 1973.

12. Cas Heilman and Keith Goldhammer, "The Psycho-Social Foundation for Career Education," *Bulletin of the National Association of Secondary School Principals* (March 1973).

13. Carnegie Commission on Higher Education, *Toward a Learning Society: Alternative Channels to Life, Work, and Service* (New York: McGraw-Hill), p. 92, 1973.

14. Willard W. Wirtz, "Education's National Manpower Policy," University of Chicago *School Review*, vol. 82, no. 1 (November 1973).

Chapter 8

1. Gene Bottoms, "The Georgia Plan for Career Education" (Address

to the Annual Teacher Education Conference, Athens, Georgia, January 18, 1973).

2. *Ibid.*

3. "Superintendent's Guide to Career Development" (Governor's Special Conference on Career Development, Macon, Georgia, October 11–12, 1972).

4. Bottoms, *op. cit.*

5. *Ibid.*

Chapter 9

1. "Executive Briefing Manual," typewritten (Los Angeles Unified School District, April 1973).

2. *Ibid.*

3. *Ibid.*

4. *Ibid.*

5. Paul N. Peters and Joseph T. McGhee, "Career Education in California." (Paper presented at the American Personnel and Guidance Association and California Personnel and Guidance Association Joint Convention, February 12, 1973.)

6. *Ibid.*

7. *Ibid.*

Chapter 10

1. Oregon Board of Education, "Goals for Elementary and Secondary Education" (Oregon State Department of Education, February 1974).

2. Oregon Board of Education, "Oregon Graduation Requirements" (Oregon State Department of Education, September 1972).

3. Quotations and excerpts from conversations with education officials in Oregon; passages from published state documents are treated without specific notes.

4. Dale Parnell, *American Vocational Journal* (December 1969).

Chapter 12

1. Bruce Reinhart, "Career Education: Concept, Components, Scope." (Address to the National Career Education Conference, Rutgers University, July 16, 1973.)

2. Keith Goldhammer, "Roles of Schools and Colleges of Education in Career Education." (Address to the National Conference on Career Education for Deans of Colleges of Education, Columbus, Ohio, April 24, 1972.)

3. Elizabeth Jane Simpson, "Career Education: Challenge to Teacher Education," *Challenge* 1 (1973).

4. Reinhart address.

5. Kenneth B. Hoyt *et al., Career Education and the Elementary School Teacher* (Salt Lake City: Olympus Publishing Company, 1973), p. 166.

6. *Ibid.,* pp. 167–71.

7. Kenneth B. Hoyt *et al., Career Education: What It Is and How to Do It,* 2nd ed. (Salt Lake City: Olympus Publishing Company, 1972), p. 131.

8. *Ibid.,* p. 125.

9. Goldhammer address.

10. *Ibid.*

11. *Ibid.*

12. Career Education Development Task Force, *Forward Plan for Career Education Research and Development* (Washington, D.C.: Education Division, National Institute of Education, Department of Health, Education, and Welfare), p. ES-2.

13. E. L. Tolbert, *Counseling for Career Development* (Boston: Houghton Mifflin, 1974), pp. 19–20.

14. Warren W. Willingham, Richard J. Ferrin, and Elsie P. Begle, *Career Guidance in Secondary Schools* (New York: College Entrance Examination Board, 1972), pp. 3–11.

Chapter 13

1. Stephen K. Bailey, "Issues and Problems in Career Education," George Washington University Seminar Series, 1973.

2. William Theodore deBary, *Columbia Reports,* (New York: Columbia University, April 1973).

3. William Theodore deBary, "General Education and the Humanities," *Seminar Reports,* Columbia University, vol. I, no. 1 (October 22, 1973).

4. *The Chronicle of Higher Education,* December 3, 1973, p. 2.

5. Nathan Glazer, "Conflicts in Schools for the Minor Professions," *Harvard Graduate School of Education Bulletin,* vol. 18, no. 2 (Spring–Summer 1974).

6. K. Patricia Cross, "The Learning Society," *The College Board Review* (Spring 1974), 22–23.

7. Brochure from Director of Admissions, Chatham College, Pittsburgh, Pa., 1974.

8. News release from the College Entrance Examination Board, March 25, 1974.

9. Bailey, *op. cit.*

10. S. Moses, *The Learning Force, etc.* (Syracuse: Educational Policy Research Center, 1970).

11. *Education Daily* (Washington, D.C.), August 27, 1973.

12. Stephen K. Bailey, "Higher Education—American Style," *American Education.*

13. *The New York Times,* February 24, 1974, p. 47.

14. "Review," *The Chronicle of Higher Education,* February 19, 1974, p. 4.

15. *Ibid.*, February 4, 1974, p. 1.

16. *Ibid.*, p. 1.

17. Peter Drucker, "What Education Needs," *Comment,* (Spring 1973).

18. Ernest L. Boyer, "Higher Education for All, through Old Age," *The New York Times,* April 8, 1974.

19. Frank Newman *et al., Report on Higher Education: The Federal Role* (Washington, D.C.: U.S. Office of Education, March 1973), pp. 26–28.

Chapter 14

1. David Rogers, "Vocational and Career Education: A Critique and Some New Directions," *Teachers College Record*, vol. 74, no. 4 (May 1973), p. 13.

2. Samuel Burt, "Collaboration at the Crossroads," in Pucinski, R., and S. Hirach (eds.), *The Courage to Change* (Englewood Cliffs, N.J.: Prentice-Hall, 1971), p. 141.

3. Kenneth B. Hoyt *et al., Career Education: What It Is and How to Do It* (Salt Lake City: Olympus Publishing Company, 1972).

4. "Career Education and the Business Man" (Washington, D.C.: Chamber of Commerce of the United States, June 1973), p. 22.

Chapter 15

1. Career Education Task Force, "Forward Plan for Career Education Research and Development" (Washington, D.C.: National Institute of Education, April 1973).

2. "NIE: Its History and Programs" (Washington, D.C.: Office of Public Information, National Institute of Education, February 28, 1974).

Chapter 16

1. "Activities in Fiscal Year 1973: Center for Career Education" (Washington, D.C.: U.S. Office of Education, November 1973).

2. "Career Education, Programs and Progress" (Washington, D.C.: U.S. Office of Education, February 1974), p. 4.

3. *Ibid.*, p. 5.

4. Elizabeth J. Simpson, "Curriculum Development, Vocational Education Amendments of 1968." (An internal technical report, U.S. Office of Education, March 27, 1974.)

5. Kenneth B. Hoyt, "An Introduction to Career Education." (A draft circulated in April 1974, Office of Career Education, U.S. Office of Education.)

6. "Plans for Office of Education Career Education Program in FY 1975." (Tentative planning document, March 1974.)

7. Constantine Menges and John Alden, "Memorandum from the Deputy Assistant Secretary for Policy Development, Education Division to Agencies of the Division" (November 28, 1974), pp. 10–12.

Index